JOURNEY

Through the Bible

JOURNEY

Through the Bible

Scott Brown

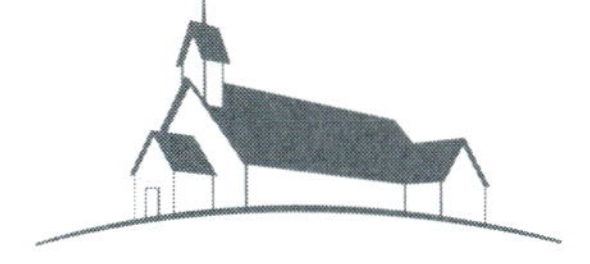

Journey Through the Bible

First Printing: November 2017

The National Center for Family-Integrated Churches
220 South White St., Wake Forest, NC 27587
www.ncfic.org

ISBN-10: 1–62418–059–0
ISBN-13: 978–1–62418–059–0

Book Design and Typography by Steadfast Design Firm

Printed in the United States of America

"Whether you have just started leading family worship or have done so for years, you will find much in Scott Brown's remarkable Journey through the Bible to equip you to open the Word with your family. It offers many helps for each book of the Bible, including a memory verse, overview, top five facts, theme, author, audience, key verses, lessons, and outline. Two especially helpful features are suggestions for how to see Christ in each book of the Old Testament and a list of study questions and answers for discussion with your family."

Dr. Joel R. Beeke

PRESIDENT, PURITAN REFORMED THEOLOGICAL SEMINARY, GRAND RAPIDS, MI

Don't forget your guide map... Journey through the Bible, written by Scott Brown, an experienced guide, who has trod the path with his wife and family through the pages of Scripture many times before. Along the way, he has recorded some of the soaring peaks to ascend and dangerous crevasses to avoid, helping both novice and experienced explorers alike. The impact of taking this Journey through the Bible during your family devotions will be incalculable in the life of your children.

Craig D. Houston

PASTOR, WESTSIDE BAPTIST CHURCH, BREMERTON, WASHINGTON

"Here Scott Brown has provided an excellent introduction to the whole Bible for families. God has given the whole Word of God to equip our children for every good work, and the should not leave home without a familiarity with all 66 books."

Kevin Swanson

DIRECTOR of the GENERATIONS MINISTRY. EXECUTIVE DIRECTOR, CHRISTIAN HOME EDUCATORS OF COLORADO. AUTHOR OF *FREEDOM* and *APOSTATE*.

"Great biblical helps for families was and their devotional times together are always necessary. Certainly, Scott Brown deserves to have us listen when we come to this subject. This is a help for the family reading the Bible together. If it encourages families to do more of that, it will serve our generation well."

Sam Waldron

DEAN and PROFESSOR of SYSTEMATIC THEOLOGY at COVENANT BAPTIST THEOLOGICAL SEMINARY, and AUTHOR of A MAN AS PRIEST

"A closed Bible is convicting no one, instructing no one, transforming no one. Yet Satan himself must retreat before the weapon of God's Word when it is wielded with faith and skill. Because the Word of God gives life (1 Peter 1:23), and the Word of God brings growth (1 Peter 2:2), there is nothing more important than to familiarize ourselves and our families with its divine message. Scott Brown's Journey Through the Bible is a helpful tool toward this end. This work is well organized, well studied, and well written. It's subject matter is nothing less than glorious."

Justin Huffman

PASTOR and AUTHOR of the DAILY DEVOTION APP and GROW: THE COMMAND TO EVER-EXPANDING JOY

"Scott Brown has carefully compiled pertinent information about each book of the Bible in an extremely accessible fashion. From overall themes, to key verses, to review questions, Journey Through the Bible is designed to aid the individual, the family, or the christian classroom in the study of God's Word. It is a worthy resource that will benefit the Kingdom of Christ."

Anthony Mathenia

PASTOR, CHRIST CHURCH-RADFORD

"Journey Through the Bible is not only excellent for the Christian who wants to be more familiar with the books of the Bible, but is an outstanding resource for parents who desire to instruct their children in this way. Originally written for this purpose, this volume should be in the home of every believer as a tool to equip us better to know, understand, and apply God's blessed Word to our lives. I recommend it enthusiastically!"

Pastor Rob Ventura

PASTOR, GRACE COMMUNITY BAPTIST CHURCH, NORTH PROVIDENCE, RI, CO-AUTHOR of *A PORTRAIT OF PAUL* and *SPIRITUAL WARFARE*

"As a parent who regularly leads my family in reading the Bible, I have been long searching for a resource that could help my children with comprehension and meditation. Scott Brown's Journey Through the Bible is gold mine of valuable tools to aid families in studying Scripture together. It is everything I've been seeking: helpful background information, practical application, hymns, memory verses, study questions, and more for each book of the Bible. There is nothing more powerful for my family's spiritual life than understanding and meditating upon Scripture, and Journey Through the Bible helps us do just that. I will be using this book with my own family and recommending it to others!"

Scott Aniol, PhD

CHAIR of the WORSHIP MINISTRY DEPARTMENT at SOUTHWESTERN BAPTIST THEOLOGICAL SEMINARY. FOUNDER OF RELIGIOUS AFFECTIONS MINISTRIES

"Disciple-makers are more concerned with giving people all that Jesus taught, than teaching just parts of the Bible. Scott has given the church a necessary tool, exploring major themes and formulating the necessary questions, with a clear focus on Christ. This book can be used as a framework for those who desire to study the whole Bible systematically. Every pastor should have it on his desk and recommend it to his new converts and families in the church."

Malamulo Chindongo

PASTOR, ANTIOCH BAPTIST CHURCH in BLANTYRE, MALAWI

We want to express special thanks to the many people who participated in the hard work of editing and proofreading.

Colton Neifert, Isaac Burke, Jonathan Tanaka, Will Arterburn, Joah Carpenter, Deborah Brown, Claudia Brown, David Brown, John Morganti, Robert Bosley, and Taman Turbinton. We also loved the design and layout provided by the team at Steadfast Design Firm.

Table of Contents

Dear Reader,

This book is a product of our family worship times as we read the Bible together as a family.

As our children were growing up, our family made it our practice to read the Bible from cover to cover. We did this for many years. Some of our children even learned how to read through our times of studying God's Word as a family.

Our family took turns reading Scripture. The little ones would repeat one or two words that we taught them to pronounce. Those who could read would read one to five verses and the best readers would read five verses each. We would read around four chapters per day, usually in the morning.

As each year passed, I kept adding to a document that contained introductory information about each book. I used this document to provide my family with background information and other things I thought were important about each book. By the time our children were adults, I had over 400 pages of notes. These notes documented the following kinds of information:

1. The historical context of each book of the Bible.
2. The questions I asked them.
3. An explanation of the meaning of each book.
4. A list of the important matters of each book.
5. A list of key memory verses.
6. A basic outline of each book.

This book is a compilation of the notes I have used over the years as a private individual, a father, and a pastor.

How *to* Use *this* Book

This book is designed to be a concise teaching tool that will help you study the books of the Bible – from Genesis to Revelation – with your family.

As you read through each book of the Bible, I suggest that you do the following:

1. **Read** the overview that explains the meaning and significance of the book to your family.
2. **Listen** to the audio message on jttb.co before reading each book.
3. **Memorize** the short theme that captures the message of the book.
4. **Sing** the hymn which communicates the primary message of the book. Continue to sing it several times while reading through each book.
5. **Learn** one or more of the suggested memory verses.
6. **Explain** the context of each book.
7. **Review** the critical facts of each book.
8. **Walk** through the provided outline of each book so that everyone can see where the storyline is going.
9. **Show** how each Old Testament book points (ahead) to Jesus Christ.

Preface

Everyone needs to take multiple journeys through the Bible in their lifetime. This book is designed to help you walk through the Bible and understand the *context*, *purpose*, and *message* of each book. You will also find corresponding *study questions*, *lessons*, and even *hymns* to sing as you progress on your journey.. Most importantly, you will see how the entire Bible points to the Good Shepherd, our Lord Jesus Christ. He is the one we need to see on each page.

You will notice that I've included study questions you can use for yourself, your children, or your study group. These questions arose out of my own reading the Bible to my children over the years. Each year, I would add questions to ask them to help them understand what I felt was important.

Our family tried to read the Bible together aloud each year for many years and I hope that your experience will be the same. This one thing I know: Everything in this world will try to stop you from reading your Bible cover to cover. I have seen this firsthand. Reading through the Bible requires rhythmical regularity. It requires setting aside other good things. It will not happen without a genuine love for the Words of God. It requires a genuine conviction of the beauty and perfection of God to complete the task.

One of my favorite books on the inspiration and authority of Scripture is Louis Gaussen's "God Breathed." In this book, he speaks of the beauty, the grandeur, the depth, and the height of the Bible:

> *The Bible, in fact, has lessons for all conditions; it brings upon the scene both the lowly and the great; it reveals equally to both the love of God,*

> *and unveils in both the same miseries, it addresses itself to children; and it is often children that show us there the way to Heaven and the great things of Jehovah. It addresses itself to shepherds and herdsmen; and it is often shepherds and herdsmen who lift up their voices there, and reveal to us the character of God. It speaks to kings and to scribes, and it is often kings and scribes that teach us there man's wretchedness, humiliation, confessions of conscience, pouring forth of prayer in secret, travels, proverbs, revelations often depths of the heart, the holy courses pursed by a child of God, weaknesses unveiled, falls, recoveries, inward experiences, parables, familiar letters, theological treatises, sacred commentaries on some ancient Scripture, national chronicles, military annals, political statistics, descriptions of God, portraits of angles, celestial visions, practical counsels, rules, of life, solution of cases of conscience, judgments of the Lord, sacred hymns, predictions of future events, narratives of what passed during the days preceding our creation, sublime odes, inimitable pieces of poetry; all this is found there by turns; and all this meets our view in the most delightful variety, and presenting a whole whose majesty, like that of a temple, is overpowering.*[1]

In short, the Bible is a perfect book for a family. It speaks to every possible situation a family will encounter. More than that, it covers all their future encounters as well.

The Bible is lyrical, historical, narrative, and musical. It is sufficient. It is perfect. It is living bread. It is spirit and it is life. It is what your family needs.

Please receive this exhortation to take up and read the Bible from Genesis to Revelation many times while your children are in your home. You will never regret it.

1. François Samuel Robert Louis Gaussen and John W. Robbins, *God-breathed: the divine inspiration of the Bible* (Unicoi, TN: The Trinity Foundation, 2001), 64.

The Old Testament

4004 B.C.
Creation

Flood
2348 B.C.

2000 B.C.
Abraham

Exodus
1445 B.C.

1000 B.C.
David

Sennacherib
722 B.C.

586 B.C.
Nebuchadnezzar

Birth of Christ
5 B.C.

This Is My Father's World

WORDS: Maltbie D. Babcock, 1902; *alt.*
MUSIC: "Terra Beata"; English melody; *arr. by* Franklin L. Sheppard, *pub.* 1915. Public Domain.

for more resources go to ***jttb.co/genesis***

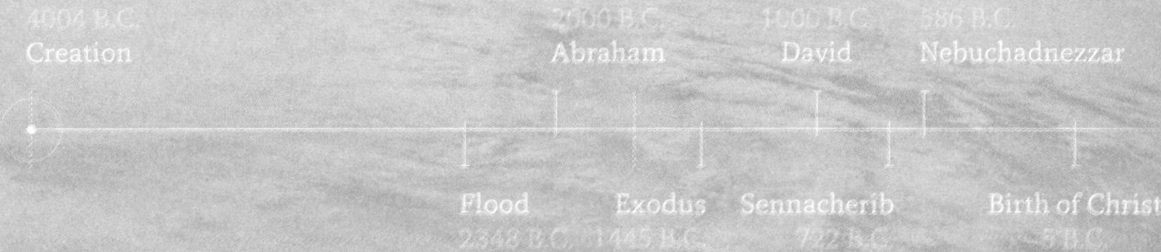

Journey through

Genesis

THEME	AUTHOR	TIME OF WRITING
Beginnings	Moses	1445–1405 B.C.

MEMORY VERSE

"In the beginning God created the heavens and the earth."

Genesis 1:1

OVERVIEW

Genesis is the book of beginnings – the beginning of the universe, the atmosphere, the biosphere, man, animals, evil, marriage, family, work, and covenants. Genesis reports on the first murder, the origin of diverse languages at the Tower of Babel, and the origin of the nations that resulted. It exposes the beginnings of sin and its results. It prescribes the nature of marriage, manhood, and womanhood. It displays the judgment of God – banishment from the garden, the flood, and the destruction of Sodom and Gomorrah. These are types of the final judgement. There are 165 passages from Genesis quoted in the New Testament. Christ quoted Genesis six times. If you reject the historicity of Genesis, you have thrown away the historicity of the entire Bible and the integrity of Jesus Christ Himself.

Top 5 Facts to Remember

1. God created everything in six, 24-hour days (Gen. 1:31–2:3).[1]
2. God commanded the first man and woman to "be fruitful and multiply," and to take dominion over the earth (Gen. 1:28).
3. As a result of Adam's transgression, sin and death came into the world (Gen. 3).[2]
4. God judged the world by a great flood, but He preserved Noah and his family (Gen. 6–8).
5. Abraham was justified by faith (Gen. 15:6).[3]

Theme: Beginnings

In Genesis, God is glorifying Himself as the *Creator* of all things, so that He might demonstrate His superior goodness in the salvation sinners, the damnation of the wicked, and for the preservation of His people for His eternal glory, and their eternal joy.

1. See also Ex. 20:11; 31:17.
2. See also Rom. 5:12–19; 1 Cor. 15:21–22.
3. See Rom. 4; Gal. 3:5–7.

Author: Moses

The clear and consistent teaching of Scripture is that Moses wrote the Pentateuch (Genesis, Exodus, Leviticus, Numbers, and Deuteronomy[4]). The Bible confirms Mosaic authorship in the following ways:

1. The Pentateuch itself tells us that Moses wrote things down and even authored books—books that were clearly meant to serve as covenant documents for the children of Israel.[5] If the books Moses wrote and delivered were not the books that we find in the Pentateuch today, then we would be left with the rather absurd conclusion that his books somehow disappeared from the Israelite community and were replaced with the works of some other author.

2. Biblical authors often refer to the Pentateuch as "the Book of Moses,"[6] "the Law of Moses,"[7] "the Book of the Law of Moses,"[8] or some other title that includes Moses' name.[9] These titles would strongly imply Mosaic authorship.

3. Many biblical writers explicitly name Moses as the author of the Pentateuch.[10]

In the final analysis, one cannot deny Mosaic authorship of the Pentateuch without calling the bulk of the Bible's testimony into question.

4. The last few chapters of Deuteronomy (which record the completion of the "Book of the Law" and the death of Moses) were obviously written by someone other than Moses (probably Joshua, who made at least one addition to the "Book of the Law" himself; see Josh. 24:26).

5. Ex. 24:4, 7; Num. 33:2; Deut. 17:18; 28:58, 61; 29:20–21, 27; 30:10; 31:9–13, 22, 24–26.

6. 2 Chron. 25:4; 35:12; Ezra 6:18; Neh. 13:1; Mark 12:26.

7. 1 Kings 2:3; 2 Kings 23:25; 2 Chron. 23:18; 30:16; Ezra 3:2; 7:6; Dan. 9:11, 13; Luke 2:22; 24:44; John 7:23; Acts 13:39; 28:23; 1 Cor. 9:9.

8. Josh. 8:31; 23:6; 2 Kings 14:6; Neh. 8:1.

9. Luke 16:29, 31; 24:27; 2 Cor. 3:15; Heb. 10:28.

10. Josh. 8:32; 2 Chron. 34:14; Neh. 8:14; 10:28–29; Mal. 4:4; Mark 7:10; 10:3–5; Luke 20:37; John 1:17, 45; 5:45–47; 7:19; Acts 15:21; Rom. 10:5, 19.

Time of Writing: 1445–1407 B.C.

Genesis was written sometime between Israel's Exodus from Egypt (1445–1447 B.C.)[11] and Moses' death (1405 B.C.).

Key Verses

"Then God said, 'Let Us make man in Our image, according to Our likeness; let them have dominion over the fish of the sea, over the birds of the air, and over the cattle, over all the earth and over every creeping thing that creeps on the earth.' So God created man in His own image; in the image of God He created him; male and female He created them."

Genesis 1:26–27

"And I will put enmity
Between you and the woman,
And between your seed and her Seed;
He shall bruise your head,
And you shall bruise His heel."

Genesis 3:15

"Joseph said to them, 'Do not be afraid, for am I in the place of God? But as for you, you meant evil against me; but God meant it for good, in order to bring it about as it is this day, to save many people alive.' "

Genesis 50:19–20

11. For more on how these dates are calculated, see "Time of Events" at the back of this book.

Lessons

1. Stand firm on what the Word of God says about the origins of the universe. God created everything in six, 24-hour days.
2. Genesis lays the foundation for the rest of Scripture. If you distort the teachings of Genesis, you distort the teachings of the entire Bible.
3. God works out all things—even the evil actions of men—for His glory and the good of His people.

Christ in Genesis

I. The Creator of All Things

The fact that Jesus Christ created all things is clearly taught in the New Testament.[12] The Genesis creation account itself—written long before the New Testament—records the Creator speaking as a plurality of persons: "Then God said, 'Let Us make man in Our image, according to Our likeness.' "[13] This Scripture shows us that, while God alone made the world, all three persons of the Trinity were involved.[14]

II. The Seed of the Woman

When cursing the serpent in Genesis 3:15, God foretold the coming of Christ:

"And I will put enmity
Between you and the woman,
And between your seed and her Seed;
He shall bruise your head,
And you shall bruise His heel."

12. John 1:3; 1:10; Col. 1:16–17; Heb. 1:2.
13. Gen. 1:26 (see also Gen. 3:22; 11:7).
14. Prov. 8.

This verse predicts three details of Christ's coming:

1. His incarnation—that He should be the seed of the woman.
2. His sufferings and death, symbolized in the bruising of His heel by the serpent.
3. His victory over Satan, pictured in His bruising of the serpent's head.

III. The Seed of Abraham, Isaac, and Jacob

The Lord promised Abraham,[15] Isaac,[16] and Jacob[17] that He would bless all the nations of the earth through their seed. Both Peter[18] and Paul[19] recognized the fulfillment of these promises in Christ.

IV. Other Types of Christ

1. Melchizedek (Gen. 14:18–20)
2. The Sacrificed Son—Isaac (Gen. 22:1–19)
3. The Betrayed, Suffering, and Exalted Servant—Joseph (Gen. 37; 39–50)
4. A King from the line of Judah (Gen. 49:10)

15. Gen. 22:18.
16. Gen. 26:4.
17. Gen. 28:14.
18. Acts 3:25.
19. Gal. 3:8.

Outline

I. **Creation and the Fall (Gen. 1–11)**

A. Creation (Gen. 1–2)

B. The Fall (Gen. 3–5)

C. The Flood and Noah's Descendants (Gen. 6–9)

D. The Nations are Scattered (Gen. 10–11)

II. **The Call of Abraham and the Patriarchs (Gen. 12–50)**

A. The Abrahamic Covenant (Gen. 12:1–22:19)

B. Isaac and Rebekah (Gen. 22:20–25:11)

C. The Generations of Ishmael (Gen. 25:12–18)

D. The Generations of Isaac (Gen. 25:19–35:29)

E. The Generations of Esau (Gen. 36:1–37:1)

F. The Generations of Jacob (Gen. 37:2–50:26)

Study Questions

What is the central theme of the book of Genesis?

Beginnings.

What are the four major events that take place in the book of Genesis?

1. Creation (Gen. 1–2).
2. The Fall (Gen. 3).
3. The Flood (Gen. 6–8).

4. The Tower of Babel (Gen. 11:1–9).

Who are some of the major figures that appear in the book of Genesis?

1. Adam
2. Noah
3. Abraham
4. Isaac
5. Jacob
6. Joseph

CHAPTERS 1–5

How many days did it take God to create the whole universe and everything in it?

Six, 24-hour days (Gen. 1:31–2:3).

What was God's assessment of creation when He looked upon it?

It was very good (Gen. 1:31).

In what way were Adam and Eve made different than the animals?

They were made in the image of God (Gen. 1:26–27).

How did God create Eve?

He caused a deep sleep to fall upon Adam and made Eve from one of his ribs (Gen. 2:21–22).

What are the three kinds of trees that God placed in the Garden of Eden?

1. Trees that were pleasant to the sight and good for food.

2. The tree of life.

3. The tree of the knowledge of good and evil (Gen. 2:9).

What was God's command to Adam regarding the trees?

Adam could eat of every tree of the garden, except for the tree of the knowledge of good and evil (Gen. 2:16–17).

What was the consequence if Adam disobeyed God by eating of the tree of the knowledge of good and evil?

Death (Gen. 2:17).

Whom did Satan deceive: Adam or Eve?

Eve (Gen. 3:1–6).

What was the lie that Satan told Eve?

"You will not surely die" (Gen. 3:4).

What did Eve observe when she looked at the tree of the knowledge of good and evil?

1. It was good for food.

2. It was pleasant to the eyes.

3. It was a tree desirable to make one wise (Gen. 3:6).

How was the serpent cursed?

He would travel on his belly, and be bruised by the Seed of the woman (Gen. 3:14–15).

How was the woman cursed?

She would experience pain in childbirth, and be ruled by her imperfect husband (Gen. 3:16).[20]

How was the man cursed?

He would find his work to be more toilsome, because God had cursed the ground for his sake (Gen. 3:17–19).

Where did God send the man and the woman after the fall?

He sent them out of the Garden of Eden (Gen. 3:23–24).

Who said, "Am I my brother's keeper?"

Cain (Gen. 4:9).

Why did Cain kill Abel?

Because Abel's works were righteous and his own were evil (Gen. 4:3–8; 1 John 3:12).

What did Cain say about the judgment that God brought upon him?

"My punishment is greater than I can bear" (Gen. 4:13–14).

Who took the place of Abel?

Seth (Gen. 4:25).

20. It should be noted that the woman was originally created to be a helper comparable to the man (Gen. 2:18), so it would be wrong to infer from this text that wives are only under the authority of their husbands because of the fall. Rather, Eve's punishment was that her husband, being fallen, would no longer rule over her with perfect wisdom and love; yet she would be obligated to submit to him anyway. This is consistent with the teaching of the Apostle Paul, who would not "permit a woman to teach or to have authority over a man," citing both Eve's place in the created order (1 Tim. 2:13), as well as her sin (v14).

Why did Enoch not see death?

Because he walked with God (Gen. 5:24; Heb. 11:5).

How old was Methuselah when he died?

Nine hundred and sixty-nine years old (Gen. 5:27).

What did Noah's father say at his birth?

"This one will comfort us concerning our work and the toil of our hands, because of the ground which the Lord has cursed" (Gen. 5:29).

CHAPTERS 6–10

How old was Noah when the flood came?

Six hundred years old (Gen. 7:6).

How old was Noah when he died?

Nine hundred and fifty years old (Gen. 9:29).

What was the behavior of the people in Noah's day?

Their wickedness was great, and their thoughts were evil continually (Gen. 6:5).

What was Noah's moral character?

He was a just man who walked with God (Gen. 6:9).

How many people survived the flood?

Eight people: Noah, his three sons, his wife, and his sons' wives (Gen. 7:7, 13).[21]

How long were Noah and his family in the ark?

One year and ten days (Gen. 7:11; 8:13–19).

Where did the ark come to rest?

On the mountains of Ararat (Gen. 8:4).

What did the dove bring back when Noah sent it out the second time?

A freshly plucked olive leaf (Gen. 8:11).

What did Noah do as soon as he came out of the ark?

He built an altar and offered sacrifices to God (Gen. 8:20).

What covenant did God make with Noah after the flood?

He promised to never again destroy all flesh with a flood (Gen. 9:8–11).

What was the sign of God's covenant with Noah?

The rainbow (Gen. 9:12–17).

What was the curse put upon Ham's son, Canaan?

He would be a "servant of servants" to his brothers (Gen. 9:25–27).

21. See also 1 Pet. 3:20.

Who was Nimrod?

He was "a mighty hunter before the Lord" (Gen. 10:9).

Who led the construction of the Tower of Babel?

Nimrod (Gen. 10:10).

CHAPTERS 11–15

Why did the people start building the Tower of Babel?

They wanted to make a name for themselves (Gen. 11:4).

Who said, "Come let Us go down and there confuse their language, that they may not understand one another's speech"?

The Lord (Gen. 11:6–7).

What did God say when He called Abram?

He told Abram to leave his father's country and journey to a land that He would show him. He promised to bless Abram, make of him a great nation, and bless all the families of the earth through him (Gen. 12:1–3).

Why did Abram go to Egypt?

Because there was a famine in the land (Gen. 12:10).

What sin did Abram commit in Egypt?

Fearing for his life, Abram told Sarai to say that she was his sister (Gen. 12:11–13).

What was the conflict between Abram and Lot?

They each had so much livestock that the land was not able to support them both (Gen. 13:6–7).

What did Abram propose in order to resolve the conflict?

That he and Lot separate (Gen. 13:8–9).

What was the first thing Abram did when he moved to Hebron?

He built an altar there to the Lord (Gen. 13:18).

Who was Melchizedek, King of Salem?

He was the priest of God Most High (Gen. 14:18).

What did the king of Sodom offer Abram?

The plunder of Sodom (Gen. 14:21).

Finish the verse: "Do not be afraid, Abram ..."

"I am your shield, your exceedingly great reward" (Gen. 15:1).

CHAPTERS 16–20

What did Sarai tell Abram to do in order to have children?

She told him to take her maid, Hagar, as his wife (Gen. 16:2).

How did Sarai treat her maid, Hagar?

She dealt harshly with her (Gen. 16:6).

What was the name of Hagar's child?

Ishmael (Gen. 16:15).

What kind of a man did God say Ishmael would be?

A wild man (Gen. 16:12).

Why did God change Abram's name to Abraham?

Because of His promise to make of Abraham "a father of many nations" (Gen. 17:5).

How old were Abraham and Sarah when God told them that they would have a son?

Abraham was one hundred years old and Sarah was ninety (Gen. 17:17, 24).

What was Sarah's reaction when God announced that she would have a child in her old age?

She laughed within herself (Gen. 18:12).

What did Abraham name the son that Sarah bore to him?

Isaac (Gen. 21:3).

What does the name "Isaac" mean?

"He laughs."

How old were Abraham and Ishmael when they were both circumcised?

Abraham was ninety-nine, and Ishmael was thirteen (Gen. 17:24–25).

What was God's purpose for Abraham's life?

That he would command his descendants to keep the way of the Lord (Gen. 18:19).

How many righteous people in Sodom would have been sufficient to spare the city?

Ten (Gen. 18:32).

How did God warn Lot about the destruction of Sodom?

He sent two angels into the city (Gen. 19:1, 12–13).

What did the angels do to the evil men who were trying to break into Lot's house?

They struck them with blindness (Gen. 19:11).

What happened to Lot's wife when she looked back?

She became a pillar of salt (Gen. 19:26).

What were the names of the sons of Lot's daughters, and what nations descended from them?

Moab, the father of the Moabites, and Ben-Ammi, the father of the Ammonites (Gen. 19:36–38).

What did Abraham do while he was staying in Gerar?

He told everyone that Sarah was his sister (Gen. 20:2).

In what way did God punish Abimelech for taking Sarah to himself?

He closed up all the wombs of Abimelech's household (Gen. 20:17–18).

CHAPTERS 21–25

What was Ishmael's skill?

Archery (Gen. 21:20).

Where was Sarah buried after her death?

In the cave of the field of Machpelah, in the land of Canaan (Gen. 23:19).

How did Abraham find a wife for Isaac?

He sent his oldest servant to his own country, to find a wife for Isaac there (Gen. 24:2–4).

What was the test that Abraham's servant created to help him find a wife for Isaac?

He asked the Lord to show him the right woman by her offering to give his camels a drink (Gen. 24:12–14).

What did Rebekah's brother and mother say when they blessed her?

"Our sister, may you become
The mother of thousands of ten thousands;
And may your descendants possess
The gates of those who hate them" (Gen. 24:60).

How old was Isaac when he got married?

Forty years old (Gen. 25:20).

Who was Isaac's favorite son?

Esau (Gen. 25:28).

Who was Rebekah's favorite son?

Jacob (Gen. 25:28).

CHAPTERS 26–40

Which son received the blessing, and how did he obtain it?

Jacob received the blessing by deceiving his father, Isaac (Gen. 27:1–29).

Why did Simeon and Levi kill the Shechemites?

Because Shechem had violated their sister, Dinah (Gen. 34:2, 31).

What did Jacob give to Joseph that caused his brothers to hate him?

A tunic of many colors (Gen. 37:3–4).

What did Jacob's other sons call Joseph when he came to see them?

"This dreamer" (Gen. 37:19).

What did Joseph dream about the first time?

He dreamed that he and his brothers were all binding sheaves in the field, and that his brothers' sheaves all bowed down to his own sheaf (Gen. 37:7).

What did Joseph dream about the second time?

He dreamed that the sun, the moon, and the eleven stars all bowed down to him (Gen. 37:9).

What did Jacob's other sons do to Joseph?

They stripped him of his tunic, cast him into a pit, and then sold him into slavery (Gen. 37:23–28).

How old was Joseph when his brothers threw him into the pit?

Seventeen years old (Gen. 37:2).

Which one of Jacob's sons tried to save Joseph?

Reuben (Gen. 37:21–22).

Why wasn't Reuben able to save Joseph from being sold into slavery?

Because Joseph's other brothers sold him while Reuben was away (Gen. 37:28–30).

How much money did Joseph's brothers sell him for?

Twenty shekels of silver (Gen. 37:28).

What did Jacob's other sons do with Joseph's multi-colored coat?

They dipped it in the blood of a goat, to make Jacob think that a wild animal had devoured Joseph (Gen. 37:31).

What did God do to Judah's sons, Er and Onan?

He killed them (Gen. 38:7–10).

To whom did the Ishmaelites sell Joseph?

Potiphar, the captain of Pharaoh's guard (Gen. 39:1).

To what position did Potiphar promote Joseph?

Overseer of his house (Gen. 39:4).

Why did Potiphar promote Joseph?

He saw that the Lord was with him, and caused everything he did to prosper (Gen. 39:3).

What was Joseph's life like in prison?

The Lord gave him favor in the sight of the keeper of the prison, who committed all the other prisoners to Joseph's hand (Gen. 39:21–23).

Who was in prison with Joseph?

Two of Pharaoh's officers: the chief butler and the chief baker (Gen. 40:1–4).

What did Pharaoh's butler dream about?

He dreamed that he was pressing grapes into Pharaoh's cup from a vine that had three branches, and giving the wine to Pharaoh (Gen. 40:9–11).

What did Pharaoh's baker dream about?

He dreamed that he had three baskets full of baked goods on his head, which the birds ate (Gen. 40:16–17).

How long after the cupbearer's release from prison did he tell Pharaoh about Joseph?

Two years (Gen. 40:23–41:1, 9–13).

CHAPTERS 41–45

What caused the cupbearer to remember Joseph?

Pharaoh's dreams, which his magicians and wise men were unable to interpret (Gen. 41:8–9).

What happened in Pharaoh's first dream?

He was standing by the river when suddenly seven fat cows came out of the water. Then seven thin and ugly cows came out and ate up the fat cows, but remained just as thin and ugly as before (Gen. 41:17–21).

What happened in Pharaoh's second dream?

He saw seven heads of grain grow up healthy, which were then devoured by seven withered and thin heads (Gen. 41:22–24).

What was Joseph's advice to Pharaoh?

That he set a wise man over the land of Egypt, and collect food to prepare for the seven years of famine (Gen. 41:33–36).

How much food did Joseph tell Pharaoh to gather during the seven plentiful years?

One-fifth of the produce of the land (Gen. 41:34).

Why did Pharaoh promote Joseph over his house and people?

He recognized that the Spirit of God was in Joseph, and that no one was as discerning and wise as him (Gen. 41:38–39).

How old was Joseph when Pharaoh put him in power?

Thirty years old (Gen. 41:46).

Why did Joseph name his first son "Manasseh"?

Because God had made him forget all his toil and all his father's house (Gen. 41:51).

Why did Joseph name his second son "Ephraim"?

Because God had caused him to be fruitful in the land of his affliction (Gen. 41:52).

Why did Jacob send his sons to Egypt?

Because the famine was severe, and he had heard that there was grain in Egypt (Gen. 41:56–42:2).

Why didn't Jacob send Benjamin with them?

He feared that some calamity might befall him (Gen. 42:4).

What did Joseph do to his brothers when they came to Egypt?

He accused them of spying, demanded that they bring their youngest brother to him, imprisoned them, bound Simeon, filled their sacks, and sent them home to get Benjamin (Gen. 42).

What did Joseph's brothers find in their sacks on the way home?

Their money (Gen. 42:27–28).

Who was Jacob speaking of when he said, "But his bow remained in strength"?

Joseph (Gen. 49:22–24).

How long did the Egyptians mourn Jacob's death?

Seventy days in Egypt (Gen. 50:3), and then seven more days in Canaan (Gen. 50:10).

How did Joseph respond to his brothers when they feared his revenge?

He comforted and spoke kindly to them, pointing to the good that God had accomplished through their evil actions (Gen. 50:19–21).

How many generations of Ephraim's children did Joseph see?

Three generations (Gen. 50:23).

How old was Joseph when he died?

One hundred and ten years old (Gen. 50:26).

When I See the Blood

WORDS and MUSIC: John G. Foote, *pub.* 1892; *alt. by* E. A. H, *pub.* 1909. Public Domain

for more resources go to ***jttb.co/exodus***

4004 B.C.
Creation

2000 B.C.
Abraham

1000 B.C.
David

586 B.C.
Nebuchadnezzar

Flood
2348 B.C.

Exodus
1445 B.C.

Sennacherib
722 B.C.

Birth of Christ
5 B.C.

Journey through

Exodus

THEME

Deliverance

AUTHOR

Moses

TIME OF WRITING

1445–1405 B.C.

MEMORY VERSES

5 *And I have also heard the groaning of the children of Israel whom the Egyptians keep in bondage, and I have remembered My covenant.*

6 *Therefore say to the children of Israel: "I am the Lord; I will bring you out from under the burdens of the Egyptians, I will rescue you from their bondage, and I will redeem you with an outstretched arm and with great judgments."*

Exodus 6:5–6

OVERVIEW

Exodus displays the primary biblical imagery for deliverance from bondage. Someone once said that when God wants to change history, he does not start with a battle, he starts with a baby. The book of Exodus opens with a people in bondage and the birth of a baby - Moses.

Exodus declares the doctrines of enslavement, deliverance, judgment, revelation, law, worship, Sabbath, and covenant. The Exodus is the premier symbol of redemption in the Old Testament as the cross is the symbol in the New Testament. Exodus presents the gospel before the law and the Passover tells of the efficacy of the shedding of blood. The book of Exodus centers around three main events and locations: the Passover in Egypt, the crossing through the Red Sea in the wilderness, and the giving of the law on Mount Sinai.

Top 5 Facts to Remember

1. God delivered His people from their bondage with the purpose that they would serve Him.[1]
2. God raised up Pharaoh to demonstrate His power in him.[2]
3. For the children of Israel, redemption came *before* the giving of the Law.[3]
4. The Israelites quickly turned to worshipping a golden calf, and as a result, three thousand of them died.[4]
5. God gave very detailed instructions about how Israel was to worship Him.[5]

Theme: Deliverance

In Exodus, God is glorifying Himself as the *Deliverer* so that He might demonstrate His superior goodness in the salvation sinners, the damnation of the wicked, and for the preservation of His people for His eternal glory, and their eternal joy.

Author: Moses

The clear and consistent teaching of Scripture is that Moses wrote the Pentateuch (Genesis, Exodus, Leviticus, Numbers, and Deuteronomy). For more information on Pentateuchal authorship, see the authorship section for *Genesis*.

1. Ex. 7:16; 8:1, 20; 9:1, 13; 10:3.
2. Ex. 9:16; Rom. 9:17.
3. Ex. 14:30; 20:1–17.
4. Ex. 32.
5. Ex. 25–31; 34–40.

Time of Writing: 1445–1405 B.C.

Exodus was written sometime between Israel's Exodus from Egypt (1445 B.C.)[6] and Moses' death (1405 B.C.). Exodus records events that took place near the end of Moses' life,[7] making 1445–1405 B.C. the most likely time of writing.

Key Verses

"I will make a difference between My people and your people. Tomorrow this sign shall be."

Exodus 8:23

"Then Moses called for all the elders of Israel and said to them, 'Pick out and take lambs for yourselves according to your families, and kill the Passover lamb. And you shall take a bunch of hyssop, dip it in the blood that is in the basin, and strike the lintel and the two doorposts with the blood that is in the basin. And none of you shall go out of the door of his house until morning. For the Lord will pass through to strike the Egyptians; and when He sees the blood on the lintel and on the two doorposts, the Lord will pass over the door and not allow the destroyer to come into your houses to strike you.' "

Exodus 12:21–23

"And the Lord went before them by day in a pillar of cloud to lead the way, and by night in a pillar of fire to give them light, so as to go by day and night."

Exodus 13:21

6. For more on how these dates are calculated, see "Time of Events" at the back of this book.
7. For instance, Ex. 16:35 records Israel's wandering in the wilderness for 40 years. Therefore, Exodus must have been written after these years of wandering were completed (no earlier than 1445–1405 B.C., the same year that Moses died).

"Now therefore, if you will indeed obey My voice and keep My covenant, then you shall be a special treasure to Me above all people; for all the earth is Mine."

Exodus 19:5

"Now the Lord descended in the cloud and stood with him there, and proclaimed the name of the Lord. And the Lord passed before him and proclaimed, 'The Lord, the Lord God, merciful and gracious, longsuffering, and abounding in goodness and truth, keeping mercy for thousands, forgiving iniquity and transgression and sin, by no means clearing the guilty, visiting the iniquity of the fathers upon the children and the children's children to the third and the fourth generation.'"

Exodus 34:5–7

Lessons

1. For the Israelites, redemption came before the giving of the Law. This is symbolic of the way that God has always saved His people. Justification always precedes sanctification.

2. We should always be ready to repent and run from idolatry. Idolatry causes severe and often irreversible damage. If you play with idols, they will destroy you.

3. God is a better Master than Pharaoh. Pharaoh is a picture of Satan. He doesn't let you rest, he oppresses you, he demands bricks without giving you any straw, but God is a better Master. He says, "Come to Me, all you who labor and are heavy laden, and I will give you rest. Take My yoke upon you and learn from Me, for I am gentle and lowly in heart, and you will find rest for your souls. For My yoke is easy and My burden is light" (Matt. 11:28–30).

Christ in Exodus

I. Moses

In many ways, Moses is a type of Christ. As infants, both Moses and Jesus were saved from the mass-murder plots of civil leaders.[8] Like Moses, Jesus came to deliver God's people from slavery.[9] Like Moses, Jesus performed miracles. Like Moses, Jesus acted as a lawgiver. As Moses interceded for Israel, Jesus now intercedes on behalf of the church.[10]

II. The Passover Lamb

Christ's death was pictured in the killing of the Passover lamb more than 1,400 years before it took place.[11] According to Paul, Christ is "our Passover" (1 Cor. 5:7). Just as the blood of a lamb saved the firstborn children from death in the plague, so the blood of Jesus Christ, the Lamb of God, saved His people from God's wrath. Just as the Lord passed over the houses of the Hebrews, so He also "passed over the sins that were previously committed," justifying "the one who has faith in Jesus" (Rom. 3:25–26).

III. Other Types of Christ

1. Israel's Deliverance from Slavery
2. The Manna
3. The Water from the Rock
4. The Tabernacle
5. The High Priest

8. Ex. 1:22–2:10; Matt. 2:13–18.
9. Ex. 3:9–10; Rom. 6:5–7, 18.
10. Ex. 32:9–14; 1 Tim. 2:5; 1 John 2:1.
11. Ex. 12:3–7.

Outline

I. **Redemption: Deliverance from Bondage (Ex. 1–18)**

A. The Call of Moses and God's Showdown with Pharaoh (Ex. 1–11)

B. The Passover and the Deliverance from Bondage (Ex. 12–13)

C. The Crossing of the Red Sea and Deliverance from Death (Ex. 14–18)

II. **Revelation from God: Instructions from Sinai (Ex. 19–40)**

A. The Giving of the Law and the Deliverance from the World, the Flesh, and the Devil (Ex. 19–34)

B. The Construction of the Tabernacle and the Worship of God (Ex. 35–40)

Study Questions

CHAPTERS 1–5

What is the theme of the book of Exodus?

Deliverance.

What are the three major events that occur in the book of Exodus?

1. The Passover.
2. The crossing of the Red Sea.
3. The giving of the Law on Mount Sinai.

What are the two major sections that divide the book of Exodus, and what is the focus of each?

1. Chapters 1–18, which focus on Israel's deliverance from bondage.
2. Chapters 19–40, which focus on the giving of the Law at Mount Sinai.

What are the three primary geographical locations mentioned in the book of Exodus?

1. Egypt.
2. The wilderness.
3. Mount Sinai.

What happened when the Egyptians afflicted the children of Israel?

The more they afflicted them, the more they multiplied and grew (Ex. 1:12).

What was the name of Moses' father-in-law?

Jethro (Ex. 3:1).

How did the midwives disobey Pharaoh?

They refused to kill the male Hebrew children (Ex. 1:15–17).

What did God do to the midwives when they refused to obey Pharaoh?

He dealt well with them (Ex. 1:20).

Why did Moses flee Egypt?

Because Pharaoh wanted to kill him (Ex. 2:11–15).

Where did Moses live after he fled from Egypt?

Midian (Ex. 2:15).

How did God appear to Moses when he was in Horeb?

In a burning bush (Ex. 3:2).

What was the Lord's response when Moses objected to God's command by saying he was "slow of speech and slow of tongue"?

"Who has made man's mouth? Or who makes the mute, the deaf, the seeing, or the blind? Have not I, the Lord? Now therefore, go, and I will be with your mouth and teach you what you shall say" (Ex. 4:11–12).

Who did God appoint as a spokesman for Moses?

Aaron, his brother (Ex. 4:14–16).

What did the Lord seek to do to Moses at the encampment?

He sought to kill him (Ex. 4:24).

What did Zipporah (Moses' wife) do and say to him when she was angry?

She circumcised her son, and said to Moses, "Surely you are a husband of blood to me" (Ex. 4:24–26).

How did Pharaoh make the work harder for the children of Israel?

He stopped giving them straw to make brick, and demanded that they produce the same number of bricks as before (Ex. 5:7–8).

CHAPTERS 6–15

What was Moses and Aaron's message to Pharaoh?

That he should send the children of Israel out of his land (Ex. 7:2).

What did God say He would do when Moses and Aaron delivered the message to Pharaoh?

He would harden Pharaoh's heart, and multiply His signs and wonders in the land of Egypt (Ex. 7:3).

How old were Moses and Aaron when they spoke with Pharaoh?

Moses was 80, and Aaron was 83 (Ex. 7:7).

What was the first miracle that Moses and Aaron performed before Pharaoh?

Aaron cast down his rod, and it became a serpent (Ex. 7:10).

What did Pharaoh command his sorcerers and wise men to do in response?

To cause their rods to become serpents, like Aaron's rod (Ex. 7:11–12).

What did Aaron's serpent do to the other serpents?

It swallowed them (Ex. 7:12).

How many plagues did God send upon Egypt?

Ten.

What were the ten plagues?

1. Water turned to blood (Ex. 7:14–25).
2. Frogs (Ex. 8:1–15).
3. Lice (Ex. 8:16–19).
4. Flies (Ex. 8:20–32).
5. Livestock diseased (Ex. 9:1–7).
6. Boils (Ex. 9:8–12).
7. Hail (Ex. 9:13–35).

8. Locusts (Ex. 10:1–20).

9. Darkness (Ex. 10:21–29).

10. The death of the firstborn (Ex. 11; 12:29–30).

Where was blood found during the first plague?

Throughout all the land of Egypt, even in buckets and pitchers (Ex. 7:19).

Where were the frogs found during the second plague?

In Pharaoh's house, in his bedroom, on his bed, in the houses of his servants, on his people, in his ovens, and in his kneading bowls (Ex. 8:3–4).

Where did the lice come from for the third plague?

God formed them from the dust of the land (Ex. 8:17).

Where did the flies infest during the fourth plague?

Pharaoh's house, his servants' houses, and all the land of Egypt (Ex. 8:24).

What happened to the livestock of Egypt during the fifth plague?

All of them died (Ex. 9:6).

What happened to the livestock of the children of Israel during the fifth plague?

Not one died (Ex. 9:6).

What happened to the people and animals of Egypt during the sixth plague?

They broke out in boils (Ex. 9:10).

What did God send on the land of Egypt for the seventh plague?

Thunder, hail, and fire (Ex. 9:23–25).

What did the servants of Pharaoh who feared the Lord do when they heard that God would send hail on the land?

They made their servants and livestock flee to the houses (Ex. 9:20).

Was there any hail where the children of Israel lived?

No (Ex. 9:26).

Why did God continue to harden Pharaoh's heart when he heard about the tenth plague?

To show His power, and declare His name in all the earth (Ex. 9:16).

What did the locusts do to the land of Egypt during the eighth plague?

They covered the face of the whole land, and ate everything green which had survived the hail (Ex. 10:14–15).

What happened when darkness came upon the land of Egypt?

The Egyptians could not see one another, nor did anyone rise from his place (Ex. 10:22–23).

During the plague of darkness, what was different about the place where the children of Israel lived?

They all had light in their dwellings (Ex. 10:23).

What was the last plague that God placed upon Egypt?

He struck all the firstborn in the land of Egypt (Ex. 12:29).

Why did God continue to harden Pharaoh's heart when he was informed of the tenth plague?

To multiply His wonders in the land of Egypt (Ex. 11:9).

How were the Israelites supposed to dress and act when they ate the Passover meal?

Each person was to eat the Passover with a belt on his waist, his sandals on his feet, and his staff in his hand (Ex. 12:11).

How did God command the Israelites to celebrate the Passover?

He commanded the Hebrews and their children to observe it as an ordinance forever, to remind them of their deliverance from Egypt (Ex. 12:24–27).

What kinds of animal could the children of Israel use for the Passover?

Either a sheep or a goat (Ex. 12:5).

What did the Hebrews do with the blood of the lambs?

They put it on the doorposts and lintel of their houses (Ex. 12:7, 22).

What happened when the Lord saw the blood on the houses of the children of Israel?

He passed over them, and did not kill their firstborn (Ex. 12:13).

What was the extent of the death of the firstborn during the tenth plague?

There was not a house without someone dead (Ex. 12:29–30).

How many Hebrews left Egypt with Moses?

600,000 men, besides women and children (Ex. 12:37).

How many of Jacob's descendants came to Egypt originally?

Seventy persons (Ex. 1:5).

Why did God lead the children of Israel around the land of the Philistines?

He knew they would change their minds when they saw war, and return to Egypt (Ex. 13:17).

How did God lead the children of Israel in the way they were supposed to go?

He went before them in a pillar of cloud by day, and a pillar of fire by night (Ex. 13:21–22).

Why did God harden Pharaoh's heart after the children of Israel left Egypt?

To gain honor over Pharaoh and his army, so the Egyptians would know that He is the Lord (Ex. 14:4).

What did the children of Israel say to Moses when they saw Pharaoh and his army drawing near to them?

They accused him of leading them into the wilderness to die (Ex. 14:10–12).

What did Moses say to the Israelites when Pharaoh and his army were drawing near?

He told them to stand still, and see the salvation of the Lord (Ex. 14:13–14).

What did God command Moses to do to the Red Sea?

To divide the sea with his rod (Ex. 14:16).

Why did God cause the Egyptians to pursue the children of Israel through the Red Sea?

To gain honor over Pharaoh and his army, so the Egyptians would know that He is the Lord (Ex. 14:17–18).

What did God do to the Egyptian chariots as they pursued the children of Israel?

He took off their wheels (Ex. 14:25).

How did the children of Israel respond after the crossing of the Red Sea, and the traumatic death of Pharaoh and the Egyptian army?

They feared the Lord, and believed Him and His servant Moses (Ex. 14:31).

What did Moses and the Israelites do after the crossing of the Red Sea?

They sang a song to the Lord (Ex. 15:1–21).

What difficulty did the Israelites face when they entered the Wilderness of Shur and Marah?

They couldn't find any fresh water to drink (Ex. 15:22–23).

What does the name, "Marah" mean?

"Bitter" (Ex. 15:23).

What did the Lord do at Marah to make the water drinkable?

He showed Moses a tree, which he cast into the waters, and made them sweet (Ex. 15:25).

What was God's promise to the children of Israel concerning the plagues He had brought upon Egypt?

If they obeyed Him, He would put none of those diseases on them (Ex. 15:26).

CHAPTERS 16–20

What was the manna like that God gave to the children of Israel?

It was a small round substance, as fine as frost on the ground (Ex. 16:14). It was like white coriander seed, and the taste of it was like wafers made with honey (Ex. 16:31).

Why did God give the children of Israel manna?

To test them, to see whether they would walk in His law or not (Ex. 16:4).

What other food source did God give the children of Israel?

Quails (Ex. 16:13).

How many days per week did God provide the manna?

Six days a week (Ex. 16:26).

What happened to the manna if it was left overnight?

It bred worms and stank (Ex. 16:20).

How long did God provide the manna?

Forty years, until the Israelites came to the land of Canaan (Ex. 16:35).

What happened at the place that became known as Massah and Meribah?

The people complained because there was no water to drink, so Moses struck the rock in Horeb, which caused water to flow from it (Ex. 17:1–7).

What did Moses do that determined whether Israel or Amalek prevailed?

When he held up his hand, Israel prevailed; and when he let down his hand, Amalek prevailed (Ex. 17:11–12).

What advice did Jethro give to Moses when he saw his heavy responsibility?

He told Moses to judge the great matters himself, and appoint able men to judge the small matters (Ex. 18:21–22).

What did God promise the Israelites at Mt. Sinai on the condition that they obeyed Him?

They would be a special treasure to Him above all people (Ex. 19:5).

What was Israel's response to God?

"All that the Lord has spoken we will do" (Ex. 19:8).

Which chapter records the first giving of the Ten Commandments?

Chapter 20.

What are the Ten Commandments, in order?

1. You shall have no other gods before Me (v. 3).
2. You shall not make for yourself a carved image (vv. 4–6).
3. You shall not take the name of the Lord your God in vain (v. 7).
4. Remember the Sabbath day, to keep it holy (vv. 8–11).
5. Honor your father and your mother (v. 12).
6. You shall not murder (v. 13).
7. You shall not commit adultery (v. 14).
8. You shall not steal (v. 15).
9. You shall not bear false witness against your neighbor (v. 16).
10. You shall not covet your neighbor's house (v. 17).

What kind of altar did God command the Israelites to build?

An altar of either earth or stone, but not hewn stone (Ex. 20:24–25).

CHAPTERS 21–40

What effect does a bribe have on people?

It blinds the discerning and perverts the words of the righteous (Ex. 23:8).

Who did God appoint to minister as priests?

Aaron and his sons: Nadab, Abihu, Eleazar, and Ithamar (Ex. 28:1).

What was engraved on the golden plate fastened to Aaron's turban?

"Holiness to the Lord" (Ex. 28:36–38).

Why was Bezalel such a skilled craftsman?

Because he was filled with the Spirit of God (Ex. 31:2–5).

Why did the children of Israel ask Aaron to make gods for them?

Because they saw that Moses was delayed in coming down from the mountain (Ex. 32:1).

Who led the effort to make the golden calf?

Aaron did (Ex. 32:2–4).

How did Aaron make the golden calf?

He told all the people to give him their golden earrings, which he melted down and molded into a calf (Ex. 32:2–4).

What did Aaron say about the golden calf he created?

"This is your god, O Israel, that brought you out of the land of Egypt" (Ex. 32:4).

What was the Lord's response when the children of Israel turned to idolatry?

He told Moses that He would consume the people, and make a great nation of him instead (Ex. 32:7–10).

What was Moses' plea to God?

He begged Him to spare the people, and remember the oath that He had sworn to Abraham, Isaac, and Israel (Ex. 32:11–13).

What was the Lord's response after Moses pleaded with Him?

He relented from the harm which He said He would do to His people (Ex. 32:14).

What were the Ten Commandments written on?

Two tablets of stone (Ex. 32:15; 34:4, 28).

Who wrote the Ten Commandments?

God did (Ex. 32:16).

What was Moses' response when he saw the golden calf and the people dancing?

He became angry, and broke the two tablets of stone (Ex. 32:19).

What was the name of the tent that God commanded Moses to set up outside the camp?

The tabernacle of meeting (Ex. 33:7).

What happened when Moses entered the tabernacle?

The pillar of cloud descended and stood at the door of the tabernacle, and the Lord talked with Moses (Ex. 33:9).

What did God say about His character when Moses went up on Mt. Sinai the second time?

"The Lord, the Lord God, merciful and gracious, longsuffering, and abounding in goodness and truth, keeping mercy for thousands, forgiving iniquity and transgression and sin, by no means clearing the guilty, visiting the iniquity of the fathers upon the children and the children's children to the third and the fourth generation" (Ex. 34:6–7).

What did God say when Moses asked to see His glory?

He told Moses that he could see His back, but not His face (Ex. 33:19–23).

How did the people respond when Moses came down from Mt. Sinai with the new tablets?

They were afraid to come near him, because the skin of his face shone (Ex. 34:29–30).

What did Moses do to his face when he spoke with the people?

He put a veil over it (Ex. 34:33–35).

Who were the master craftsmen chosen by God to build the tabernacle?

Bezalel the son of Uri, and Aholiab the son of Ahisamach (Ex. 35:30–35).

What happened when the cloud that covered the tabernacle was taken up?

The children of Israel would travel onward (Ex. 40:36).

Holy, Holy, Holy

WORDS: Reginald Heber, 1826. MUSIC: “Nicaea”; John B. Dykes, *pub.* 1861. Public Domain.

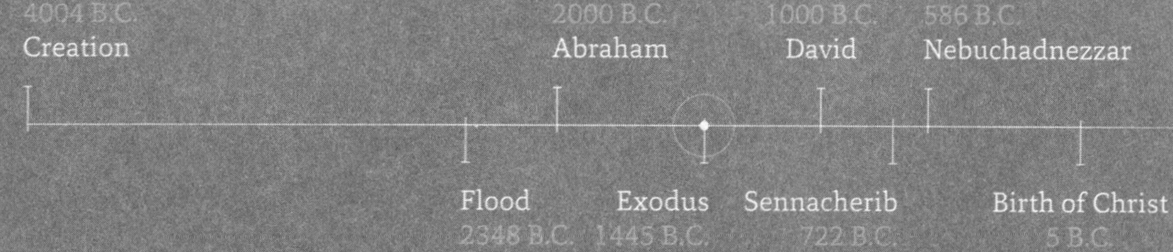

Journey through

Leviticus

THEME	AUTHOR	TIME OF WRITING
Holiness	Moses	1445–1405 B.C.

MEMORY VERSE

"And you shall be holy to Me, for I the Lord am holy, and have separated you from the peoples, that you should be Mine."

Leviticus 20:26

OVERVIEW

In Exodus, Moses instructed the Israelites *where* to worship, but Leviticus tells them *how* to worship. Exodus begins with enslaved sinners, but Leviticus begins with saved saints. In Leviticus, we encounter the doctrine of holiness: holy clothing, holy sacrifices, holy places, holy days, holy law, and a holy nation.

There are two kinds of holiness: personal holiness relating to sin, illustrated by the sacrifice of animals for the forgiveness of sin, and personal holiness relating to lifestyle, illustrated by living differently from neighboring nations to signify their separateness as a chosen nation.

Top 5 Facts to Remember

1. God commanded the children of Israel to offer five kinds of offerings: (1) the burnt offering, (2) the grain offering, (3) the peace offering, (4) the sin offering, and (5) the trespass offering.

2. Animals that were sacrificed to God had to be "without blemish."

3. The Israelites were commanded to observe seven feasts: (1) the Passover, (2) the Feast of Unleavened Bread, (3) the Feast of Firstfruits, (4) the Feast of Weeks, (5) the Feast of Trumpets, (6) the Day of Atonement, and (7) the Feast of Tabernacles.

4. The Lord killed Nadab and Abihu (two of Aaron's sons) for worshipping in a way that He had not commanded them (Lev. 10:1–2).

5. Leviticus 19:18, "You shall love your neighbor as yourself," was cited by our Lord. He called it the second greatest commandment (Matt. 22:34–40; Mark 12:29–31).

Theme: Holiness

In Leviticus, God is glorifying Himself as *holy* so that He might demonstrate His superior goodness in the salvation sinners, the damnation of the wicked, and for the preservation of His people for His eternal glory, and their eternal joy.

Author: Moses

The clear and consistent teaching of Scripture is that Moses wrote the Pentateuch (Genesis, Exodus, Leviticus, Numbers, and Deuteronomy). For more information on Pentateuchal authorship, see the authorship section for *Genesis*.

Time of Writing: 1445–1405 B.C.

Leviticus was written sometime between Israel's Exodus from Egypt (1445 B.C.)[1] and Moses' death (1405 B.C.).

1. For more on how these dates are calculated, see "Time of Events" at the back of this book.

Key Verses

"And Moses said to Aaron, 'Go to the altar, offer your sin offering and your burnt offering, and make atonement for yourself and for the people. Offer the offering of the people, and make atonement for them, as the Lord commanded.' "

Leviticus 9:7

"Then Nadab and Abihu, the sons of Aaron, each took his censer and put fire in it, put incense on it, and offered profane fire before the Lord, which He had not commanded them. So fire went out from the Lord and devoured them, and they died before the Lord."

Leviticus 10:1–2

"For I am the Lord your God. You shall therefore consecrate yourselves, and you shall be holy; for I am holy. Neither shall you defile yourselves with any creeping thing that creeps on the earth."

Leviticus 11:44

"For the life of the flesh is in the blood, and I have given it to you upon the altar to make atonement for your souls; for it is the blood that makes atonement for the soul."

Leviticus 17:11

Lessons

1. Due to our sinfulness, there is an infinite gap between God and man. Only the shed blood of Jesus Christ can bridge that gap.
2. Substitutionary atonement is the basis of our fellowship with God.
3. Worshipping in the way God has prescribed is often costly.

Christ in Leviticus

I. The High Priest

In Leviticus 16, the Lord gave Moses very detailed instructions about how the high priest would atone for the sins of the people. Once a year, on the Day of Atonement, the high priest would enter the Holy Place with sweet incense and the blood of sacrificed animals. The author of Hebrews explained the fulfillment of this picture in Christ: "But Christ came as High Priest of the good things to come ... For Christ has not entered the holy places made with hands, which are copies of the true, but into heaven itself, now to appear in the presence of God for us; not that He should offer Himself often, as the high priest enters the Most Holy Place every year with blood of another—He then would have had to suffer often since the foundation of the world; but now, once at the end of the ages, He has appeared to put away sin by the sacrifice of Himself" (Heb. 9:11, 24–26).

II. The Five Sacrifices

The five sacrifices which the Israelites were commanded to offer—the burnt offering,[2] the grain offering,[3] the peace offering,[4] the sin offering,[5] and the trespass offering[6]—were all given as symbols of Christ's sacrifice for the elect. The Apostle Paul taught this when he encouraged the Ephesians to "walk in love, as Christ also has loved us and given Himself for us, an offering and a sacrifice to God for a sweet-smelling aroma" (Eph. 5:2).

2. Lev. 1; 6:8–13; 7:8.
3. Lev. 2; 6:14–23; 7:9–10.
4. Lev. 3; 7:11–21, 28–34.
5. Lev. 4; 6:24–30.
6. Lev. 5; 7:1–7.

III. The Seven Feasts

The seven feasts which the Israelites were commanded to observe—the Passover,[7] the Feast of Unleavened Bread,[8] the Feast of Firstfruits,[9] the Feast of Weeks,[10] the Feast of Trumpets,[11] the Day of Atonement,[12] and the Feast of Tabernacles[13]—are all symbolic of the spiritual feast that Christians have in Christ. Jesus Himself said, "I am the living bread which came down from heaven. If anyone eats of this bread, he will live forever; and the bread that I shall give is My flesh, which I shall give for the life of the world" (John 6:51).

Outline

I. **Sacrifice: How One Obtains Fellowship with God (Lev. 1–17)**

- A. Laws on Offerings (Lev. 1–7)
- B. The Mediator (Lev. 8–10)
- C. Purification – Laws on Ritual Impurity (Lev. 11–15)
- D. Propitiation – The Day of Atonement (Lev. 16)
- E. Blood Sacrifice – Life Is in the Blood (Lev. 17)

II. **Sanctification: How One Maintains Fellowship with God (Lev. 18–27)**

- A. Laws on Living as a Holy People (Lev. 18–20)

7. Lev. 23:5.
8. Lev. 23:6–8.
9. Lev. 23:9–14.
10. Lev. 23:15–21.
11. Lev. 23:23–25.
12. Lev. 23:26–32.
13. Lev. 23:33–44.

B. Laws on Showing Reverence for Holy Things (Lev. 21–24)

C. Laws Anticipating Life in the Promised Land (Lev. 25–27)

Study Questions

CHAPTERS 1–10

What is the theme of Leviticus?

Holiness. There are two kinds of holiness spoken of in Leviticus:

1. Personal holiness relating to sin, illustrated by the sacrifice of animals for the forgiveness of sin.
2. Personal holiness relating to lifestyle, illustrated by living a life set apart unto God and in a way that was different than the pagan nations.

When did Moses write Leviticus?

Sometime between 1445 and 1405 B.C.

What does Leviticus teach us about sin?

The death of a substitute is necessary for the forgiveness of sins.

What does Leviticus teach us about the worship of God?

Only God's laws and standards can regulate His worship.

What is the emphasis of chapters 1–10?

Holy worship inside the tabernacle.

What is the emphasis of chapters 11–27?

Holy living outside the tabernacle.

When did the events in Leviticus occur?

After the building of the tabernacle (Lev. 1:1; cf. Ex. 40).

What were the five kinds of sacrifices that God commanded the Israelites to offer?

1. The burnt offering (Lev. 1; 6:8–13; 7:8).
2. The grain offering (Lev. 2; 6:14–23; 7:9–10).
3. The peace offering (Lev. 3; 7:11–21, 28–34).
4. The sin offering (Lev. 4; 6:24–30).
5. The trespass offering (Lev. 5; 7:1–7).

How were the people instructed to make restitution with the trespass offering?

Anyone who committed a trespass was to offer a ram without blemish, and make restitution for the harm that he had done, with one-fifth added to it (Lev. 5:15–16).

Who were Nadab and Abihu?

Sons of Aaron (Lev. 10:1).

What did Nadab and Abihu do, and what was the consequence for their actions?

They offered profane fire before the Lord, and were consumed by fire that went out from Him (Lev. 10:1–2).

CHAPTERS 11–27

What happened on the Day of Atonement?

The high priest would make atonement for the people by offering sacrifices to God (Lev. 16).

Besides the Sabbath, what feasts did God command Israel to observe?

1. The Passover (Lev. 23:5).
2. The Feast of Unleavened Bread (vv. 6–8).
3. The Feast of First Fruits (vv. 9–14).
4. The Feast of Weeks (vv. 15–21).
5. The Feast of Trumpets (vv. 23–25).
6. The Day of Atonement (vv. 26–32).
7. The Feast of Tabernacles (vv. 33–44).

What was the sin of the son of Shelomith, and what was his punishment?

His sin was blaspheming the name of the Lord, and his punishment was death by stoning (Lev. 24:10–23).

When the year of Jubilee arrived, what happened to land that had been sold?

It was returned to the original owner (Lev. 25:23–34).

What is the significance of the ritual states described in Leviticus?

In Leviticus, there are three ritual states described: unclean/impure, clean/pure, and holy. It is important to note that ritual states are distinct from moral states in that ritual states cover things that are not sinful. For instance, a person would be unclean if they touched a corpse or gave birth to a child but they would not be sinning. These classifications were meant to teach us that we are set aside for holiness.

Leviticus makes it clear that there is a distinction between pure and impure, holy and unholy. Every activity is either holy or unholy. In fact, there is no situation in life where you do not need reconciliation with God because everything is affected by the fall. We should see our need for Christ in all things and be grateful for God's mercy.

Guide Me, O Thou Great Jehovah

WORDS: William Williams, *pub.* 1745; *tr. by* Peter Williams, *pub.* 1771.
MUSIC: "Cwm Rhondda"; John Huges, 1907. Public Domain.

*Alternate text. †Descriptions of Jesus

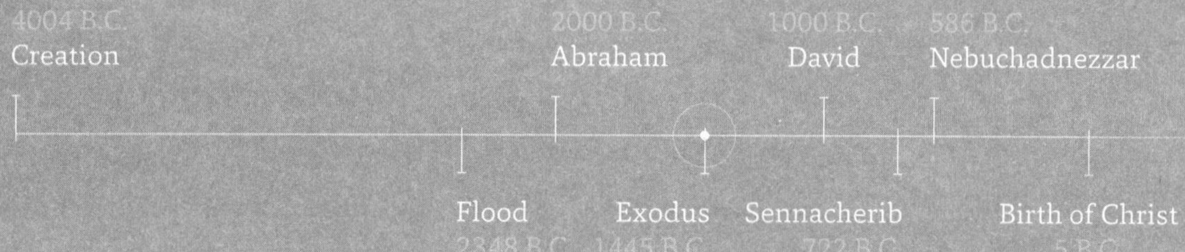

Journey through

Numbers

THEME	AUTHOR	TIME OF WRITING
Wilderness Wanderings	Moses	1445–1405 B.C.

MEMORY VERSES

24 The Lord bless you and keep you; 25 the Lord make His
face shine upon you, and be gracious to you; 26 the Lord lift
up His countenance upon you, and give you peace.

Numbers 6:24–26

OVERVIEW

The book of Numbers describes 40 years of disobedience by the Israelites as they wandered in the wilderness. If you want to be a disobedient nomad, here is what it looks like – idolatry, complaining, fear and disobedience. Numbers also includes two numberings of this disobedient people across two generations in chapters 1 and 26 and two sets of instructions in chapters 5–9 and 21–36.

You will also notice the centrality of the presence of God, as God places the Tabernacle, the place of His presence, in the middle of all the tribes. This served as the central focus of the people in the wilderness and made it clear that God would never leave or forsake His people.

Top 5 Facts to Remember

1. Because the people were not willing to enter the Promised Land (Num. 14:1–10), God sentenced them to forty years of wandering in the wilderness (Num. 14:33–34).

2. When the children of Israel learned that they would not be allowed to enter the Promised Land, they decided to go up anyway, only to be driven back by the Amalekites and the Canaanites (Num. 14:39–45).

3. When the Lord sent fiery serpents among the people, He told Moses to make a bronze serpent and put it on a pole. Whenever someone was bitten, if he looked at the bronze serpent, he lived (Num. 21:4–9).

4. When the king of Moab asked Balaam to curse the people of God, God would not allow it, but caused Balaam to bless them three times instead (Num. 22–24).

5. The Reubenites, the Gadites, and half the tribe of Manasseh asked for permission to remain on the eastern side of the Jordan, which Moses granted on one condition—that they help drive the Canaanites out of the Promised Land (Num. 32).

Theme: Wilderness Wanderings

In Numbers, God is glorifying Himself through the wanderings of the Israelites in the wilderness, so that He might demonstrate His superior goodness in the salvation sinners, the damnation of the wicked, and for the preservation of His people, both for His eternal glory, and their eternal joy.

Author: Moses

The clear and consistent teaching of Scripture is that Moses wrote the Pentateuch (Genesis, Exodus, Leviticus, Numbers, and Deuteronomy). For more information on Pentateuchal authorship, see the authorship section for Genesis.

Time of Writing: 1445–1405 B.C.

The book of Numbers was written sometime between Israel's Exodus from Egypt (1445 B.C.)[1] and Moses' death (1405 B.C.). Numbers records events that took place near the end of Moses' life,[2] making 1445–1405 B.C. the most likely time of writing.

Key Verses

"Then the Lord spoke to Moses, saying, 'Speak to the children of Israel: "When a man or woman commits any sin that men commit in unfaithfulness against the Lord, and that person is guilty, then he shall confess the sin which he has committed. He shall make restitution for his trespass in full, plus one-fifth of it, and give it to the one he has wronged. But if the man has no relative to whom restitution may be made for the wrong, the restitution for the wrong must go to the Lord for the priest, in addition to the ram of the atonement with which atonement is made for him. Every offering of all the holy things of the children of Israel, which they bring to the priest, shall be his. And every man's holy things shall be his; whatever any man gives the priest shall be his."' "

Numbers 5:5–10

"Now when the people complained, it displeased the Lord; for the Lord heard it, and His anger was aroused. So the fire of the Lord burned among them, and consumed some in the outskirts of the camp."

Numbers 11:1

"Now while the children of Israel were in the wilderness, they found a man gathering sticks on the Sabbath day. And those who found him gathering sticks

1. For more on how these dates are calculated, see "Time of Events" at the back of this book.
2. For instance, Moses says in Num. 32:13 that Israel had already wandered in the wilderness for 40 years. If the 40 years of wandering began in 1445 B.C., then Numbers could have been written no earlier than 1445–1405 (the same year that Moses died).

brought him to Moses and Aaron, and to all the congregation. They put him under guard, because it had not been explained what should be done to him. Then the Lord said to Moses, 'The man must surely be put to death; all the congregation shall stone him with stones outside the camp.' So, as the Lord commanded Moses, all the congregation brought him outside the camp and stoned him with stones, and he died."

Numbers 15:32–36

Lessons

1. The worship of God ought to be central in the lives of His people.
2. If God desires to bless His people, nothing will stop Him.

Christ in Numbers

I. The Bronze Serpent

When many of the Israelites were dying from the bites of fiery serpents, the Lord said to Moses, "Make a fiery serpent, and set it on a pole; and it shall be that everyone who is bitten, when he looks at it, shall live" (Num. 21:8). Jesus Christ predicted His own fulfillment of this verse: "And as Moses lifted up the serpent in the wilderness, even so must the Son of Man be lifted up, that whoever believes in Him should not perish but have eternal life" (John 3:14–15). Like the Israelites, every unregenerate man is a dying man, infected with the poison of sin. Like the bronze serpent that Moses lifted up on a pole, Christ was lifted up on a cross. As the bitten person who looked at the bronze serpent lived, so the sinner that looks to Jesus Christ for salvation will have eternal life.

II. Balaam's Prophecy

When Balak wanted Balaam to curse the Israelites, God would not allow it, and caused Balaam to bless them instead. After he had blessed the children of Israel three times, Balaam prophesied of the coming Christ in Numbers 24:17:

"I see Him, but not now;
I behold Him, but not near;
A Star shall come out of Jacob;
A Scepter shall rise out of Israel,
And batter the brow of Moab,
And destroy all the sons of tumult."

Balaam's prophecy was fulfilled 1,400 years later, when the wise men saw Jesus' star in the east, and came to worship Him (Matt. 2:1–2).

III. Other Types of Christ

1. The Water from the Rock (Num. 20)
2. The Cities of Refuge (Num. 35:6–28)

Outline

I. The Old Generation (Num. 1–12)

II. Twelve Spies and Punishment (Num. 13–19)

III. A New Generation Enters the Promised Land (Num. 20–36)

Study Questions

CHAPTERS 1–10

What is the theme of Numbers?

Wilderness Wanderings.

On which side of the tabernacle did each of the twelve tribes camp?

1. Judah, Issachar, and Zebulun camped on the east side.

2. Reuben, Simeon, and Gad camped on the south side.
3. Levi camped in the center with the tabernacle.
4. Ephraim, Manasseh, and Benjamin camped on the west side.
5. Dan, Asher, and Naphtali camped on the north side. (Num. 2)

What was the Nazarite vow?

1. To abstain from all products of the grapevine.
2. To grow long hair.
3. To not go near any dead body. (Num. 6:1–8)

What did God want Aaron the priest to say when he blessed the children of Israel?

"The Lord bless you and keep you;
The Lord make His face shine upon you,
And be gracious to you;
The Lord lift up His countenance upon you,
And give you peace"

Numbers 6:24–26

How long did the Levites continue their service in the tabernacle of meeting?

25 years - starting at 25 years old and ending at 50 (Num. 8:23–26).

How did the Lord lead the children of Israel through the wilderness?

With a cloud by day and with fire by night (Num. 9:15–23).

How did God punish the children of Israel for grumbling and complaining in Numbers 11:1?

He consumed some of them with fire.

What did God say when Moses questioned the feasibility of providing the people with food?

"Has the Lord's arm been shortened? Now you shall see whether what I say will happen to you or not" (Num. 11:23).

What did the Lord do to the people when they yielded to craving?

He struck them with a very great plague (Num. 11:33–34).

What was Miriam and Aaron's reason for speaking against Moses?

He had married an Ethiopian woman (Num. 12:1).

What affliction came upon Miriam for her sin against Moses?

She became leprous (Num. 12:10).

What did the twelve spies bring back from their trip?

A large cluster of grapes, some pomegranates, and some figs (Num. 13:23).

What report did the spies bring back about the Promised Land?

They said that the land flowed with milk and honey, but that the inhabitants were strong (Num. 13:27–29).

What did Caleb encourage the people to do after they heard the report?

To go up at once and take possession of the land (Num. 13:30).

What did the other ten spies say after hearing Caleb's proposal?

"We are not able to go up against the people, for they are stronger than we" (Num. 13:31).

Why were the Israelites not allowed to enter the Promised Land?

Because, notwithstanding the wonders that God had done for them in Egypt, they put Him to the test ten times, and did not heed His voice (Num. 14:20–23).

What was God's promise to Caleb?

That he would enter the Promised Land, and that his descendants would inherit it (Num. 14:24).

How was the man punished who gathered sticks on the Sabbath?

He was stoned to death (Num. 15:32–36).

What was the sin of Korah, Dathan, and Abiram?

They rebelled against the authority of Moses and Aaron (Num. 16:1–3, 12–14).

How were Dathan and Abiram punished for their rebellion?

The ground swallowed them up (Num. 16:25–34).

How were Korah and his remaining followers punished?

Fire came out from the Lord and consumed them (Num. 16:35).

CHAPTERS 21–36

Why did God send fiery serpents among the people?

Because they spoke against Him and against Moses (Num. 21:4–6).

What did Moses make to save those who were bitten?

A bronze serpent on a pole (Num. 21:8–9).

Who was Balaam the son of, and where did he live?

He was the son of Beor, and he lived in Pethor (Num. 22:5).

What did Balak want Balaam to do?

To curse the children of Israel (Num. 22:4–6).

Why did Balaam's donkey refuse to obey?

She saw the Angel of the Lord standing in the way with a sword in His hand (Num. 22:23–27).

What did the Angel of the Lord tell Balaam to do?

To go with the princes of Balak, but only speak what he was told by the Angel of the Lord (Num. 22:35).

What did Balaam do when he took up his oracle the first time?

Instead of cursing Israel, he blessed them bountifully (Num. 23:5–12).

Who did God choose to take the place of Moses?

Joshua the son of Nun (Num. 27:18–19).

To whom did Moses say, "But if you do not do so, then take note, you have sinned against the Lord; and be sure your sin will find you out"?

The children of Gad and Reuben (Num. 32:6, 23).

Trust and Obey

WORDS: John H. Sammis, 1887. MUSIC: Daniel B. Towner, 1887. Public Domain

for more resources go to **jttb.co/deuteronomy**

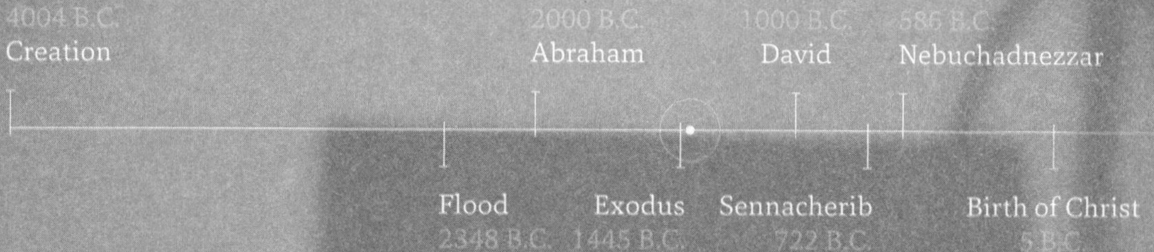

Journey through

Deuteronomy

THEME

Heartfelt Obedience to the Law of God

AUTHOR

Moses

TIME OF WRITING

1445–1405 B.C.

MEMORY VERSE

"Oh, that they had such a heart in them that they would fear Me and always keep all My commandments, that it might be well with them and with their children forever!"

Deuteronomy 5:29

OVERVIEW

The book of Deuteronomy is comprised of three sermons delivered by Moses in the last month of his life. Just before he died, he delivered laws of love to govern the Israelites. The glory of the gospel is on every page and the cross is demanded in every chapter. God requires perfect obedience, holiness, and justice, which are only found in Jesus Christ, the Son of God, who is provided as our substitute. Jesus Christ, who kept every law, imputed His obedience to unworthy sinners.

A broad range of issues are covered in the book of Deuteronomy. You will find lessons in leadership in chapter 1:9–18, responsibility for community in chapter 3:12–33, education by parents in chapter 4:9–10, poverty, homelessness, debt, drug abuse, honesty in business, management of money, welfare, personal hygiene, marriage, sexuality, conservation, care of the elderly, human rights, child abuse, injustice, dangers of the occult, and the safety of your house.

Top 5 Facts to Remember

1. The word "Deuteronomy" literally means, "second law."

2. Deuteronomy 6:4–5, "The Lord is one ... love the Lord your God with all your heart," was quoted by Jesus. He called it the greatest commandment (Matt. 22:34–38; Mark 12:28–30).

3. The Lord directed Moses to teach the children of Israel a song (commonly called the "Song of Moses"), to serve as a testimony against them when they broke His covenant (Deut. 31:16–22, 30; 32:1–44).

4. Moses told the children of Israel to set aside three cities of refuge so that anyone who killed his neighbor unintentionally could flee there (Deut. 19:1–7).

5. Moses was 120 years old when he died (Deut. 34:7).

Theme: Heartfelt Obedience to the Law of God

In Deuteronomy, God is glorifying Himself through heartfelt obedience to His laws, so that He might demonstrate His superior goodness in the salvation sinners, the damnation of the wicked, and for the preservation of His people, both for His eternal glory, and their eternal joy.

Author: Moses

The clear and consistent teaching of Scripture is that Moses wrote the Pentateuch (Genesis, Exodus, Leviticus, Numbers, and Deuteronomy[1]). For more information on Pentateuchal authorship, see the authorship section for Genesis.

1. The last few chapters of Deuteronomy (which record the completion of the "Book of the Law" and the death of Moses) were obviously written by someone other than Moses (probably Joshua, who made at least one addition to the "Book of the Law" himself; see Josh. 24:26).

Time of Writing: 1445–1405 B.C.

Most of Deuteronomy was written in 1445–1405 B.C.,[2] during the last 39 days of Moses' life.[3] Joshua probably completed the book sometime between Moses' death and his own death (no later than 1405 B.C.).

Key Verses

"Hear, O Israel: The Lord our God, the Lord is one! You shall love the Lord your God with all your heart, with all your soul, and with all your strength.

"And these words which I command you today shall be in your heart. You shall teach them diligently to your children, and shall talk of them when you sit in your house, when you walk by the way, when you lie down, and when you rise up. You shall bind them as a sign on your hand, and they shall be as frontlets between your eyes. You shall write them on the doorposts of your house and on your gates."

Deuteronomy 6:4–9

"I call heaven and earth as witnesses today against you, that I have set before you life and death, blessing and cursing; therefore choose life, that both you and your descendants may live."

Deuteronomy 30:19

2. For more on how these dates are calculated, see "Time of Events" at the back of this book.

3. Moses must have written Deuteronomy sometime between his speech on the 1st day of the 11th month (Deut. 1:3), and the crossing of the Jordan just 69 days later (Josh. 4:19). Since we are told that that Moses died at least 30 days before the crossing of the Jordan (Deut. 34:8), that leaves us with a 39-day window in which Moses could have written Deuteronomy (with the last few chapters being added by another author, probably Joshua).

"Now see that I, even I, am He,
And there is no God besides Me;
I kill and I make alive;
I wound and I heal;
Nor is there any who can deliver from My hand."

Deuteronomy 32:39

Lessons

1. God's people are chosen because of His love, not because of their righteousness.
2. Obedience to God's law brings blessing, and disobedience brings cursing.

Christ in Deuteronomy

I. A Prophet like Moses

In Deuteronomy 18:15–19, Moses told the children of Israel about a coming Prophet like himself: "The Lord your God will raise up for you a Prophet like me from your midst, from your brethren. Him you shall hear." The Apostle Peter saw the fulfillment of this prophecy in Jesus (Acts 3:19–23).

II. The Requirements of the Law

Our need for atonement is demonstrated on every page of Deuteronomy since no one has ever been able to keep the commandments perfectly. Deuteronomy requires perfect obedience, perfect holiness, and perfect justice – requirements that only Jesus Christ was able to perform.

Outline

I. **Moses' First Speech (Deut. 1–4)**

II. **Moses' Second Speech (Deut. 5–26)**

- A. The Summary (Deut. 5)
- B. The Expositions (Deut. 6:1–26:15)
  1. The First Commandment (Deut. 6–11)
  2. The Second Commandment (Deut. 12–13)
  3. The Third Commandment (Deut. 14–15)
  4. The Fourth Commandment (Deut. 16:1–17)
  5. The Fifth Commandment (Deut. 16:18–18:22)
  6. The Sixth Commandment (Deut. 19:1–22:8)
  7. The Seventh Commandment (Deut. 22:9–23:18)
  8. The Eighth Commandment (Deut. 23:19–25:12)
  9. The Ninth Commandment (Deut. 25:13–19)
  10. The Tenth Commandment (Deut. 26:1–15)
- C. The Conclusion (Deut. 26:16–19)

III. **Moses' Third Speech (Deut. 27:1–31:13)**

IV. **The Last Day of Moses' Life (Deut. 31:14–33:29)**

V. **Moses Sees the Promised Land (Deut. 34)**

Study Questions

CHAPTERS 1–10

What does the word "Deuteronomy" mean?

"Second law."

What is the central verse of Deuteronomy?

"Oh, that they had such a heart in them that they would fear Me and always keep all My commandments, that it might be well with them and with their children forever!" (Deut. 5:29).

What is the theme of Deuteronomy?

Heartfelt obedience to the Law of God.

How does Moses summarize the Law of God in Deuteronomy 10?

Fear the Lord, walk in all His ways, love Him, serve Him with all your heart and with all your soul, and keep His commandments and statutes (Deut. 10:12–13).

Why did the Lord drive out the nations before the Israelites?

To punish them for their wickedness and to fulfill the word which He swore to Abraham, Isaac, and Jacob (Deut. 9:4–5).

CHAPTERS 11–20

How many witnesses were required to put someone to death?

Two or three witnesses (Deut. 17:6).

Why didn't the Levites receive a portion of the inheritance?

Because the Lord was their inheritance (Deut. 18:1–2).

What does the Lord think about those who practice witchcraft?

They are an abomination to Him (Deut. 18:10–12).

What is the proper method for determining whether someone is a false prophet?

If his prediction does not come to pass, then he is a false prophet (Deut. 18:20–22).

What kinds of men were exempt from going to war?

1. He who had built a new house and had not dedicated it (Deut. 20:5).
2. He who had planted a vineyard and had not eaten of it (Deut. 20:6).
3. He who was betrothed to a woman and had not married her (Deut. 20:7).
4. He who was fearful and fainthearted (Deut. 20:8).

CHAPTERS 21–34

What was the punishment for stubborn and rebellious sons?

Death by stoning (Deut. 21:18–21).

What was an Israelite supposed to do if he saw his brother's animal going astray?

Return it to his brother, or keep it at his own house until his brother came looking for it (Deut. 22:1–3).

What restrictions does God place on the way men and women dress?

A woman should not wear anything that pertains to a man, nor should a man put on a woman's garment (Deut. 22:5).

What was a man prohibited from doing in his first year of marriage?

He was not allowed to go out to war or be charged with any business (Deut. 24:5).

How often were the priests supposed to read the Law to the people?

Every seven years (Deut. 31:10–11).

What did Moses tell the Israelites to command their children?

To be careful to observe all the words of God's law (Deut. 32:45–46).

What did God show Moses right before he died?

The Promised Land (Deut. 34:1–4).

How old was Moses when he wrote Deuteronomy?

One hundred and twenty years old (Deut. 34:7).[4]

What was unique about Moses' relationship with God?

God knew him "face to face" (Deut. 34:10).

4. Moses wrote Deuteronomy sometime during the last 39 days of his life (see Time of Events).

Onward, Christian Soldiers

WORDS: Sabine Baring-Gould, 1865.
MUSIC: "St. Gertrude"; Arthur S. Sullivan, 1871. Public Domain.

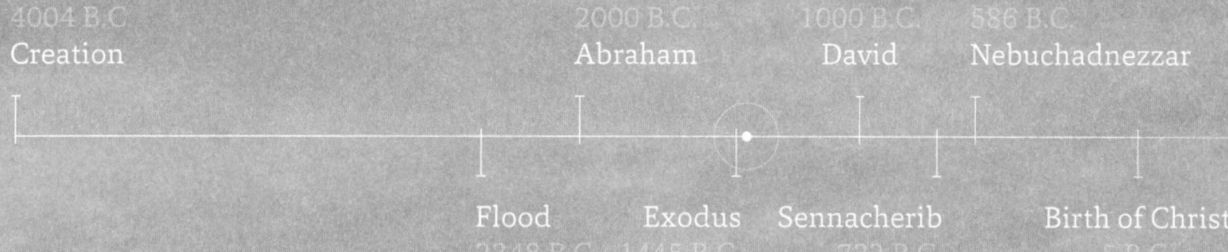

Journey through

Joshua

THEME

Victory Through Obedience

AUTHOR

Joshua

TIME OF WRITING

1405–1385 B.C.

MEMORY VERSE

8 This Book of the Law shall not depart from your mouth, but you shall meditate in it day and night, that you may observe to do according to all that is written in it. For then you will make your way prosperous, and then you will have good success.

9 Have I not commanded you? Be strong and of good courage; do not be afraid, nor be dismayed, for the Lord your God is with you wherever you go.

Joshua 1:1

OVERVIEW

Victory comes by faith in God and obedience to His word, not military power or numerical superiority. Faithful obedience is the victory. This truth is communicated through the lives of the people you will meet in this book, such as Joshua, Caleb, Rahab, Achan, the Canaanites, the Gibeonites, the Anakim, Eleazer, and Phinehas.

The Israelities, led by Joshua, are victorious over their enemies against all odds. They conquer and divide the Promised Land which demonstrates the faithfulness of God toward His people by keeping His promises.

Top 5 Facts to Remember

1. Rahab was David's great-great-grandmother, which places her in Christ's genealogy (Matt. 1:1, 5–6).
2. When the Israelites started eating the produce of Canaan, the manna that God had given them for 40 years ceased (Josh. 5:10–12).
3. Under Joshua, the Israelites defeated and possessed the land of 31 kings (Josh. 12).
4. The Gibeonites tricked Joshua into making peace with them by pretending to be from a far country (Josh. 9).
5. When Joshua was pursuing the Amorites, the Lord caused the sun to stand still for about a whole day (Josh. 10:12–13).

Theme: Victory Through Obedience

In Joshua, God is glorifying Himself through victory through obedience, so that He might demonstrate His superior goodness in the salvation sinners, the damnation of the wicked, and for the preservation of His people for His eternal glory, and their eternal joy.

Author: Joshua

While the book of Joshua does not clearly identify its author, it does tell us that Joshua himself wrote words "in the Book of the Law of God" (Josh. 24:26), making Joshua a likely candidate. Also, the book bears the marks of eyewitness testimony.[1] While a secondary author could have drawn from Joshua's memoirs to produce the book in its final form, the fact that Joshua himself wrote his ac-

1. Note the references to "we" and "us" in Josh. 5:1 and 5:6 respectively, and the assertion in Josh. 6:25 that Rahab the harlot was still alive at the time of writing.

count "in the Book of the Law of God" makes it highly unlikely that a secondary author would have taken it upon himself to edit Joshua's work. Therefore, it is reasonable to conclude that Joshua himself wrote the book that bears his name.

Time of Writing: 1405–1385 B.C.

Joshua would have written his book sometime between Moses' death (1405 B.C.)[2] and his own death[3] (no later than 1385 B.C.).

Key Verses

"And those twelve stones which they took out of the Jordan, Joshua set up in Gilgal. Then he spoke to the children of Israel, saying: 'When your children ask their fathers in time to come, saying, "What are these stones?" then you shall let your children know, saying, "Israel crossed over this Jordan on dry land"; for the Lord your God dried up the waters of the Jordan before you until you had crossed over, as the Lord your God did to the Red Sea, which He dried up before us until we had crossed over, that all the peoples of the earth may know the hand of the Lord, that it is mighty, that you may fear the Lord your God forever.' "

Joshua 4:20–24

"Behold, this day I am going the way of all the earth. And you know in all your hearts and in all your souls that not one thing has failed of all the good things which the Lord your God spoke concerning you. All have come to pass for you; not one word of them has failed."

Joshua 23:14

2. For more on how these dates are calculated, see "Time of Events" at the back of this book.

3. Josh. 24:29–33 (which records the death of Joshua, the behavior of the people after his death, the burying of Joseph's bones, and the death of Eleazar) was obviously written later (the exact date is uncertain).

"And if it seems evil to you to serve the Lord, choose for yourselves this day whom you will serve, whether the gods which your fathers served that were on the other side of the River, or the gods of the Amorites, in whose land you dwell. But as for me and my house, we will serve the Lord."

Joshua 24:15

Lessons

1. True victory comes through faith and obedience.
2. God always keeps His promises.
3. God is sovereign over all things.
4. God punishes nations for their wickedness.
5. It is the duty of every father to tell the next generation the great things that God has done.

Christ in Joshua

I. Joshua

Joshua is a type of Christ. Like Joshua, who led the Israelities into the Promised Land, Christ will lead God's people to "new heavens and a new earth in which righteousness dwells" (2 Pet. 3:13). The name *Jesus* comes from transliterating the Hebrew name *Joshua* into Greek.

II. Other Types of Christ

1. The Promised Land
2. The Commander of the Lord's Army (Josh. 5:13–15)

Outline

I. **Entering the Land (Josh. 1–5)**

II. **Conquering the Land (Josh. 6–12)**

III. **Dividing the Land (Josh. 13–24)**

Study Questions

CHAPTERS 1–10

What is the theme of the book of Joshua?

Victory Through Obedience.

What is the key verse in the book of Joshua?

"This Book of the Law shall not depart from your mouth, but you shall meditate in it day and night, that you may observe to do according to all that is written in it. For then you will make your way prosperous, and then you will have good success. Have I not commanded you? Be strong and of good courage; do not be afraid, nor be dismayed, for the Lord your God is with you wherever you go" (Josh. 1:8–9).

What command is given three times to Joshua in the first chapter?

Be strong and of good courage (Josh. 1:6, 7, 9).

Where did Rahab hide the spies?

With the stalks of flax on the roof of her house (Josh. 2:6).

How did Rahab help the spies escape from the city?

She let them down by a rope through her window (Josh. 2:15).

How did Rahab mark her house to distinguish it from the other houses in Jericho?

She bound a scarlet cord in her window (Josh. 2:17–18, 21).

What happened when the priests who were carrying the ark stepped into the Jordan River?

The waters upstream stood still, and all Israel crossed over on dry ground (Josh. 3:14–17).

Why did Joshua command twelve men to build a stone memorial?

As a reminder to tell the next generation what God had done (Josh. 4:4–7).

Why did Joshua circumcise the men who were born in the wilderness?

Because their fathers had not circumcised them like they were commanded (Josh. 5:4–5).

When did God stop giving Israel manna?

The day after they started eating the produce of Canaan (Josh. 5:12).

Why was Joshua commanded to take off his sandals?

Because he was standing on holy ground (Josh. 5:15).

How many times were the Israelites supposed to march around Jericho each day?

Once each day for six days, and then seven times on the seventh day (Josh. 6:3–4).

What happened to the wall of Jericho when the people shouted with a great shout?

It fell down flat (Josh. 6:20).

Who was spared from destruction in Jericho?

Rahab and her family (Josh. 6:22–23).

What did Joshua say about the man who would rebuild Jericho?

"Cursed be the man before the Lord who rises up and builds this city Jericho; he shall lay its foundation with his firstborn, and with his youngest he shall set up its gates" (Josh. 6:26).

What was the sin that Achan committed?

He took of the accursed things (Josh. 7:1).

What three things did Achan covet and take?

1. A beautiful Babylonian garment.
2. Two hundred shekels of silver.
3. A wedge of gold weighing fifty shekels (Josh. 7:21).

What was the punishment that Achan received for his sin?

The Israelites stoned him with stones, burned him with fire, and buried him under a great heap of stones (Josh. 7:24–26).

What lie did the Gibeonites tell Joshua?

That they had come from a far country (Josh. 9:3–13).

Why did Joshua make a covenant with the Gibeonites?

Because he had not asked for counsel from the Lord (Josh. 9:14–15).

What did Joshua do when he learned the Gibeonites had lied to him?

He cursed them, and made them woodcutters and water carriers (Josh. 9:22–23).

How did God make Israel victorious when they defended the Gibeonites?

He routed the Amorites before Israel, cast down large hailstones on them as they fled, and caused the sun to stand still while the Israelites pursued them (Josh. 10:10–14).

CHAPTERS 11–24

Why didn't any cities besides Gibeon attempt to make peace with Israel?

Because the Lord had hardened their hearts (Josh. 11:19–20).

How many kings did Israel defeat during the conquest of Canaan?

Thirty-one (Josh. 12).

How did Joshua divide the inheritance?

He sent men to survey the land and divide it into seven parts, and then cast lots for each tribe (Josh. 18:3–10).

How was Israel supposed to protect those who killed someone accidentally?

By appointing cities of refuge (Josh. 20:1–6).

Who said, "As for me and my house, we will serve the Lord"?

Joshua (Josh. 24:2, 15).

How old was Joshua when he died?

110 years old (Josh. 24:29).

Take My Life and Let It Be Consecrated

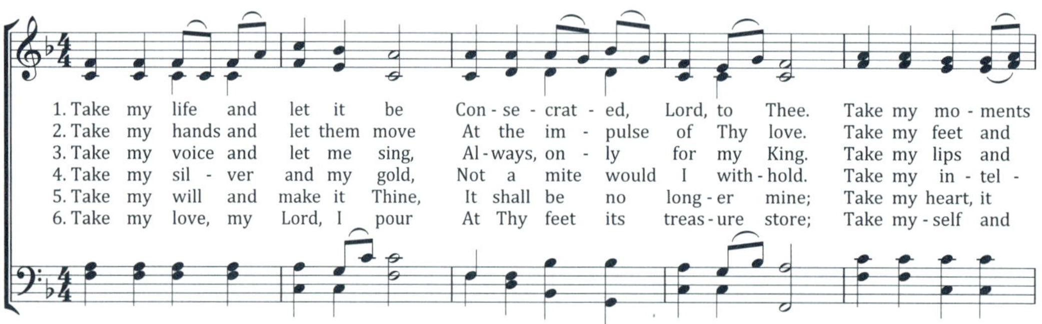

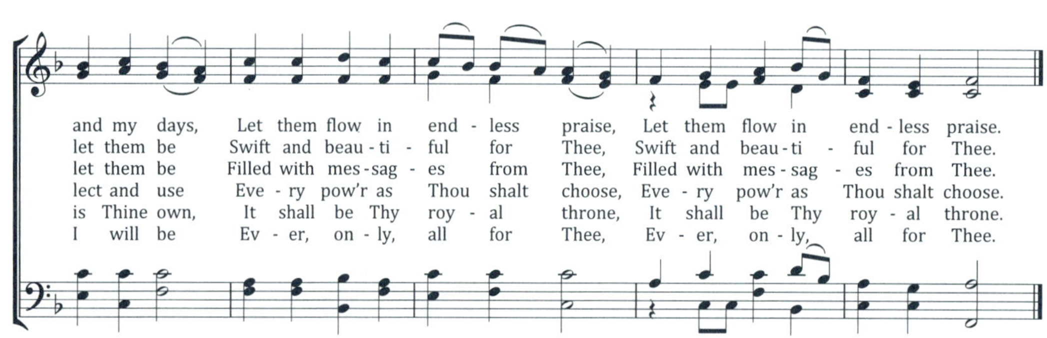

WORDS: Frances R. Havergal, 1874.
MUSIC: "Hendon"; Henri A. C. Malan, 1827; *har. by* Lowell Mason, 1841. Public Domain.

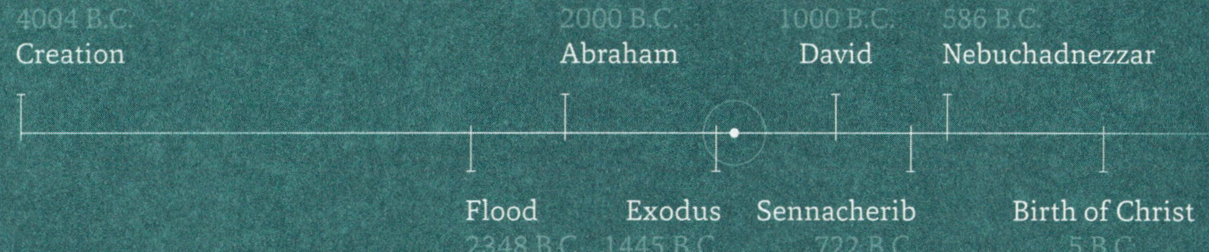

Journey through

Judges

THEME

Disobedience

AUTHOR

Probably Samuel

TIME OF WRITING

1043 B.C.

MEMORY VERSE

"In those days there was no king in Israel; everyone did what was right in his own eyes."

Judges 21:25

OVERVIEW

The book of Judges displays, in graphic form, the tragedy of autonomy. It shows what it looks like when every man does what is right in his own eyes. In the book of Joshua, we observed faithfulness and the rest God gave His people on every side. The book of Judges shows us what disobedience looks like and the effects of doing what is right in your own eyes. It is violent, unsettling, and even embarrassing to read in certain places. It records family feuds, civil wars, sexual abuse, radical immaturity, and unspeakable violence that occurred over a 350-year timeframe. Judges provides us with one of the most dramatic warnings in the Bible.

Top 5 Facts to Remember

1. To deliver Israel from Eglon, king of Moab, God raised up a left-handed man named Ehud who assassinated Eglon with a cubit-long dagger (Judg. 3:12–30).
2. When the Lord gave Barak victory over Sisera, not a single man of Sisera's army survived (Judg. 4:15–16).
3. Jael, Heber's wife, killed Sisera by driving a tent peg through his temple (Judg. 4:21).
4. To prevent the Israelites from taking any credit for their victory, the Lord made Gideon send most of his army away, reducing its size from 32,000 to 300 men (Judg. 7:1–8).
5. When a young lion attacked Samson, the Spirit of the Lord came upon him, and he tore the lion apart with his bare hands (Judg. 14:5–6).

Theme: Disobedience

In Judges, God is glorifying Himself through disobedience, so that He might demonstrate His superior goodness in the salvation sinners, the damnation of the wicked, and for the preservation of His people for His eternal glory, and their eternal joy.

Author: *Probably* Samuel

The Scriptures are silent on the authorship of Judges, though Jewish tradition attributes the book to Samuel.[1]

1. According to the Babylonian Talmud (a written collection of Jewish rabbinic tradition), "Samuel wrote his book, Judges, and Ruth." See Michael Levi Rodkinson, The Babylonian Talmud: Book 7 (Vols. XIII. and XIV.): Tract Baba Bathra (Last Gate) (Seattle, WA: Amazon Digital Services LLC, 2012), 45.

Time of Writing: 1043 B.C.

The author of Judges implies that he is writing after Israel's transition to a monarchy,[2] making 1051B.C. (the beginning of Saul's reign)[3] the earliest possible time of writing. The Jebusites still occupied Jerusalem at the time Judges was written,[4] making the date of their expulsion by David[5] (1004 B.C.) the latest possible time of writing. Therefore, it is reasonable to conclude that Judges was written sometime between 1051 and 1003 B.C.

Key Verses

"Then the children of Israel did evil in the sight of the Lord, and served the Baals; and they forsook the Lord God of their fathers, who had brought them out of the land of Egypt; and they followed other gods from among the gods of the people who were all around them, and they bowed down to them; and they provoked the Lord to anger. They forsook the Lord and served Baal and the Ashtoreths. And the anger of the Lord was hot against Israel. So He delivered them into the hands of plunderers who despoiled them; and He sold them into the hands of their enemies all around, so that they could no longer stand before their enemies."

Judges 2:11–14

"And when the Lord raised up judges for them, the Lord was with the judge and delivered them out of the hand of their enemies all the days of the judge; for the

2. Note the author's repeated assertion that Israel was without a king "in those days" (Judg. 17:6; 18:1; 19:1; 21:25). Why would he emphasize the lack of a king unless Israel's form of government had changed by his own time?
3. For more on how these dates are calculated, see "Time of Events" at the back of this book.
4. Judg. 1:21.
5. 2 Sam. 5:6–9; 1 Chron. 11:4–8.

Lord was moved to pity by their groaning because of those who oppressed them and harassed them."

Judges 2:18

Lessons

1. It is tragic when people seek to do what is right in their own eyes.
2. There is much blessing in repenting of your sin and turning to the Lord.
3. Idolatry is a serious sin and all men have a duty to flee from it.
4. God pours out His wrath on wicked nations.

Christ in Judges

The judges were raised up as shadows of the coming Christ. While the judges were sent to deliver an undeserving people from their enemies, Christ was sent to deliver an undeserving people from their sins.

Outline

I. **Living with the Canaanites (Judg. 1:1–3:4)**

   A. Israel's Failure to Complete the Conquest (Judg. 1)

   B. God's Judgement on Israel (Judg. 2:1–3:4)

II. **War with the Canaanites (Judg. 3:5–16:31)**

   A. The Mesopotamian Invasion (Judg. 3:5–11)

   B. The Moabite Invasion (Judg. 3:12–31)

   C. The Canaanite Invasion (Judg. 4–5)

D. The Midianite Invasion (Judg. 6:1–10:5)

E. The Ammonite Invasion (Judg. 10:6–12:15)

F. The Philistine Invasion (Judg. 13–16)

III. Living like the Canaanites (Judg. 17–21)

A. The Sin of Idolatry (Judg. 17–18)

B. Sins of Immorality (Judg. 19)

C. The Sin of Civil War (Judg. 20–21)

Study Questions

CHAPTERS 1–5

Why were King Adoni-Bezek's thumbs and big toes cut off?

Because he had done the same to 70 other kings (Judg. 1:6–7).

What was the spiritual condition of the people of Israel?

They did not know the Lord nor the work which He had done for Israel (Judg. 2:10).

What did the people do instead of listening to their judges?

They played the harlot with other gods (Judg. 2:17).

How did God judge Israel when they did evil after Othniel's death?

He strengthened Eglon king of Moab against them (Judg. 3:12).

How did Ehud kill Eglon?

He stabbed him with a dagger (Judg. 3:16–22).

How did Ehud escape?

He went out through the porch and locked the doors of the upper room behind him (Judg. 3:23–26).

How did Ehud and the children of Israel defeat Moab?

They seized the fords of the Jordan which led to Moab (Judg. 3:27–30).

Who was Deborah?

She was a prophetess, the wife of Lapidoth, and a judge of Israel (Judg. 4:4).

How did Jael kill Sisera?

She drove a tent peg through his temple (Judg. 4:21).

Which chapter of Judges contains the song of Deborah?

Judges 5.

CHAPTERS 6–10

What did Gideon cite as evidence that he was not fit to be a judge?

His clan was the weakest in Manasseh and he was the least in his father's house (Judg. 6:15).

What was the name of the altar that Gideon built?

"The-Lord-Is-Peace" [6] (Judg. 6:24).

6. Hebrew YHWH Shalom.

What did God command Gideon to destroy in his father's house?

The altar of Baal and the wooden image beside it (Judg. 6:25–26).

What was the first sign that Gideon asked God to do with the piece of fleece?

That there would be dew on the fleece alone (Judg. 6:36–38).

What was the second sign?

That there would be dew on everything except the fleece (Judg. 6:39–40).

Why did God reduce the size of Gideon's army?

So Israel would not be able to claim any glory for its deliverance (Judg. 7:2).

How did God reduce the size of Gideon's army?

He commanded Gideon to send home all who were afraid, and then all who got down on their knees to drink water (Judg. 7:3–7).

What did the people of Israel do with the ephod that Gideon made?

They played the harlot with it (Judg. 8:27).

What crime did Abimelech commit?

He murdered all his brothers except one (Judg. 9:5).

What was the point of Jotham's parable?

That the men of Shechem had acted wickedly and foolishly in making Abimelech king (Judg. 9:7–20).

What did God send between Abimelech and Shechem that led to Abimelech's downfall?

A spirit of ill will (Judg. 9:23).

What did the men of Shechem do to those who were passing on their way to Abimelech?

They robbed them (Judg. 9:25).

Why did Abimelech ask his armorbearer to kill him?

So no one would say, "A woman killed him" (Judg. 9:53–54).

How did God repay the wickedness of Abimelech?

By bringing his reign to an end and causing him to die a violent death (Judg. 9:53–56).

Who was raised up by God to be a judge after the death of Abimelech?

Tola, the son of Puah, the son of Dodo, a man of Issachar (Judg. 10:1–2).

Which judge had "thirty sons who rode on thirty donkeys"?

Jair (Judg. 10:3–4).

CHAPTERS 11–21

Who was Jephthah?

The son of Gilead and a mighty man of valor (Judg. 11:1).

Why did Jephthah's half-brothers drive him out?

Because he was the son of a harlot (Judg. 11:1–2).

Who was the victim of Jephthah's foolish vow?

His daughter (Judg. 11:10–31, 34–40).

What was Samson's riddle?

"Out of the eater came something to eat,
And out of the strong came something sweet" (Judg. 14:14).

Why did Samson's wife trick him into giving her the answer?

Because the Philistines had threatened to burn her and her father's house with fire (Judg. 14:15–16).

What did Samson use to kill 1,000 Philistines?

The jawbone of a donkey (Judg. 15:14–17).

What did the lords of the Philistines tell Delilah to do?

To find out what caused Samson's strength (Judg. 16:5).

How did Delilah get Samson to tell her the cause of his strength?

She pestered him daily with her words and pressed him (Judg. 16:16–17).

What did Delilah do when she found out the source of Samson's strength?

She called for the lords of the Philistines, and had Samson's hair shaved off while he was asleep (Judg. 16:18–19).

What did the Philistines do to Samson when they saw his strength was gone?

They put out his eyes, bound him with bronze fetters, and made him a grinder in the prison (Judg. 16:21).

How did Samson kill 3,000 Philistines?

He collapsed their temple on them by pushing on the two middle pillars (Judg. 16:25–30).

What do we learn from the account of Samson regarding the kind of people God uses to accomplish His will?

God uses sinful people to accomplish his purposes.

What moral guidance did the people follow during the period of the judges?

Everyone did what was right in his own eyes (Judg. 21:25).

My Redeemer

WORDS: Philip P. Bliss, 1876. MUSIC: James McGranahan, 1877. Public Domain.

Journey through

Ruth

THEME

A Kinsman Redeemer

AUTHOR

Unknown

TIME OF WRITING

1030–1010 B.C

MEMORY VERSE

16 *But Ruth said: "Entreat me not to leave you, or to turn back from following after you; for wherever you go, I will go; and wherever you lodge, I will lodge; your people shall be my people, and your God, my God.*
17 *Where you die, I will die, and there will I be buried. The Lord do so to me, and more also, if anything but death parts you and me."*

Ruth 1:16–17

OVERVIEW

The book of Ruth begins with a famine and ends with a baby in order to demonstrate how God reorders what was disorderly in the lives of ordinary people. Their trials and tears and trauma turn out for the good of all mankind. The worst things happened, but the best things were happening behind the scenes in the plan of God. This beautiful story illustrates how God preserves His people through dark times, tragic situations, apostasy, and rebellion through a "Kinsman Redeemer".

Top 5 Facts to Remember

1. The story of Ruth and Boaz took place "in the days when the judges ruled" (Ruth 1:1).
2. When given the opportunity to leave, Ruth decided to stay with Naomi (Ruth 1:8–17).
3. To make Ruth's gleaning easier, Boaz commanded his servants to let grain fall from their bundles on purpose (Ruth 2:15–16).
4. Everyone in Bethlehem knew Ruth to be a virtuous woman (Ruth 3:11).
5. Ruth was David's great-grandmother, which places her in Christ's genealogy (Ruth 4:13–22; Matt. 1:1, 5–6).

Theme: A Kinsman Redeemer

In Ruth, God is glorifying Himself through loyalty, so that He might demonstrate His superior goodness in the salvation sinners, the damnation of the wicked, and for the preservation of His people for His eternal glory, and their eternal joy.

Author: *Unknown*

The Scriptures are silent on the authorship of Ruth, though Jewish tradition attributes the book to Samuel.[1] However, this seems unlikely, since David—who is mentioned by name in the text[2]—did not assume office until after Samuel's death.

Time of Writing: 1030–1010 B.C.

The book mentions David by name,[3] but not Solomon, which means Ruth was probably written sometime before David's reign (1010–970 B.C.).[4]

Key Verses

"And Boaz answered and said to her, 'It has been fully reported to me, all that you have done for your mother-in-law since the death of your husband, and how

1. According to the Babylonian Talmud (a written collection of Jewish rabbinic tradition), "Samuel wrote his book, Judges, and Ruth." See Michael Levi Rodkinson, The Babylonian Talmud: Book 7 (Vols. XIII. and XIV.): Tract Baba Bathra (Last Gate) (Seattle, WA: Amazon Digital Services LLC, 2012), 45.
2. Ruth 4:17, 22.
3. Ruth 4:17, 22.
4. For more on how these dates are calculated, see "Time of Events" at the back of this book.

you have left your father and your mother and the land of your birth, and have come to a people whom you did not know before. The Lord repay your work, and a full reward be given you by the Lord God of Israel, under whose wings you have come for refuge.' "

Ruth 2:11–12

"And he said, 'Who are you?' So she answered, 'I am Ruth, your maidservant. Take your maidservant under your wing, for you are a close relative.' "

Ruth 3:9

"So Boaz took Ruth and she became his wife; and when he went in to her, the Lord gave her conception, and she bore a son . . . And they called his name Obed. He is the father of Jesse, the father of David."

Ruth 4:13, 17b

Lessons

1. God preserves His people through trials and dark times.
2. God rewards women of virtue.
3. The gospel is for all people, regardless of culture or nationality.

Christ in Ruth

I. **Boaz**

Boaz is a type of Christ. Like Boaz was to Ruth, Christ is our Kinsman Redeemer, having purchased us "with His own blood."[5]

5. Acts 20:28.

II. The Line of David

Jesus Christ came through the line of David, and David was Ruth's great-grandson.[6]

Outline

I. Loyalty Through Tragedy and Anguish (Ruth 1)

A. Tragedy (Ruth 1:1–5)

B. Ruth's Opportunity to Leave Naomi (Ruth 1:6–15)

C. Ruth Decides to Stay with Naomi (Ruth 1:16–18)

D. Ruth Returns with Naomi (Ruth 1:19–22)

II. Love (Ruth 2)

A. Boaz Meets Ruth (Ruth 2:1–7)

B. Boaz Provides for Ruth (Ruth 2:8–23)

III. Marriage (Ruth 3)

A. Naomi Seeks Redemption for Ruth (Ruth 3:1–5)

B. Ruth Obeys Naomi (Ruth 3:6–9)

C. Boaz Desires to Redeem Ruth (Ruth 3:10–18)

IV. Lineage (Ruth 4)

A. Boaz Marries Ruth (Ruth 4:1–12)

B. Ruth Bears a Son (Ruth 4:13)

6. Ruth 4:13–22; Matt. 1:1, 5–6.

C. Naomi Receives a New Family (Ruth 4:14–16)

D. Ruth Becomes David's Great-Grandmother (Ruth 4:17–22)

Study Questions

In what time period did the story of Ruth take place?

In the days when the judges ruled (Ruth 1:1).

What was the name of Naomi's husband?

Elimelech (Ruth 1:2).

What were the names of Naomi's two sons?

Mahlon and Chilion (Ruth 1:2).

What was the sign that the Lord had visited His people?

The end of the famine (Ruth 1:6).

How was Ruth related to Naomi?

She was Naomi's daughter-in-law (Ruth 1:22).

Why did Naomi tell her daughters-in-law to leave her?

Because she had no more sons for them to marry (Ruth 1:11–13).

What was Ruth's response when Naomi told her to leave?

She refused to go (Ruth 1:16–17).

Who was Boaz?

A relative of Naomi's husband, and a man of great wealth (Ruth 2:1).

All Hail the Power of Jesus Name!

WORDS: Edward Perronet, pub.1780; *alt. by* John Rippon.
MUSIC: "Diadem"; James Ellor, 1838. Public Domain.

for more resources go to ***jttb.co/samuel***

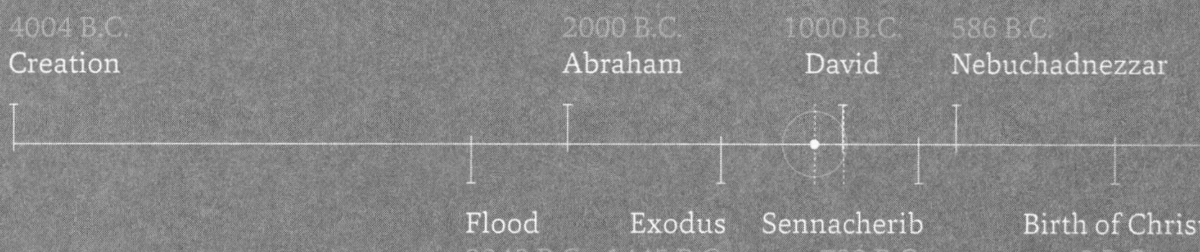

Journey through

1 & 2 Samuel

THEME

Obedience Over Sacrifice

AUTHOR

Unknown

TIME OF WRITING

931–722 B.C.

MEMORY VERSE

*22 So Samuel said: "Has the Lord as great delight in burnt
offerings and sacrifices, as in obeying the voice of the Lord?
Behold, to obey is better than sacrifice, and to heed than the
fat of rams. 23 For rebellion is as the sin of witchcraft, and
stubbornness is as iniquity and idolatry. Because you have
rejected the word of the Lord, He also has rejected you from
being king."*

1 Samuel 15:22–23

OVERVIEW

1 and 2 Samuel present the transition of leadership from the judges to the kings and was written during a period that spanned 931–722 B.C. At the beginning of 1 Samuel, the Philistines are ruling. They had been afflicting the people of God for 40 years according to the book of Judges. At the end of 2 Samuel, King David is on his throne. The nation has passed from being harried and harassed by the pagans to a nation with a God-fearing king on the throne. The contrast is further seen in the change of priests who are leading the worship of God. Eli is the priest at the beginning of 1 Samuel but, by the end, there are faithful priests ordering the house of God. The message throughout is that heartfelt obedience is better than heartless sacrifice.

Top 5 Facts to Remember

1. When the Philistines captured the ark of God, they placed it in the temple of their idol, Dagon. However, when the Philistines came back the next morning, Dagon had fallen on his face before the ark. The Philistines set Dagon back up, but when they came back the next morning, he had fallen down again, and this time his head and hands had broken off (1 Sam. 5:2–4).

2. When Samuel became old, the Israelites asked that he appoint a king so they could be like the other nations (1 Sam. 8:4–5).

3. Although David could have easily killed King Saul on at least two occasions, he refused to do so because Saul was "the Lord's anointed" (1 Sam. 24:10; 26:23).

4. David reigned in Hebron for seven and a half years, and in Jerusalem for thirty-three years (2 Sam. 5:4–5).

5. The Lord struck Uzzahh dead for taking hold of the ark (2 Sam. 6:6–7).

Theme: Obedience over Sacrifice

In 1 and 2 Samuel, God is glorifying Himself through kingdoms, so that He might demonstrate His superior goodness in the salvation sinners, the damnation of the wicked, and for the preservation of His people for His eternal glory, and their eternal joy.

Author: *Unknown*

The Scriptures are silent on the authorship of 1 & 2 Samuel. According to Jewish tradition, the book was started by Samuel and finished by Gad the Seer and Nathan the Prophet[1] (both of whom served as prophets during the time of David). However, this theory seems unlikely, since the author appears to be writing sometime after the reign of Solomon (see Time of Events).

Time of Writing: 931–722 B.C.

The author implies that he is writing after the division of Judah and Israel into separate kingdoms,[2] which took place after Solomon's death in 931 B.C.[3] The book was probably completed before the destruction of the northern kingdom in 723 B.C., since this event is never mentioned or alluded to in the text.

Key Verses

"But now your kingdom shall not continue. The Lord has sought for Himself a man after His own heart, and the Lord has commanded him to be commander over His people, because you have not kept what the Lord commanded you."

1 Samuel 13:14

1. According to the Babylonian Talmud (a written collection of Jewish rabbinic tradition), "Samuel wrote his book, Judges, and Ruth. . . . But is it not written: 'And Samuel died'? The book was finished by Gad the seer and Nathan the prophet." See Michael Levi Rodkinson, The Babylonian Talmud: Book 7 (Vols. XIII. and XIV.): Tract Baba Bathra (Last Gate) (Seattle, WA: Amazon Digital Services LLC, 2012), 45–46.

2. Note the author's reference to "the kings of Judah" in 1 Sam. 27:6, which would be a rather strange title to use if one king still ruled both Israel and Judah. However, if the author of Samuel was writing after the division of the kingdom, then mentioning the kings of Judah would make perfect sense, as it would serve to distinguish them from the kings of Israel.

3. For more on how these dates are calculated, see "Time of Events" at the back of this book.

"Then Jonathan said to the young man who bore his armor, 'Come, let us go over to the garrison of these uncircumcised; it may be that the Lord will work for us. For nothing restrains the Lord from saving by many or by few.'"

1 Samuel 14:6

"Therefore You are great, O Lord GOD. For there is none like You, nor is there any God besides You, according to all that we have heard with our ears."

2 Samuel 7:22

Lessons

1. True satisfaction is found in God alone.
2. Sometimes God teaches us a lesson by granting us what we wrongfully desire.
3. Who you worship and how you worship matters.
4. God will defeat His enemies, even if they are giants.
5. Obedience is better than sacrifice.
6. We should honor the civil authorities that God has placed over us.
7. God is sovereign over history.

Christ in 1 & 2 Samuel

I. **Samuel**

Samuel is a type of Christ. We read that Samuel "grew in stature, and in favor both with the Lord and men" (1 Sam. 2:26), and the same is said of Christ (Luke 2:52). Like Samuel, Jesus prophesied against the corrupt religious leaders of

His day.[4] Like Samuel—who served as a righteous judge over the nation of Israel[5]—Jesus will righteously judge the world, separating the sheep from the goats (Matt. 25:31–46).

II. David

David is a type of Christ. Like King David, King Jesus leads His people to victory over their enemies.

III. Other Types of Christ

1. The Anointed King (1 Sam. 2:10)
2. The Seed of David (2 Sam. 7:12–16)

Outline

1 SAMUEL

1. Samuel: Israel's Last Judge (1 Sam. 1–8)
2. Saul: Israel's First King (1 Sam. 9–15)
3. David: A Man After God's Own Heart (1 Sam. 16–31)

2 SAMUEL

1. David's Triumphs (2 Sam. 1–10)
2. David's Trials and Tribulations (2 Sam. 11–24)

---

4. 1 Sam. 3:10–18; Matt. 23:13–39; Luke 11:42–54.
5. 1 Sam. 7:15; 12:1–5.

Study Questions

1 SAMUEL

What were the names of Elkanah's wives?

Hannah and Peninnah (1 Sam. 1:2).

Which city did Elkanah travel to in order to worship and offer sacrifices to the Lord?

Shiloh (1 Sam. 1:3).

What did Peninnah do to Hannah, since Hannah could not have children?

She provoked her severely (1 Sam. 1:5–7).

What did Elkanah say to Hannah when she would weep and not eat?

"Hannah, why do you weep? Why do you not eat? And why is your heart grieved? Am I not better to you than ten sons?" (1 Sam. 1:8).

Why did Eli think Hannah was drunk when he saw her praying?

Because she was praying silently, with only her lips moving (1 Sam. 1:12–14).

What did Hannah do with Samuel once he was weaned?

She brought him to the house of the Lord in Shiloh, and lent him to the Lord (1 Sam. 1:24–28).

What was the spiritual condition of Eli's sons?

They were corrupt, and did not know the Lord (1 Sam. 2:12).

What were the sins that Eli's sons committed when the people offered sacrifices?

They stole from the sacrifices that belonged to God (1 Sam. 2:13–16).

What did God think about the sin of Eli's sons?

He saw their sin as very great (1 Sam. 2:17).

Why did God judge Eli and his house?

Because he did not restrain his sons, but honored them more than God (1 Sam. 2:29–30; 3:12–13).

How often did the Word of the Lord come in the days of Eli?

Rarely (1 Sam. 3:1).

When Samuel answered the Lord's call, what did he say?

"Speak, for Your servant hears" (1 Sam. 3:10).

Why did Phineas' wife name her son Ichabod (Literally: Inglorious)?

Because the ark of God had been captured, and because her father-in-law and husband had died (1 Sam. 4:21–22).

What did Samuel's sons do when he made them judges over Israel?

They did not walk in his ways. Instead, they turned aside after dishonest gain, took bribes, and perverted justice. (1 Sam. 8:3).

What did Samuel say would happen if a king were to rule over Israel?

He would take a significant portion of Israel's resources for himself (1 Sam. 8:10–18).

How did Saul disobey when he attacked the Amalekites?

Though he was commanded to utterly destroy everything (1 Sam. 15:3), Saul spared King Agag and the best of the Amalekites' animals (1 Sam. 15:8–9).

Why didn't Saul obey the Lord and destroy everything?

Because he feared the people (1 Sam. 15:24).

What did God say about Eliab when he was brought forward as a candidate for king of Israel?

He rejected him, despite his impressive appearance and physical stature (1 Sam. 16:6–7).

Who was David's father?

Jesse (1 Sam. 16:19).

Why did Samuel anoint David as king?

Because the Lord commanded him to do so (1 Sam. 16:12).

What town was David from?

Bethlehem (1 Sam. 16:18).[6]

What would happen to Saul whenever David played the harp for him?

He would become refreshed and well and the distressing spirit would depart from him (1 Sam. 16:23).

6. See also John 7:42.

What was the promised reward for killing Goliath?

Great riches, marriage to the king's daughter, and exemption from taxes (1 Sam. 17:25).

Why was David confident that he could defeat Goliath?

Because the Lord had delivered him before (1 Sam. 17:37).

What was the friendship of David and Jonathan like?

The soul of Jonathan was knit to the soul of David, and Jonathan loved him as his own soul (1 Sam. 18:1).

Why did Saul want David to marry his daughter?

So she would be a snare to him (1 Sam. 18:20–21).

What did Ahimelech the priest give David to eat while he was in Nob?

The showbread (1 Sam. 21:1–6).

How many men gathered to David when he was at the cave of Adullam?

About 400 (1 Sam. 22:1–2).

What did Jonathan do for David in the Wilderness of Ziph?

He strengthened David's hand in God, told him not to fear, and made a covenant with him (1 Sam. 23:15–18).

What did David do when Saul entered his hiding place?

He secretly cut off a corner of Saul's robe (1 Sam. 24:4).

Why did David prevent his men from killing Saul?

Because he was the Lord's anointed (1 Sam. 24:6–7).

What two things did David take from Saul when he was in the Wilderness of Ziph?

His spear and his jug of water (1 Sam. 26:12).

How were David and Abishai able to get so close to Saul?

Because the Lord had caused a deep sleep to fall on Saul's men (1 Sam. 26:12).

What was Saul's response when David offered reconciliation?

He promised to harm David no more (1 Sam. 26:21).

Why did Achish give the city of Ziklag to David?

Because David had asked him for a place to dwell (1 Sam. 27:5–6).

Why did Saul consult with the witch of Endor?

Because the Lord would not answer his prayers (1 Sam. 28:6–8).

Whom did Saul request that the witch bring up?

Samuel (1 Sam. 28:11).

How did Saul die?

He was wounded by Philistine archers and then killed himself with his own sword (1 Sam. 31:3–4).

2 SAMUEL

What was David's response to the death of Saul and Jonathan?

He tore his clothes, mourned, and fasted (2 Sam. 1:11–12).

Who was the commander of Saul's army?

Abner the son of Ner (2 Sam. 2:8).

Which one of Saul's sons reigned over Israel for two years?

Ishbosheth (2 Sam. 2:10).

How was Ishbosheth murdered?

As Ishbosheth was lying on his bed, Rechab and Baanah stabbed him in the stomach, beheaded him, and made their escape (2 Sam. 4:5–8).

What was David's response to the murder of Ishbosheth?

He had Ishbosheth's murderers executed (2 Sam. 4:9–12).

How old was David when he became king, and how long was his reign?

He was thirty years old when he began to reign, and he reigned forty years (2 Sam. 5:4).

What did David do when the Philistines came searching for him?

He went down to the stronghold and inquired of the Lord (2 Sam. 5:17–19).

What happened to Uzzahh when he touched the ark?

God struck him dead (2 Sam. 6:6–7).

Where was the ark taken after Uzzahh's death?

The house of Obed-Edom the Gittite (2 Sam. 6:9–10).

What was Michal's response to David's dancing?

She despised him in her heart (2 Sam. 6:16).

What was Michal's punishment?

She had no children to the day of her death (2 Sam. 6:23).

Who was the general of David's army?

Joab the son of Zeruiah (2 Sam. 8:16).

What person in Saul's household was lame in his feet?

Mephibosheth the son of Jonathan (2 Sam. 4:4).

How did Mephibosheth become lame?

His nurse dropped him while she was fleeing from the Philistines (2 Sam. 4:4).

How did David show kindness to Mephibosheth?

He restored all of Saul's land to him and offered him a place at the king's table (2 Sam. 9:7).

How did David kill Uriah?

At David's command, Joab put Uriah on the front lines and then retreated from him. Uriah was killed in the battle, just as David had planned (2 Sam. 11:14–17).

What was the parable that Nathan told David?

Nathan spoke of a rich man with many flocks and herds, who took a poor man's only possession—one little ewe lamb (2 Sam. 12:1–4).

What was the name of the second son that Bathsheba bore to David?

Solomon (2 Sam. 12:24).

What did David do at the threshing floor of Araunah the Jebusite?

He built an altar there, and a sacrificed to the Lord (2 Sam. 24:18–25).

Oh, Worship the King

WORDS: William Kethe, *pub.*1561; *recast by* Robert Grant, *pub.*1833; *alt.*
MUSIC: "Lyons"; Joseph M. Kraus, *ca.*1785; *arr. by* William Gardiner, *pub.*1815. Public Domain.

for more resources go to **jttb.co/kings**

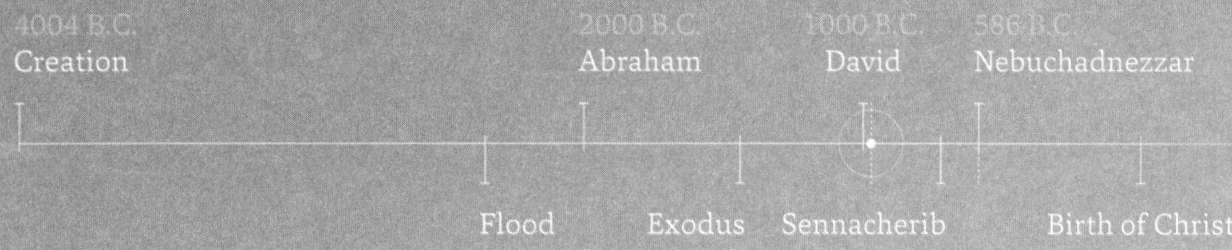

Journey through

1 & 2 Kings

THEME

A Kingdom Divided

AUTHOR

Possibly Jeremiah

TIME OF WRITING

561–538 B.C.

MEMORY VERSE

"Now it came to pass when all Israel heard that Jeroboam had come back, they sent for him and called him to the congregation, and made him king over all Israel. There was none who followed the house of David, but the tribe of Judah only."

1 Kings 12:20

OVERVIEW

These two books, spanning 450 years of history, illustrate how a kingdom divided against itself cannot stand. 1 Kings begins where 2 Samuel leaves off, during the final days of David's life at around 971 B.C. Just after Solomon's death (1 Kings 11:43), the kingdom was divided in two. Israel occupied the northern kingdom and Judah occupied the southern kingdom. The northern kingdom rejected God's pattern of worship first and was destroyed in 722 B.C. Then the southern kingdom of Judah followed in her footsteps and was destroyed by Nebuchadnezzar in 586 B.C.

Top 5 Facts to Remember

1. Solomon began building the temple 480 years after the Exodus took place (1 Kings 6:1).
2. Because of his many pagan wives, Solomon began worshipping idols in his later years (1 Kings 11:1–8).
3. After Solomon died, the kingdom of Israel became divided (1 Kings 12:1–20).

4. Naaman, the commander of the Syrian army, became a worshiper of the one true God after Elisha healed him of his leprosy (2 Kings 5:1–19).

5. When the Syrian army was close to capturing Samaria, the Lord scared the Syrians away with the sound of a great army (2 Kings 7:6–7).

Theme: A Kingdom Divided Against Itself Cannot Stand

In 1 and 2 Kings, God is glorifying Himself through a kingdom divided against itself, so that He might demonstrate His superior goodness in the salvation sinners, the damnation of the wicked, and for the preservation of His people for His eternal glory, and their eternal joy.

Author: *Possibly* Jeremiah

The Scriptures are silent on the authorship of 1 & 2 Kings, though Jewish tradition attributes the book to Jeremiah.[1]

Time of Writing: 561–538 B.C.

Jehoiachin's release from prison (561 B.C.)[2] is the last event recorded in the book of Kings,[3] and Cyrus' decree to return and build the temple (538 B.C.) is not recorded, making it likely that the book of Kings was completed sometime

1. According to the Babylonian Talmud (a written collection of Jewish rabbinic tradition), "Jeremiah wrote his book, Kings, and Lamentations." See Michael Levi Rodkinson, The Babylonian Talmud: Book 7 (Vols. XIII. and XIV.): Tract Baba Bathra (Last Gate) (Seattle, WA: Amazon Digital Services LLC, 2012), 45.

2. For more on how these dates are calculated, see "Time of Events" at the back of this book.

3. 2 Kings 25:27–30.

between these two events. However, it's possible that some sections of the book were written much earlier.

Key Verses

"Then Solomon rested with his fathers, and was buried in the City of David his father. And Rehoboam his son reigned in his place."

1 Kings 11:43

"And Elijah came to all the people, and said, 'How long will you falter between two opinions? If the Lord is God, follow Him; but if Baal, follow him.' But the people answered him not a word."

1 Kings 18:21

"Then Hezekiah prayed before the Lord, and said: 'O Lord God of Israel, the One who dwells between the cherubim, You are God, You alone, of all the kingdoms of the earth. You have made heaven and earth. Incline Your ear, O Lord, and hear; open Your eyes, O Lord, and see; and hear the words of Sennacherib, which he has sent to reproach the living God. Truly, Lord, the kings of Assyria have laid waste the nations and their lands, and have cast their gods into the fire; for they were not gods, but the work of men's hands—wood and stone. Therefore they destroyed them. Now therefore, O Lord our God, I pray, save us from his hand, that all the kingdoms of the earth may know that You are the Lord God, You alone.' "

2 Kings 19:15–19

Lessons

1. God judges those who commit idolatry.
2. God blesses those who obey His commands.
3. God is faithful to keep His covenant.
4. God judges nations that rebel against His commands.

5. Prophets have a responsibility to speak to civil leaders.

6. We should look at history in a distinctly biblical way.

Christ in 1 & 2 Kings

I. David

David is a type of Christ. Like David, Christ is a King who conquers all His enemies.

II. Solomon

Solomon is a type of Christ. Like Solomon, Christ is the Son of David. Like Solomon, Christ is a King who is full of wisdom.

Outline

I. **The United Kingdom under Solomon (1 Kings 1–11)**

II. **The Divided Kingdom—Judah and Israel (1 Kings 12 – 2 Kings 17)**

III. **The Remaining Kingdom—Judah (2 Kings 18–25)**

Study Questions

1 KINGS

Which chapters of 1 Kings cover the united kingdom under Solomon?

1 Kings 1–11.

What was the capital city of the northern kingdom?

Samaria.

What was the capital of the southern kingdom?

Jerusalem.

Who did David appoint as king over Israel before his death?

His son Solomon (1 Kings 1:32–35).

How did the people of Israel respond at Solomon's inauguration?

They rejoiced with great joy (1 Kings 1:40).

What five things did David's final charge to Solomon include?

1. To be strong and prove himself a man (1 Kings 2:2).
2. To walk in the ways of the Lord (v. 3–4).
3. To punish Joab (v. 5–6)
4. To show kindness to the sons of Barzillai (v. 7).
5. To punish Shimei (v. 8–9).

How long did David reign as king over Israel?

40 years (1 Kings 2:11).

When the Lord appeared to Solomon at Gibeon, what did Solomon ask for?

An understanding heart (1 Kings 3:9).

What was the conflict between the two harlots?

They both claimed to be the mother of the living son (1 Kings 3:16–22).

How did Solomon resolve the conflict?

He commanded his men to divide the living child in two. When one woman begged that he spare the child's life, Solomon knew that she was the real mother (1 Kings 3:23–28).

How is the wisdom of Solomon compared to the wisdom of other men in the book of Kings?

The author says that Solomon "was wiser than all men" (1 Kings 4:29–31).

How many years after the Exodus from Egypt did Solomon start building the temple?

480 years (1 Kings 6:1).

Why was the stone for the temple finished in the quarry?

So the sound of tools would not be heard in the temple (1 Kings 6:7).

Which parts of the temple did Solomon overlay with gold?

The whole temple (1 Kings 6:22).

How many years did it take Solomon to build the temple?

Seven years (1 Kings 6:38).

What was the name of the skilled craftsman who worked for King Solomon?

Huram (1 Kings 7:13–14).

How did Solomon see his life as a fulfillment of the promises that the Lord had made to David?

He built the temple, just as the Lord had promised David his father (1 Kings 8:17–21).

When Solomon prayed at the dedication of the temple, what did he say about the promises of God?

Not one word had failed (1 Kings 8:56).

What did the Lord say to Solomon when He appeared to him a second time?

The Lord promised to establish Solomon's throne forever if he and his sons obeyed, and cut off Israel from the land if they disobeyed (1 Kings 9:1–9).

What did Solomon give to Hiram, king of Tyre?

Twenty cities in the land of Galilee (1 Kings 9:10–11).

Why did the Queen of Sheba come to see Solomon?

She wanted to test him with hard questions (1 Kings 10:1).

What caused Solomon's heart to turn away to other gods?

His pagan wives (1 Kings 11:1–8).

Who were the enemies that God raised up against Solomon?

Hadad, Rezon, and Jeroboam (1 Kings 11:14, 23, 26).

What did Shemaiah say to Rehoboam?

That he should not go up and fight against the children of Israel (1 Kings 12:22–24).

How did God feed Elijah at the Brook Cherith?

Elijah drank from the brook, and was fed there by the ravens (1 Kings 17:2–6).

Where did God send Elijah when the brook dried up?

To a widow who lived in Zarephath (1 Kings 17:7–9).

How did Elijah raise the widow's son from the dead?

He stretched himself out on the child three times, and cried out to the Lord, and the Lord revived the widow's son (1 Kings 17:17–24).

When Elijah claimed that he was the only faithful Israelite remaining, what was the Lord's response?

He told Elijah that there were still 7,000 in Israel who had refused to worship Baal (1 Kings 19:10–18).

What happened to Naboth when he refused to give Ahab his vineyard?

Queen Jezebel had him executed on false charges of blasphemy (1 Kings 21:1–16).

What was Ahab's response to Micaiah's prophecy?

He threw Micaiah into prison (1 Kings 22:26–27).

2 KINGS

What did Elisha ask Elijah to give him?

A double portion of Elijah's spirit (2 Kings 2:9).

How did God take Elijah up to heaven?

By a chariot of fire in a whirlwind (2 Kings 2:11).

What miracle did Elisha perform in Jericho after Elijah's death?

He healed the bad water that was there (2 Kings 2:19–22).

How were the youths punished for mocking Elisha?

Two female bears came out of the woods and mauled forty-two of them (2 Kings 2:23–24).

What happened to the widow who was unable to pay her dead husband's creditor?

The Lord multiplied her jar of oil, so she could sell the extra oil and pay the debt (2 Kings 4:1–7).

How did Elisha revive the Shunammite's son?

He prayed to the Lord, and warmed the child's flesh with his own body (2 Kings 4:32–35).

Who was Naaman?

The commander of the Syrian army (2 Kings 5:1).

What disease did he have?

Leprosy (2 Kings 5:1).

How did Naaman learn about Elisha?

An Israelite slave girl told Naaman's wife about him (2 Kings 5:2–3).

What was Naaman's response when Elisha told him to bathe in the Jordan seven times?

He was furious (2 Kings 5:9–12).

What happened when Naaman dipped seven times in the Jordan?

His flesh was restored like the flesh of a little child (2 Kings 5:14).

What did Gehazi obtain from Naaman by lying?

Two talents of silver and two changes of garments (2 Kings 5:20–24).

What curse did Elisha pronounce on Gehazi for his sin?

He put the leprosy of Naaman on Gehazi and his descendants forever (2 Kings 5:25–27).

Why did the Syrians retreat when they were so close to capturing Samaria?

The Lord caused them to hear the noise of a great army, so they fled for their lives (2 Kings 7:6–7).

Who drove chariots furiously?

Jehu the son of Nimshi (2 Kings 9:20).

How did Jezebel die?

Her eunuchs threw her out of a window, and Jehu trampled her underfoot (2 Kings 9:30–33).

What happened when a dead man came into contact with the bones of Elisha?

He revived and stood on his feet (2 Kings 13:21).

What was the Rabshakeh's message to Hezekiah?

He mocked Hezekiah's trust in God and urged him to give a pledge to the king of Assyria (2 Kings 18:17–25).

What did Isaiah predict would happen to the king of Assyria?

He would hear a rumor, return to his own land, and fall by the sword there (2 Kings 19:7).

How many of Sennacherib's men did the Angel of the Lord kill?

185,000 (2 Kings 19:35).

Who murdered Sennacherib while he was worshiping his false god?

Two of his sons, Adrammelech and Sharezer (2 Kings 19:37).

What did Hezekiah say in his prayer when he was sick and near death?

He asked the Lord to remember how he had walked before Him in truth and with a loyal heart, and had done what was good in His sight. (2 Kings 20:1–3).

What was Manasseh's character like when he reigned over Judah?

He did evil in the sight of the Lord, and committed abominations (2 Kings 21:1–2).

How old was Josiah when he became king?

Eight years old (2 Kings 22:1).

Why did God promise Josiah that he would not see Israel's calamity?

Because his heart was tender, and because he had humbled himself, torn his clothes, and wept before the Lord (2 Kings 22:18–19).

What did Josiah do to all the idols and places of idol worship?

He destroyed them (2 Kings 23:4–20).

What made Josiah's reign unique?

No king before him or after him turned to the Lord like he did, with all his heart, soul, and might (2 Kings 23:25).

Praise to the Lord, the Almighty

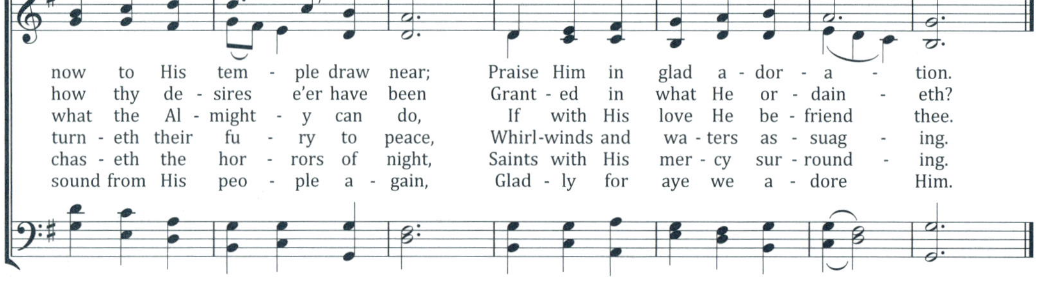

WORDS: Joachim Neander, *pub.*1680; *tr. by* Catherine Winkworth, 1863. MUSIC: "Lobe den Herren"; Unknown, *pub.*1665; *har. by* William S. Bennett, 1864. Public Domain.

for more resources go to ***jttb.co/chronicles***

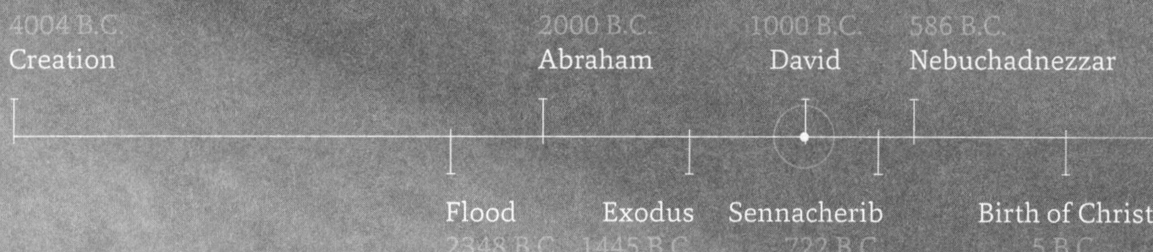

Journey through

1 & 2 Chronicles

THEME	AUTHOR	TIME OF WRITING
The Kings of Judah	*Probably* Ezra	450–430 B.C.

MEMORY VERSE

"If My people who are called by My name will humble themselves, and pray and seek My face, and turn from their wicked ways, then I will hear from heaven, and will forgive their sin and heal their land."

2 Chronicles 7:14

OVERVIEW

Here we encounter the same period of time as 1 and 2 Samuel and 1 and 2 Kings. This is similar to how the four Gospels were written by four different men of the same time period but with different perspectives. In the original Hebrew Bible, Chronicles was the final book of the Old Testament, not Malachi. The perspective of the book is that the exile is over. God's people have returned to the land. However, their enthusiasm is flagging. They have fallen into the old patterns as Ezra, Nehemiah and Haggai, Zechariah and Malachi show. God is proving that He did indeed fulfill the prophesies and the threats of Deuteronomy 28.

Top 5 Facts to Remember

1. Chapters 1–9 are devoted almost exclusively to genealogy.
2. When David sinned by commanding the Israelites to be numbered, the Lord caused 70,000 men of Israel to die in a plague (1 Chron. 21:14).
3. Solomon built the temple on Mount Moriah, exactly where David had sacrificed to the Lord after the plague (1 Chron. 21:28; 2 Chron. 3:1).
4. Solomon recognized that it was impossible to contain God in even the heaven of heavens, let alone the temple that he had built (2 Chron. 6:18).
5. In His compassion, God sent messengers to warn Judah of His coming judgment, but they despised His words (2 Chron. 36:14–16).

Theme: The Kings of Judah

In 1 and 2 Chronicles, God is glorifying Himself through the kings of Judah, so that He might demonstrate His superior goodness in the salvation sinners, the damnation of the wicked, and for the preservation of His people for His eternal glory, and their eternal joy.

Author: *Probably* Ezra

The Scriptures are silent on the authorship of 1 & 2 Chronicles, though Jewish tradition attributes the book to Ezra.[1]

1. According to the Babylonian Talmud (a written collection of Jewish rabbinic tradition), "Ezra wrote his book, and Chronicles--the order of all generations down to himself." See Michael Levi Rodkinson, The Babylonian Talmud: Book 7 (Vols. XIII. and XIV.): Tract Baba Bathra (Last Gate) (Seattle, WA: Amazon Digital Services LLC, 2012), 45.

Time of Writing: 450–430 B.C.

King Jehoiachin (also refered to as Jeconiah) began his reign over Judah in 598 B.C., and reigned until Nebuchadnezzar took him to Babylon in 597 B.C. 1 Chronicles 3:17-24 records eight generations of Jehoiachin's descendants, suggesting a time of writing during Jehoiachin's eighth generation, or between 450 and 430 B.C.

Key Verses

"And David said to Gad, 'I am in great distress. Please let me fall into the hand of the Lord, for His mercies are very great; but do not let me fall into the hand of man.' "

1 Chronicles 21:13

"Moreover all the leaders of the priests and the people transgressed more and more, according to all the abominations of the nations, and defiled the house of the Lord which He had consecrated in Jerusalem.

And the Lord God of their fathers sent warnings to them by His messengers, rising up early and sending them, because He had compassion on His people and on His dwelling place. But they mocked the messengers of God, despised His words, and scoffed at His prophets, until the wrath of the Lord arose against His people, till there was no remedy."

2 Chronicles 36:14–16

Lessons

1. God blesses obedience, and punishes disobedience.
2. We should trust in God, not man.
3. God will judge idolaters.

4. Godly rulers restore true worship and obedience to God's commands.

5. The law of God applies to civil authorities.

Christ in 1 & 2 Chronicles

I. The Kings of Judah

The focus of 1 & 2 Chronicles is the kings of Judah—Christs' genealogical line (Matt. 1:1–17). The kings of Judah also serve as types of Jesus Christ. Many of Judah's kings despised the ways of the Lord, and the few who walked in His ways did so with many imperfections; yet Christ is our perfectly-righteous King, whose kingdom will never come to an end.

II. Other Types of Christ

1. Solomon's Temple
2. Solomon's Wisdom

Outline

I. **Genealogies (1 Chron. 1–9)**

II. **The United Kingdom (1 Chron. 10 – 2 Chron. 9)**

III. **The Divided Kingdom (2 Chron. 10:1–36:21)**

IV. **The Return from Exile (2 Chron. 36:22–23)**

Study Questions

1 CHRONICLES

Who is the author of 1 & 2 Chronicles?

Probably Ezra.

What is the focus of 1 & 2 Chronicles?

The kings of Judah and their relationship to God.

Why did God kill Uzzah?

Because he touched the ark (1 Chron. 13:9–10).

What did David do with the ark after the death of Uzzah?

He placed it in the house of Obed-Edom the Gittite (1 Chron. 13:12–13).

What happened while the ark was in the house of Obed-Edom?

God blessed the house of Obed-Edom and all that he had (1 Chron. 13:14).

What was Michal's response when she saw David whirling and playing music?

She despised him in her heart (1 Chron. 15:29).

Who moved David to number Israel?

Satan (1 Chron. 21:1).[2]

When David sinned by numbering Israel, God gave him the choice of 3 punishments. What were they?

1. Famine for three years
2. Defeat by his enemies for three months.
3. A plague for three days (1 Chron. 21:9–12).

What was David's response when Ornan offered to give him his threshing floor?

He refused to take it without paying the full price (1 Chron. 21:22–25).

2 CHRONICLES

What did Solomon ask God for?

Wisdom and knowledge (2 Chron. 1:7–12).

Why did the Queen of Sheba visit Solomon?

To test him with hard questions (2 Chron. 9:1).

What was the Queen of Sheba's response when she saw Solomon's wisdom?

There was no more spirit in her (2 Chron. 9:3–4).

2. cf. 2 Sam. 24:1. Satan's wicked scheme was ultimately a part of God's plan.

How long did Solomon reign over Israel?

Forty years (2 Chron. 9:30).

Who succeeded Solomon as king over Israel?

Rehoboam his son (2 Chron. 9:31).

What did Asa pray when he went out to fight with the Ethiopians?

He acknowledged God's great power, and petitioned Him for help (2 Chron. 14:9–11).

What sins did Asa commit near the end of his reign?

He put Hanani the seer in prison, oppressed some of the people, and did not seek the Lord in his disease (2 Chron. 16:7–14).

What did Jehoshaphat do in the third year of his reign?

He sent leaders to teach the Book of the Law in the cities of Judah (2 Chron. 17:7–9).

How many prophets could Ahab find who would tell him what he wanted to hear?

Four hundred (2 Chron. 18:5).

Why did king Ahab hate the prophet Micaiah?

Because he always prophesied bad things concerning him (2 Chron. 18:7).

Did Ahab and Jehoshaphat go to battle against Ramoth Gilead?

Yes (2 Chron. 18:28).

Why did the Lord bring Judah low?

Because Ahaz king of Israel had encouraged moral decline in Judah and had been continually unfaithful to the Lord. (2 Chron. 28:19).

What kind of relationship did Hezekiah have with God?

He did what was good and right and true before the Lord his God (2 Chron. 31:20).

Who invaded Judah during Hezekiah's reign?

Sennacherib king of Assyria (2 Chron. 32:1).

What did Hezekiah say that strengthened the people?

"Be strong and courageous; do not be afraid nor dismayed before the king of Assyria, nor before all the multitude that is with him; for there are more with us than with him. With him is an arm of flesh; but with us is the Lord our God, to help us and to fight our battles" (2 Chron. 32:7–8).

What did the angel of the Lord do to the Assyrian army after Isaiah and Hezekiah prayed?

He cut down every mighty man of valor, leader, and captain (2 Chron. 32:20–21).

What was found in the temple during Josiah's reign?

The Book of the Law (2 Chron. 34:14–18).

What was Josiah's response when he heard the words of the Law?

He tore his clothes, and sent men to inquire of the Lord (2 Chron. 34:19–21).

Since when had the Passover been kept in Israel the way Josiah kept it?

Not since the days of Samuel the prophet (2 Chron. 35:18).

How did Josiah die?

He was mortally wounded in a battle with Necho king of Egypt (2 Chron. 35:20–24).

How Firm a Foundation

WORDS: Author unknown, *pub.* 1787.
MUSIC: "Foundation"; American melody, *pub.* 1832. Public Domain.

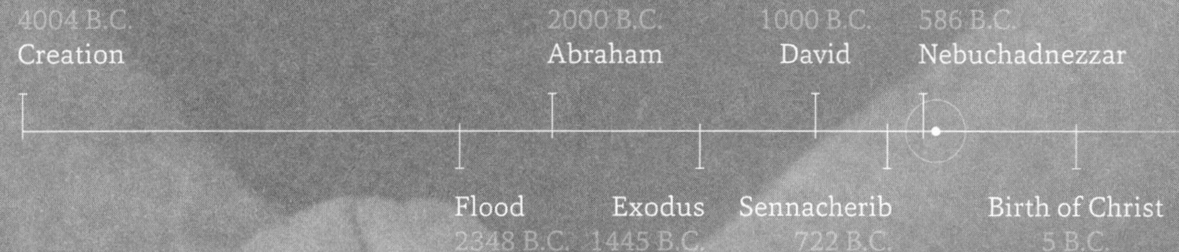

Journey through

Ezra

THEME	AUTHOR	TIME OF WRITING
Restoration	Ezra	457–444 B.C.

MEMORY VERSE

"For Ezra had prepared his heart to seek the Law of the Lord, and to do it, and to teach statutes and ordinances in Israel."

Ezra 7:10

OVERVIEW

In the book of Ezra, we observe a people returning from ruin and witness how God works for the benefit of His people to heal and restore them. The whole focus of the book is the restoration of the people through returning to true worship. This is the beginning point of all spiritual renewal and social reformation. Restoration always means a complete surrender to God. Everything must be according to the Word of God.

Top 5 Facts to Remember

1. In the first return from Babylon, Zerubbabel came to Jerusalem with 49,897 people (Ezra 2:1–2, 64–65).
2. As they sought to restore true worship, Zerubbabel and Jeshua used Scripture as their guide (Ezra 3:2, 4; 6:18).
3. Both Haggai and Zechariah prophesied during the rebuilding of the temple (Ezra 5:1; 6:14).
4. The temple was finished in the sixth year of the reign of King Darius (Ezra 6:15).
5. Ezra traveled to Jerusalem with the purpose of teaching the Law of God to the Jews (Ezra 7:10).

Theme: Restoration

In Ezra, God is glorifying Himself through the restoration of His people, so that He might demonstrate His superior goodness in the salvation sinners, the damnation of the wicked, and for the preservation of His people for His eternal glory, and their eternal joy.

Author: Ezra

The book contains a large amount of eyewitness testimony from Ezra's point of view,[1] making it very likely that he authored the other sections of the book. Ezra also incorporated several letters and legal documents into his book (which he probably obtained from the royal archives of Artaxerxes I).

Time of Writing: 457–444 B.C.

Ezra began writing after he came to Jerusalem in 457 B.C.,[2] and probably completed his book before the arrival of Nehemiah (who is not mentioned in the text) in 445 B.C.

Key Verses

"Now in the first year of Cyrus king of Persia, that the word of the Lord by the mouth of Jeremiah might be fulfilled, the Lord stirred up the spirit of Cyrus king of Persia, so that he made a proclamation throughout all his kingdom, and also put it in writing, saying,

1. Ezra 7:27–9:15.
2. For more on how these dates are calculated, see "Time of Events" at the back of this book.

'Thus says Cyrus king of Persia:

All the kingdoms of the earth the Lord God of heaven has given me. And He has commanded me to build Him a house at Jerusalem which is in Judah. Who is among you of all His people? May his God be with him, and let him go up to Jerusalem which is in Judah, and build the house of the Lord God of Israel (He is God), which is in Jerusalem. And whoever is left in any place where he dwells, let the men of his place help him with silver and gold, with goods and livestock, besides the freewill offerings for the house of God which is in Jerusalem.' "

Ezra 1:1–4

"Now the temple was finished on the third day of the month of Adar, which was in the sixth year of the reign of King Darius. Then the children of Israel, the priests and the Levites and the rest of the descendants of the captivity, celebrated the dedication of this house of God with joy. And they offered sacrifices at the dedication of this house of God, one hundred bulls, two hundred rams, four hundred lambs, and as a sin offering for all Israel twelve male goats, according to the number of the tribes of Israel. They assigned the priests to their divisions and the Levites to their divisions, over the service of God in Jerusalem, as it is written in the Book of Moses."

Ezra 6:15–18

"Now while Ezra was praying, and while he was confessing, weeping, and bowing down before the house of God, a very large assembly of men, women, and children gathered to him from Israel; for the people wept very bitterly."

Ezra 10:1

Lessons

1. Those seeking to restore true worship should expect resistance from God's enemies.
2. Christians should be people who regularly confess and repent of their sins.

3. God uses ungodly leaders to accomplish His purposes.

4. We should base our worship on the teachings of Scripture.

Christ in Ezra

Ezra and Zerubbabel are both types of Christ. Like these men, Christ came as a Restorer of true worship.

Outline

I. **The Restoration of the Temple under Zerubbabel (Ezra 1–6)**

II. **The Reformation of the People under Ezra (Ezra 7–10)**

Study Questions

Who is the author of the book of Ezra?

Ezra.

What king first commanded the rebuilding of the temple?

Cyrus king of Persia (Ezra 1:1–4).

What did Cyrus do with the articles that Nebuchadnezzar had taken from Jerusalem?

He counted them out to Sheshbazzar the prince of Judah (Ezra 1:7–8).

Who are the people listed in Ezra 2?

The Jews who returned from Babylon with Zerubbabel (Ezra 2:1–2).

What was the first thing the Jews restored when they returned to Jerusalem?

The altar of the God of Israel (Ezra 3:2–3).

Why did the people shout with a great shout?

Because the Temple's foundation had been laid (Ezra 3:11).

Who tried to discourage the Jews from rebuilding the temple?

The adversaries of Judah and Benjamin (Ezra 4:1–5).

Who commanded the Jews to rebuild the temple?

Cyrus the king of Persia (Ezra 4:3).

What was King Darius' decree?

To search the royal archives for Cyrus's decree (Ezra 5:17–6:1).

Who prophesied during the rebuilding of the temple?

Haggai the prophet and Zechariah the son of Iddo (Ezra 5:1; 6:14).

When was the temple completed?

In the sixth year of King Darius' reign (Ezra 6:15).

What feasts did the Jews keep after finishing the temple?

The Passover and the Feast of Unleavened Bread (Ezra 6:19–22).

Who was Ezra?

A descendant of Aaron, and a skilled scribe in the Law of Moses (Ezra 7:1–6).

What task did Ezra prepare his heart for?

To seek the Law of the Lord, and to do it, and to teach statutes and ordinances in Israel (Ezra 7:10).

What did the Lord put into King Artaxerxes' heart?

To beautify the house of the Lord (Ezra 7:27).

Why did Ezra proclaim a time of fasting and prayer?

To petition God for guidance and protection (Ezra 8:21–23).

What sin of the people did Ezra have to deal with?

The marrying of pagan wives (Ezra 9:1–2).

What was Ezra's response when he heard about the sin of the people?

He tore his clothes, plucked out some of the hair of his head and beard, and sat down astonished (Ezra 9:3). He then confessed the sin to God (Ezra 9:5–15).

How high had the people's iniquities risen, according to Ezra?

Higher than their heads, all the way up to the heavens (Ezra 9:6).

Who gathered to Ezra while he was crying out to the Lord?

A very large assembly of men, women, and children (Ezra 10:1).

What did Ezra tell the people who had married pagan wives to do?

To confess their sin, and separate from their pagan wives (Ezra 10:10–11).

A Mighty Fortress Is Our God

WORDS: Martin Luther, *ca.*1529; *tr.* by Frederick H. Hedge, 1853.
MUSIC: "Ein' Feste Burg"; M. L., *ca.*1529. Public Domain.

for more resources go to ***jttb.co/nehemiah***

4004 B.C. Creation
2000 B.C. Abraham
1000 B.C. David
586 B.C. Nebuchadnezzar
Flood 2348 B.C.
Exodus 1445 B.C.
Sennacherib 722 B.C.
Birth of Christ 5 B.C.

Journey through

Nehemiah

THEME

Rebuilding the Wall

AUTHOR

Nehemiah

TIME OF WRITING

424–400 B.C.

MEMORY VERSE

8 So they read distinctly from the book, in the Law of God; and they gave the sense, and helped them to understand the reading.

9 And Nehemiah, who was the governor, Ezra the priest and scribe, and the Levites who taught the people said to all the people, "This day is holy to the Lord your God; do not mourn nor weep." For all the people wept, when they heard the words of the Law.

Nehemiah 8:8–9

OVERVIEW

Nehemiah led the third and final return of the Jews to Jerusalem after their captivity. He was raised up to rebuild Judah's protective barriers – the wall and their obedience to the law of God. The Book of Nehemiah displays God's protection and preservation of His people by protecting them while they rebuilt their walls and sending men to call His people to obey His laws.

Top 5 Facts to Remember

1. Nehemiah recognized the importance of prayer, and cried out to God on many occasions.[1]

2. Sanballat, Tobiah, and Geshem's hostility towards Nehemiah began with mockery and false accusations (Neh. 2:19) but quickly escalated to violent plots (Neh. 4:7–8).

3. After Nehemiah had discovered the plot to ambush the Jewish workers, he made half of his servants stand guard with the weapons while the other half worked on the wall (Neh. 4:16).

1. Neh. 1:4–11; 2:4; 4:4–5, 9; 5:19; 6:9, 14; 13:14, 29, 31.

4. It took the Jews 52 days to repair Jerusalem's walls (Neh. 6:15).

5. Ezra and Nehemiah were contemporaries (Neh. 8:9).

Theme: Rebuilding the Wall

In Nehemiah, God is glorifying Himself through the Jews rebuilding their walls, so that He might demonstrate His superior goodness in the salvation sinners, the damnation of the wicked, and for the preservation of His people for His eternal glory, and their eternal joy.

Author: Nehemiah

Most of the book's content is Nehemiah's own eyewitness testimony,[2] making it likely that he authored the other sections. However, since Ezra and Nehemiah were treated as single book until about the 3rd century A.D., some think it more likely that Ezra authored both Ezra and Nehemiah (and incorporated Nehemiah's memoirs), or that a third author combined Ezra and Nehemiah into a single book.[3]

Time of Writing: 424–400 B.C.

The book's latest time marker is Nehemiah's return to Artaxerxes in the 32nd year of his reign[4] (424 B.C.),[5] making this the earliest possible time of writing.

2. Neh. 1–7; 12:31–13:31.

3. See F. Charles Fensham, The Books of Ezra and Nehemiah (Grand Rapids, MI: Wm. B. Eerdmans Publishing Company, 1982), 1–4.

4. Neh. 5:14; 13:6.

5. For more on how these dates are calculated, see "Time of Events" at the back of this book.

Nehemiah probably wrote his book before the end of Artaxerxes' reign (424 B.C.), since a change in Persian leadership is not mentioned or alluded to in the text.

Key Verses

"But when Sanballat the Horonite, Tobiah the Ammonite official, and Geshem the Arab heard of it, they laughed at us and despised us, and said, 'What is this thing that you are doing? Will you rebel against the king?'

So I answered them, and said to them, 'The God of heaven Himself will prosper us; therefore we His servants will arise and build, but you have no heritage or right or memorial in Jerusalem.' "

Nehemiah 2:19–20

"Therefore I positioned men behind the lower parts of the wall, at the openings; and I set the people according to their families, with their swords, their spears, and their bows. And I looked, and arose and said to the nobles, to the leaders, and to the rest of the people, 'Do not be afraid of them. Remember the Lord, great and awesome, and fight for your brethren, your sons, your daughters, your wives, and your houses.' "

Nehemiah 4:13–14

"For they all were trying to make us afraid, saying, 'Their hands will be weakened in the work, and it will not be done.' Now therefore, O God, strengthen my hands."

Nehemiah 6:9

Lessons

1. God protects and preserves His people.
2. Prayer is a vital part of the Christian life.
3. God brings revival through the faithful preaching of His word.

Christ in Nehemiah

Nehemiah is a type of Christ. While Nehemiah was sent by God to build the walls of Jerusalem, Christ was sent by His Father to build His church. Like Nehemiah, Christ cleansed the Temple.[6] Like Nehemiah, Christ wept over Jerusalem.[7]

Outline

I. **Nehemiah's Arrival in Jerusalem (Neh. 1–2)**

II. **Rebuilding the Wall (Neh. 3:1–7:3)**

III. **Records from the First Return (Neh. 7:4–73)**

IV. **Renewing the Covenant (Neh. 8–10)**

V. **Settling in the Land (Neh. 11)**

VI. **Genealogy of the Priests and Levites (Neh. 12:1–26)**

VII. **Dedicating the Wall (Neh. 12:27–43)**

VIII. **Nehemiah's Reforms (Neh. 12:44–13:31)**

6. Neh. 13:4–9; Matt. 21:12–13; Mark 11:15–17; Luke 19:45–46; John 2:13–17.

7. Neh. 1:4; Luke 19:41.

Study Questions

What was Nehemiah's response when he heard about the destruction of Jerusalem?

He wept, fasted, and prayed for many days (Neh. 1:4).

What position did Nehemiah hold?

He was the king's cupbearer (Neh. 1:11).

What did Nehemiah ask of the king?

That he would send him to rebuild Jerusalem (Neh. 2:5).

What was the response of Sanballat, Tobiah, and Geshem when they heard that the Jews were going to rebuild the wall?

They laughed at and despised the Jews (Neh. 2:19).

Who built the Sheep Gate?

Eliashib the high priest and his brethren (Neh. 3:1).

What was Sanballat's response when he heard that the people of Israel were rebuilding the wall?

He was furious and very indignant, and he mocked the Jews (Neh. 4:1).

What did Tobiah say about the strength of the new wall?

He claimed that even a fox would be able to break it down (Neh. 4:3).

Why did Nehemiah tell the people not to be afraid of their enemies?

Because the Lord was great and awesome (Neh. 4:14).

What did Nehemiah write in response to Sanballat's letter?

"No such things as you say are being done, but you invent them in your own heart" (Neh. 6:8).

What did Nehemiah ask God to do when his enemies were trying to make the people afraid?

He asked God to strengthen his hands (Neh. 6:9).

How long did it take the Jews to rebuild the wall of Jerusalem?

52 days (Neh. 6:15).

Who was Hananiah?

He was the leader of the citadel, a faithful man, who feared God more than many (Neh. 7:2).

What did God put into Nehemiah's heart after he had rebuilt the wall?

To register the people by genealogy (Neh. 7:5).

What did Ezra read before the people?

The Book of the Law of Moses (Neh. 8:1–8).

How did the people respond when they heard the words of the Law?

They all wept (Neh. 8:9).

What did the people of Israel do with the Ammonites and the Moabites after they read the Law of the Lord?

They separated from them (Neh. 13:1–3).

God Moves in a Mysterious Way

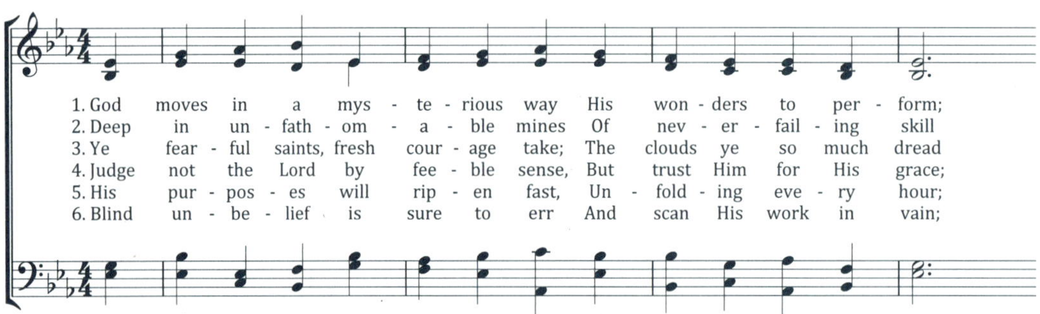

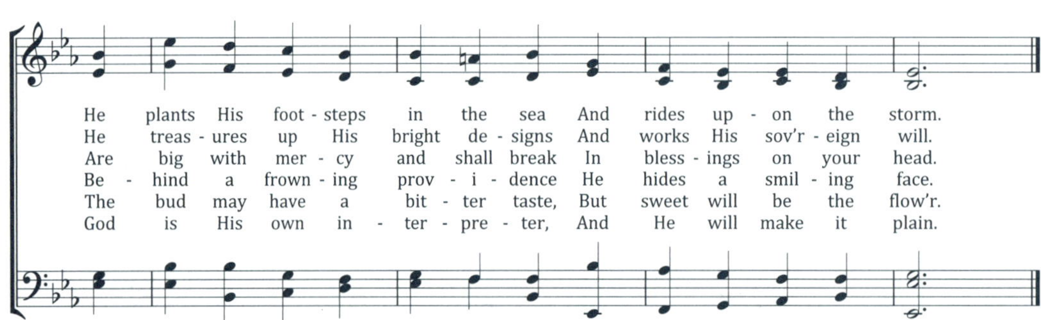

WORDS: William Cowper, 1774. MUSIC: "Dundee"; Author unknown, *pub.*1615; *har. by* Thomas Ravenscroft, 1621. Public Domain.

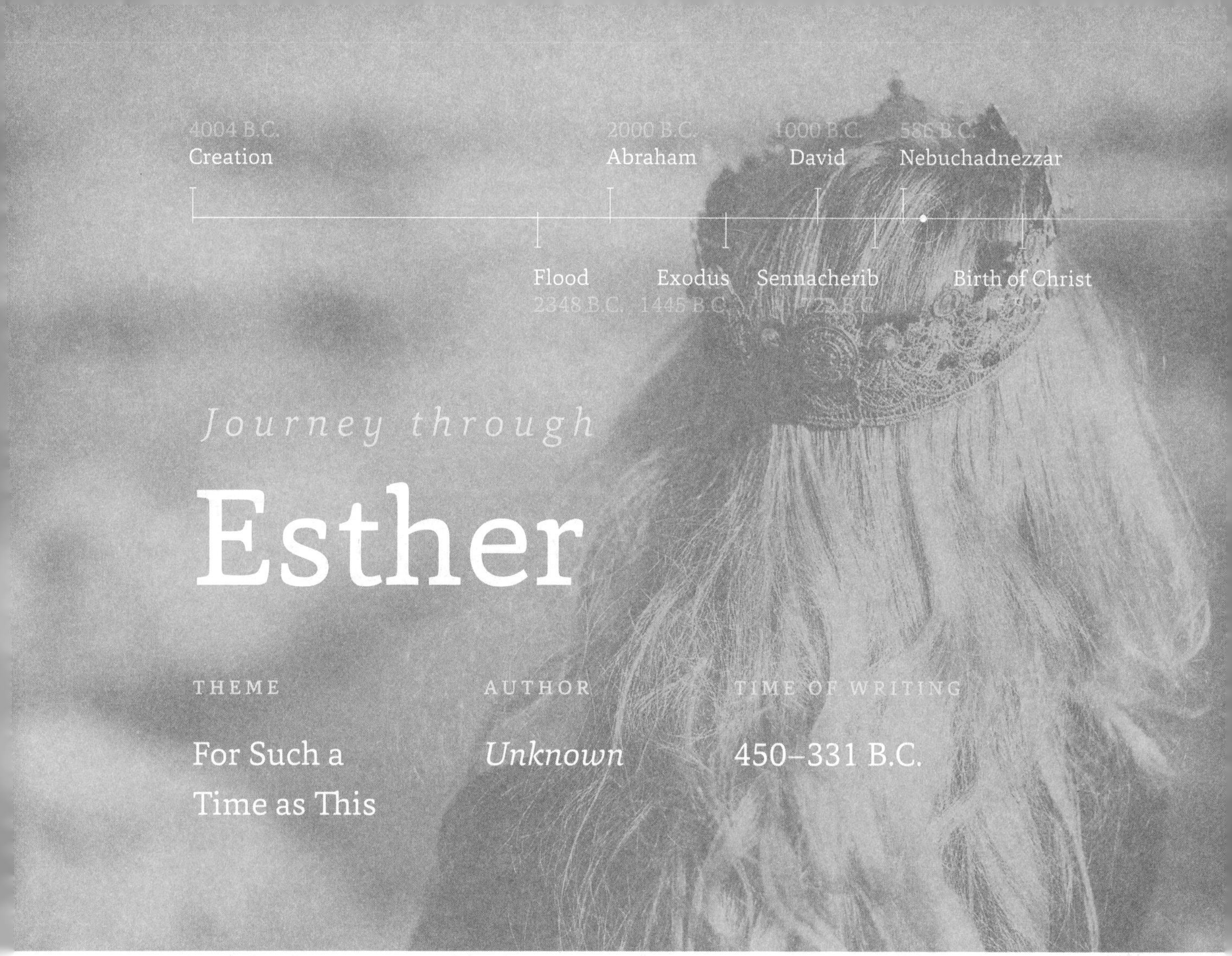

4004 B.C. Creation | 2348 B.C. Flood | 2000 B.C. Abraham | 1445 B.C. Exodus | 1000 B.C. David | 722 B.C. Sennacherib | 586 B.C. Nebuchadnezzar | 5 B.C. Birth of Christ

Journey through

Esther

THEME

For Such a Time as This

AUTHOR

Unknown

TIME OF WRITING

450–331 B.C.

MEMORY VERSE

13 And Mordecai told them to answer Esther: "Do not think
in your heart that you will escape in the king's palace any
more than all the other Jews.

14 "For if you remain completely silent at this time, relief
and deliverance will arise for the Jews from another place,
but you and your father's house will perish. Yet who knows
whether you have come to the kingdom for such a time as
this?"

Esther 4:13–14

OVERVIEW

The book of Esther reads like a novel as it tells the story of how a beautiful, Jewish orphan girl rises to wield significant power in a pagan king's court. God would ultimately use her to save the Jews from genocide. A recurring theme in Esther is that God raises up the most unlikely people to fulfill His will. Everything happens for "such a time as this."

The book of Esther makes it clear that God is in control of history even when rulers make unwise and evil decisions based on sinful motivations. Even the smallest impulses and motivations of men and women gone astray are used in the hands of God to rescue His people. God is always skillfully directing all things. He is after all, not only the God of the rulers of the kings of the earth, He is also the God of the gallows.

Top 5 Facts to Remember

1. The events recorded in the book of Esther took place after the rebuilding of the temple by Zerubbabel and Jeshua, but before the time of Ezra and Nehemiah.

2. Ahasuerus reigned over 127 provinces, from India to Ethiopia (Esth. 1:1).

3. Because of his hatred for Mordecai, Haman plotted to destroy all the Jews in the Persian Empire (Esth. 3:5–6).

4. Mordecai told Esther that if she remained silent, help for the Jews would arise from another place (Esth. 4:13–14), showing his belief in the providential care of God for His people.

5. When his plot to exterminate the Jews was exposed, Haman was hanged on the very gallows which he had made for Mordecai (Esth. 7:9–10).

Theme: For Such a Time as This

In Esther, God is glorifying Himself through His sovereign control "for such a time as this," so that He might demonstrate His superior goodness in the salvation sinners, the damnation of the wicked, and for the preservation of His people for His eternal glory, and their eternal joy.

Author: *Unknown*

No one knows who wrote the book of Esther; though Mordecai, Ezra, and Nehemiah have all been put forward as candidates.

Time of Writing: 450–331 B.C.

The author appears to be writing after Ahasuerus' reign,[1] which ended in 450 B.C.[2] Since the fall of the Persian Empire to Greece (331 B.C.) is not recorded, the book was most likely written before this event.

Key Verses

"The king loved Esther more than all the other women, and she obtained grace and favor in his sight more than all the virgins; so he set the royal crown upon her head and made her queen instead of Vashti."

Esther 2:17

"Then Haman said to King Ahasuerus, 'There is a certain people scattered and dispersed among the people in all the provinces of your kingdom; their laws are different from all other people's, and they do not keep the king's laws. Therefore it is not fitting for the king to let them remain. If it pleases the king, let a decree be written that they be destroyed, and I will pay ten thousand talents of silver into the hands of those who do the work, to bring it into the king's treasuries.' "

Esther 3:8–9

"Then King Ahasuerus said to Queen Esther and Mordecai the Jew, 'Indeed, I have given Esther the house of Haman, and they have hanged him on the gallows because he tried to lay his hand on the Jews. You yourselves write a decree concerning the Jews, as you please, in the king's name, and seal it with the king's signet ring; for whatever is written in the king's name and sealed with the king's signet ring no one can revoke.' "

Esther 8:7–8

1. In Esth. 1:1–2, great care is taken to identify exactly which Ahasuerus is being spoken of, and he is said to have sat on his throne "in those days."
2. For more on how these dates are calculated, see "Time of Events" at the back of this book.

Lessons

1. God uses people, both good and evil, to accomplish His will.
2. Everything that happens comes from the sovereign hand of God.
3. The enemies of God, no matter how powerful, can never thwart His plan.
4. God is always working to preserve His people.

Christ in Esther

If Haman had succeeded in his plot to exterminate the Jews, Christ's family line would have been cut off. Yet, we see the providence of God in preserving His people by thwarting Haman's scheme. The Devil cannot stop the work of Christ. His power is limited and his days are numbered.

Outline

I. **Esther Becomes Queen (Esth. 1–2)**

II. **Haman Plots to Destroy the Jews (Esth. 3–4)**

III. **Esther and Mordecai Defeat Haman (Esth. 5:1–8:2)**

IV. **The Jews Defeat Their Enemies (Esth. 8:3–10:3)**

Study Questions

Over how many provinces did King Ahasuerus reign?

127 (Esth. 1:1).

What did Queen Vashti do that made King Ahasuerus angry?

She refused to come at the king's command (Esth. 1:12).

According to Memucan, what effect would Vashti's rebellion have on all the women in the kingdom?

They would despise their husbands (Esth. 1:17).

What was Memucan's advice?

That King Ahasuerus give Vashti's royal position to another (Esth. 1:19).

What did the king think about Esther?

He loved her more than all the other women, and made her queen instead of Vashti (Esth. 2:17).

What did Mordecai do when all the king's servants bowed and paid homage to Haman?

He refused to do so (Esth. 3:2).

Why was Haman angry at Mordecai?

Because Mordecai would not bow or pay homage to him (Esth. 3:5).

Why did Haman ask the king to have the Jews destroyed?

Because he hated Mordecai (Esth. 3:6–9).

How did Mordecai respond when he heard about the king's decree?

He tore his clothes, put on sackcloth and ashes, went out into the midst of the city, and cried out with a loud and bitter cry (Esth. 4:1).

How did the Jews respond when they heard about the decree?

They mourned with fasting, weeping, and wailing; and many lay in sackcloth and ashes (Esth. 4:3).

What was Esther's response when Mordecai asked her to go before the king?

She told him that those who went to the king uninvited were often put to death (Esth. 4:10–11).

What was Mordecai's response?

He told Esther that if she did not help the Jews, deliverance would arise from another place, but she and her father's house would perish. (Esth. 4:13–14).

What did Esther tell Mordecai and the Jews to do?

She told them to fast for three days before she went to see the king (Esth. 4:15–17).

What did Esther say to the king?

She invited him and Haman to a banquet (Esth. 5:4).

What did Esther say to the king at the banquet?

She asked that he and Haman come to another banquet (Esth. 5:6–8).

What did Haman's wife and friends advise Haman to make?

A gallows, fifty cubits high, to hang Mordecai on (Esth. 5:14).

What did Haman do to Mordecai at the king's command?

He took the king's robe and the horse, arrayed Mordecai, led him on horseback through the city square, and proclaimed before him, "Thus shall it be done to the man whom the king delights to honor!" (Esth. 6:6–11).

What was the king's response when he heard about Haman's plot?

He was filled with wrath (Esth. 7:7).

What was done to Haman at the king's command?

He was hanged on the gallows which he had made for Mordecai (Esth. 7:9–10).

Who did Ahasuerus appoint over the house of Haman after his death?

Mordecai (Esth. 8:2).

What did the king's second decree say?

It permitted the Jews to destroy, kill, and annihilate all the forces of any people or province that would attack them, on the 13th day of the 12th month (Esth. 8:9–12).

What was the response of the Jews to the second decree?

They had joy and gladness, a feast, and a holiday (Esth. 8:17).

What did the Jews do to those who attacked them?

They overpowered and defeated them with a great slaughter (Esth. 9:1–5).

What was Mordecai's position at the end of the book of Esther?

He was second-in-command of the kingdom (Esth. 10:3).

Day by Day

WORDS: Karolina W. Sandell-Berg, 1865; *tr. by* Andrew L. Skoog.
MUSIC: "Blott en Dag"; Oskar Ahnfelt, 1872. Public Domain.

for more resources go to ***jttb.co/job***

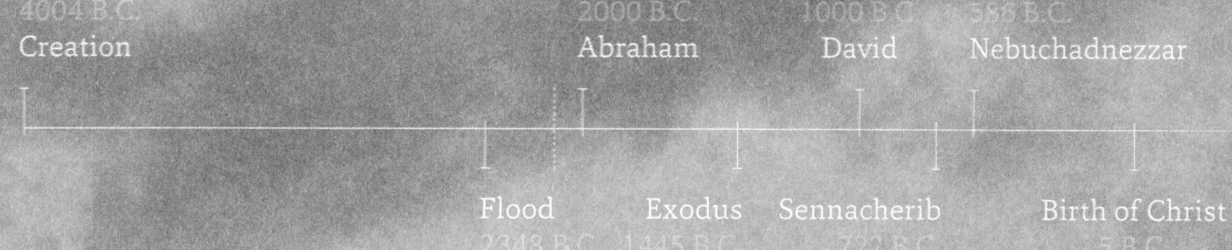

Journey through

Job

THEME

Suffering

AUTHOR

Unknown

TIME OF WRITING

Unknown

MEMORY VERSE

"Though He slay me, yet will I trust Him. Even so, I will defend my own ways before Him."

Job 13:15

OVERVIEW

The book of Job answers one of the most common and important questions: Why do the righteous suffer? Thankfully, God places high priority on answering this question by giving 42 chapters of Scripture to walk us through both the questions and the answers regarding suffering.

The book of Job also explains what we ought to learn about suffering. Job teaches us that we ought not to be presumptuous as we counsel our friends who are suffering. It is clear that through Job's suffering, God was doing something very different than what Job's friends thought.

Top 5 Facts to Remember

1. Job regularly offered sacrifices on behalf of his children (Job 1:5).
2. Satan was ultimately dependent on God for his power against Job (Job 1:9–12; 2:4–7).
3. Because he was the youngest, Elihu waited to speak until he saw that both Job and his friends were in error (Job 32:2–10).
4. Although Job wanted to question God, God was the one who questioned him (Job 38:1–42:6).
5. After the Lord had finished testing Job, He blessed him with twice as many possessions as he had owned before (Job 1:3; 42:12).

Theme: Suffering

In Job, God is glorifying Himself through suffering, so that He might demonstrate His superior goodness in the salvation sinners, the damnation of the wicked, and for the preservation of His people for His eternal glory, and their eternal joy.

Author: *Unknown*

We don't know who wrote the Book of Job, though many theories exist.

Time of Writing: *Unknown*

Job is one of the earliest books of the Bible, with the events taking place around 2000 B.C. sometime before or during the patriarchal period. He lived in the land of Uz or Edom, southeast of the Dead Sea, in the region of modern northern Arabia.

The events recorded in the book of Job most likely took place before or during

Abraham's time. Evidence for this includes Job's rather long lifespan[1] and the way he functioned as priest of his family.[2] The exact date of when the book of Job was written is uncertain.

Key Verses

"Then Job arose, tore his robe, and shaved his head; and he fell to the ground and worshiped. And he said:
'Naked I came from my mother's womb,
And naked shall I return there.
The Lord gave, and the Lord has taken away;
Blessed be the name of the Lord.'
In all this Job did not sin nor charge God with wrong."

Job 1:20–22

"As for the Almighty, we cannot find Him;
He is excellent in power,
In judgment and abundant justice;
He does not oppress.
Therefore men fear Him;
He shows no partiality to any who are wise of heart."

Job 37:23–24

"Then Job answered the Lord and said:
'I know that You can do everything,
And that no purpose of Yours can be withheld from You.
You asked, "Who is this who hides counsel without knowledge?"
Therefore I have uttered what I did not understand,
Things too wonderful for me, which I did not know.
Listen, please, and let me speak;

1. Job 42:16; cf. Gen. 25:7.
2. Job 1:5.

You said, "I will question you, and you shall answer Me."
'I have heard of You by the hearing of the ear,
But now my eye sees You.
Therefore I abhor myself,
And repent in dust and ashes.' "

Job 42:1–6

Lessons

1. God providentially allows His people to go through times of trial and suffering.
2. We should be willing to trust the Lord—whose plan is infinitely wise—regardless of our circumstances.

Christ in Job

In the midst of his suffering, Job spoke prophetically of a living, personal Redeemer who would stand at last on the earth (Job 19:23–27).

Outline

I. **God Brings Tragedy Upon Job (Job 1–2)**

II. **The Debates Between Job and His Friends (Job 3–26)**

 A. The First Cycle of Analysis (Job 3–14)

  1. Job Speaks (Job 3)
  2. Eliphaz Speaks (Job 4–5), and Job Responds (Job 6–7)
  3. Bildad Speaks (Job 8), and Job Responds (Job 9–10)

4. Zophar Speaks (Job 11), and Job Responds (Job 12–14)

B. The Second Cycle of Analysis – Job 15–21

1. Eliphaz Speaks (Job 15), and Job Responds (Job 16–17)
2. Bildad Speaks (Job 18), and Job Responds (Job 19)
3. Zophar Speaks (Job 20), and Job Responds (Job 21)

C. The Third Cycle of Analysis (Job 22–26)

1. Eliphaz Speaks (Job 22), and Job Responds (Job 23–24)
2. Bildad Speaks (Job 25), and Job Responds (Job 26)

D. Job's Final Defense (Job 27–31)

E. Elihu Speaks (Job 32–37)

III. God Speaks to Job and Questions Him (Job 38:1–42:6)

IV. God Speaks to Job's Friends (Job 42:7–11)

V. God Blesses Job (Job 42:12–17)

Study Questions

Where did Job and his family live?

The land of Uz (Job 1:1).

How does the author describe Job's character?

He was a man who was blameless and upright, one who feared God and shunned evil (Job 1:1).

What would Job do on behalf of his sons after the days of feasting?

He would offer burnt offerings for them, in case any of them had sinned (Job 1:5).

What did Satan say Job would do if he lost everything?

Curse God to His face (Job 1:11).

What was Job's response to the death of his children and the loss of all his possessions?

He tore his robe, shaved his head, fell to the ground, and worshiped God (Job 1:20–22).

What did Satan say Job would do if God afflicted his body?

Curse God to His face (Job 2:5).

What was Job's response when his wife told him to curse God?

He told her that she was speaking like a foolish woman (Job 2:10).

Who were Job's three friends?

Eliphaz, Bildad, and Zophar (Job 2:11).

What was Job's response when God spoke to him?

He realized that he could not answer God's questions (Job 40:3–5; 42:1–6).

What did Job do after God was finished speaking to him?

He repented (Job 42:6).

What did the Lord say to Job's friends?

He told them that He was angry with them, and commanded them to offer sacrifices for themselves (Job 42:7–8).

How did the Lord bless Job towards the end of his life?

He gave him twice as much livestock as before, seven more sons and three more daughters, and many more days of life (Job 42:12–15).

How many generations of his children did Job get to see?

Four generations (Job 42:16).

JOB

The Lord is My Shepherd

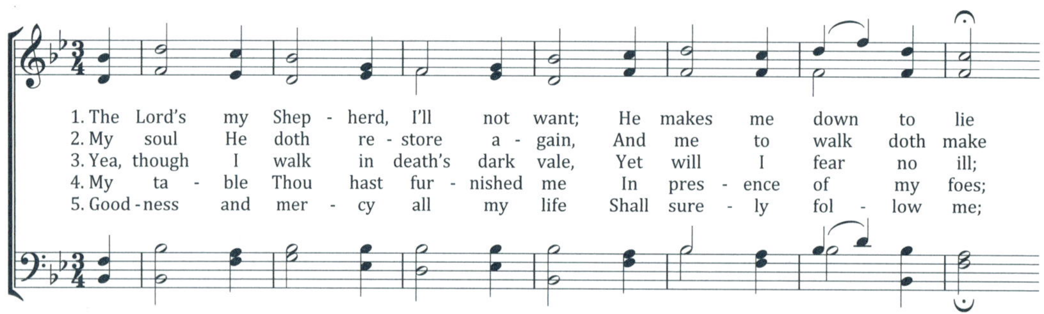

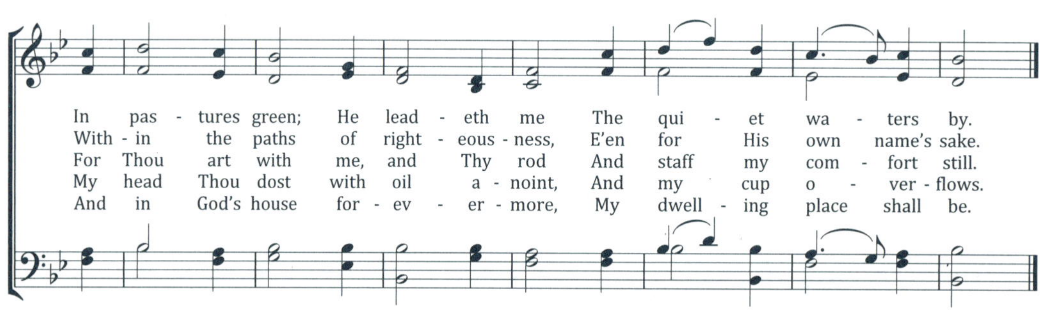

WORDS: Scripture; *alt. by* Francis Rous, *pub.*1650. MUSIC: "Ballerma"; François H. Barthélémon; *arr. by* Robert Simpson, *pub.*1833. Public Domain.

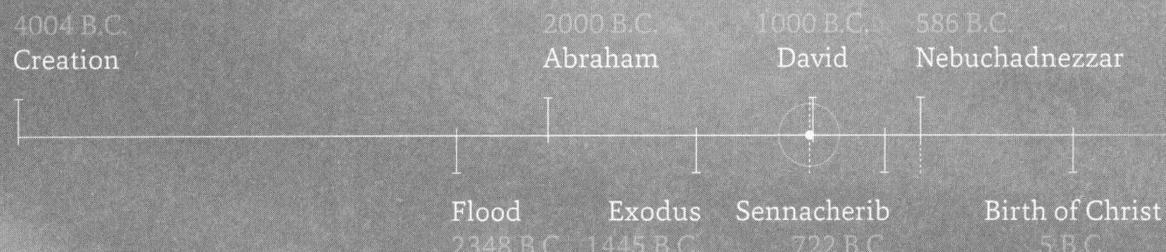

Journey through

Psalms

THEME

Worship

AUTHORS

Multiple

TIME OF WRITING

1410–450 B.C.

MEMORY VERSE

1 Blessed is the man who walks not in the counsel of the un-
godly, nor stands in the path of sinners, nor sits in the seat
of the scornful; 2 But his delight is in the law of the Lord,
and in His law he meditates day and night. 3 He shall be
like a tree planted by the rivers of water, that brings forth
its fruit in its season, whose leaf also shall not wither; and
whatever he does shall prosper.

Psalms 1:1–3

OVERVIEW

"Let everything that has breath praise the Lord." This phrase characterizes what is meant to be the supreme effect of reading the Psalms. The focus of the Psalms is worship through all the events and ups and downs of life. Psalms is comprised of 150 songs that span from Moses to the post-exilic period and they reflect a vast array of human experiences such as joy, sorrow, abandonment, atonement, tears, renewal, refuge, rest, war, peace, fear, failure, hope, enemies, love, lamentation, praise, and judgment.

In short, the book of Psalms is one of the great poetical books of the Old Testament. Interestingly, there are only five Old Testament books that do not seem to have any poetry. They are: Leviticus, Ruth, Ezra, Haggai, and Malachi.

Top 5 Facts to Remember

1. The heavens declare the glory of God (Ps. 19:1).
2. The man who delights in God's law is blessed (Ps. 1:1–2).
3. Jesus quoted the first line of Psalm 22 (a psalm which predicted His death) while on the cross (Matt. 27:46; Mar. 15:34).
4. The longest chapter in the Bible is Psalm 119, which contains 176 verses.
5. Psalm 2 speaks of how vain it is for nations to exalt themselves against Christ (cf. Acts 4:24–30).

Theme: Worship at All Times

In the book of Psalms, God is glorifying Himself through worship at all times, so that He might demonstrate His superior goodness in the salvation sinners, the damnation of the wicked, and for the preservation of His people for His eternal glory, and their eternal joy.

Authors: *Multiple*

The Psalms are the product of multiple authors. The Bible clearly identifies the authors of 101 psalms (mostly through the headings of particular psalms, but also through other passages of Scripture).

1. David wrote 75 psalms.[1]
2. Asaph wrote 12 psalms.[2]

1. 73 psalms name David as their author (Ps. 3–9; 11–32; 34–41; 51–65; 68–70; 86; 101; 103; 108–110; 122; 124; 131; 133; 138–145), while 2 additional psalms (Ps. 2 and Ps. 95) are attributed to him in Acts 4:25–26 and Heb. 4:7.
2. Ps. 50; 73–83.

3. The Sons of Korah wrote 11 psalms (including Ps. 88, which they coauthored with Heman the Ezrahite)[3]

4. Solomon wrote Psalms 72 and 127.

5. Ethan the Ezrahite wrote Psalm 89.

6. Moses wrote Psalm 90.

The Bible does not clearly identify the author(s) of the remaining 48 psalms. However, the fact that Psalms 96, 105, and 106 bear similarities to a Davidic psalm recorded in 1 Chron. 16:7–36 suggest that they are Davidic in origin.

Time of Writing: 1410–450 B.C.

Psalm 90 (authored by Moses and probably the oldest Psalm) was written sometime between 1445 and 1405 B.C.[4] The Book of Psalms was probably completed by Ezra's time (424 B.C.).

Key Verses

"The law of the Lord is perfect, converting the soul;
The testimony of the Lord is sure, making wise the simple;
The statutes of the Lord are right, rejoicing the heart;
The commandment of the Lord is pure, enlightening the eyes;
The fear of the Lord is clean, enduring forever;
The judgments of the Lord are true and righteous altogether.
More to be desired are they than gold,
Yea, than much fine gold;
Sweeter also than honey and the honeycomb.

3. Ps. 42; 44–49; 84–85; 87–88.

4. For more on how these dates are calculated, see "Time of Events" at the back of this book.

Moreover by them Your servant is warned,
And in keeping them there is great reward."

Psalm 19:7–11

"The Lord is my shepherd;
I shall not want.
He makes me to lie down in green pastures;
He leads me beside the still waters.
He restores my soul;
He leads me in the paths of righteousness
For His name's sake."

Psalm 23:1–3

"Create in me a clean heart, O God,
And renew a steadfast spirit within me.
Do not cast me away from Your presence,
And do not take Your Holy Spirit from me.
"Restore to me the joy of Your salvation,
And uphold me by Your generous Spirit.
Then I will teach transgressors Your ways,
And sinners shall be converted to You."

Psalm 51:10–13

Lessons

1. We ought to delight in the law of God.
2. We ought to recognize God's glory in the heavens.
3. The Word of God is pure, sure, perfect, and sufficient.
4. We ought to center our lives on praising the Lord.
5. We ought to trust in the sovereign hand of God.

Christ in Psalms

I. **God's Anointed King (Ps. 2)**

II. **The Resurrection (Ps. 16:9–10)**

III. **The Crucifixion (Ps. 22)**

IV. **The Good Shepherd (Ps. 23)**

V. **Hated Without Cause (Ps. 69:4)**

VI. **Sitting at the Right Hand of God (Ps. 110:1)**

VII. **The Priesthood of Melchizedek (Ps. 110:4)**

VIII. **The Cornerstone (Ps. 118:22–23)**

Outline

I. **Book I (Ps. 1–41)**

II. **Book II (Ps. 42–72)**

III. **Book III (Ps. 73–89)**

IV. **Book IV (Ps. 90–106)**

V. **Book V (Ps. 107–150)**

Study Questions

How many psalms did David write?

Seventy-four.

How many psalms did Asaph write?

Twelve.

Which psalm did Moses write?

Psalm 90.

Which psalms are labeled "Songs of Ascent"?

Psalms 120–134.

Which psalms did the sons of Korah write?

Psalms 42; 44–49; 84–85; 87–88.

Which psalms did Solomon write?

Psalms 72 and 127.

Which psalm did Ethan the Ezrahite write?

Psalm 89.

The psalms are divided into how many books?

Five.

Which psalm magnifies the Word of God?

Psalm 119.

How many different sections are there in Psalm 119?

Twenty-two.

Which psalm speaks of Christ's suffering?

Psalm 22.

After his sin with Bathsheba was exposed, what psalm did David write?

Psalm 51.

Which Psalm is called "A Song for the Sabbath day"?

Psalm 92.

What is the message of Psalm 1?

God blesses the way of the godly man and curses the way of the ungodly man.

What is the message of Psalm 23?

The Lord is a good Shepherd.

What is the message of Psalm 150?

Praise the Lord!

Which psalms are included in each of the five books?

Book I – Ps. 1–41
Book II – Ps. 42–72
Book III – Ps. 73–89
Book IV – Ps. 90–106
Book V – Ps. 107–150

O Word of God Incarnate

WORDS: William W. How, 1867; *alt.* MUSIC: "Munich"; Author unknown, *pub.*1693; *har. by* Felix Mendelssohn, 1847. Public Domain.

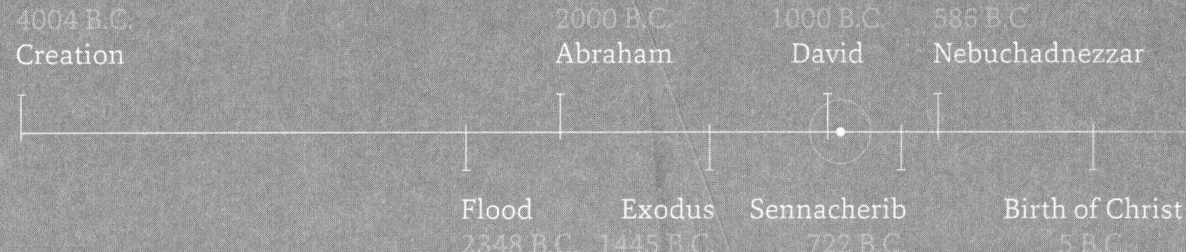

Journey through

Proverbs

THEME	AUTHORS	TIME OF WRITING
Wisdom	*Multiple*	971–686 B.C.

MEMORY VERSE

"The fear of the Lord is the beginning of knowledge, but fools despise wisdom and instruction."

Proverbs 1:7

OVERVIEW

Proverbs is a teacher's manual, written by a father, to a father for the instruction of his sons and daughters. The Proverbs are more accurate than economists, more insightful than sociologists, more practical than your teachers, more helpful than your own heart, and more enlightening than your personal experience. A proverb is a simple phrase to explain a complex subject.

Top 5 Facts to Remember

1. Proverbs 31 shows us what a virtuous woman looks like.
2. The fear of the Lord is the beginning of knowledge and wisdom (Prov. 1:7; 9:10).
3. A woman who fears the Lord will be praised (Prov. 31:30).
4. The house of the immoral woman is the way to hell (Prov. 7:27).
5. Rebuke is more effective for a wise man than a hundred blows on a fool (Prov. 17:10).

Theme: Wisdom

In Proverbs, God is glorifying Himself through wisdom, so that He might demonstrate His superior goodness in the salvation sinners, the damnation of the wicked, and for the preservation of His people for His eternal glory, and their eternal joy.

Authors: *Multiple*

A plurality of authors and copyists took part in producing the book of Proverbs:

1. Solomon.[1]
2. The men of Hezekiah, king of Judah.[2]
3. The wise.[3]
4. Agur the son of Jakeh.[4]
5. King Lemuel.[5]

Time of Writing: 971–686 B.C.

Many of the Proverbs were either written or collected by Solomon sometime during his reign (971–931 B.C.).[6] The book was probably put into its final form during the reign of Hezekiah (716–687 B.C.).

1. Prov. 1:1; 10:1; 25:1.
2. Prov. 25:1.
3. Prov. 22:17; 24:23.
4. Prov. 30:1.
5. Prov. 31:1.
6. For more on how these dates are calculated, see "Time of Events" at the back of this book.

Key Verses

"Trust in the Lord with all your heart,
And lean not on your own understanding;
In all your ways acknowledge Him,
And He shall direct your paths."

Proverbs 3:5–6

"Who can find a virtuous wife?
For her worth is far above rubies.
The heart of her husband safely trusts her;
So he will have no lack of gain."

Proverbs 31:10–11

Lessons

1. "The fear of the Lord is the beginning of knowledge" (Prov. 1:7).
2. Trust in the Lord rather than your own inclinations.
3. Flee from the temptations of the adulterous woman.

Christ in Proverbs

I. **Wisdom (Prov. 8)**

II. **The Son of God (Prov. 30:4)**

Outline

I. **The Proverbs of Solomon (Prov. 1:1–22:16)**

II. **The Words of the Wise (Prov. 22:17–24:34)**

III. **More Proverbs of Solomon (Prov. 25–29)**

IV. **The Words of Agur (Prov. 30)**

V. **The Words of Lemuel (Prov. 31)**

Study Questions

What verse summarizes the book of Proverbs?

"The fear of the Lord is the beginning of knowledge,
But fools despise wisdom and instruction" (Prov. 1:7).

The book of Proverbs tells the sluggard to consider the ways of what insect?

The ant (Prov. 6:6–8).

What are the seven things which are an abomination to the Lord?

1. A proud look.
2. A lying tongue.

3. Hands that shed innocent blood.

4. A heart that devises wicked plans.

5. Feet that are swift in running to evil.

6. A false witness who speaks lies.

7. One who sows discord among brethren (Prov. 6:16–19).

Which chapter of Proverbs contrasts Wisdom with the foolish woman?

Proverbs 9.

Which chapter of Proverbs contains the words of Agur?

Proverbs 30.

Where is the virtuous woman described in Proverbs?

Proverbs 31:10–31.

Be Thou My Vision

WORDS: *attr. to* Dallan Forgaill; *tr. by* Mary E. Byrne, *pub.*1905; *arr. by* Eleanor H. Hull, 1912.
MUSIC: "Slane"; Irish melody; *har.* Public Domain.

for more resources go to ***jttb.co/ecclesiastes***

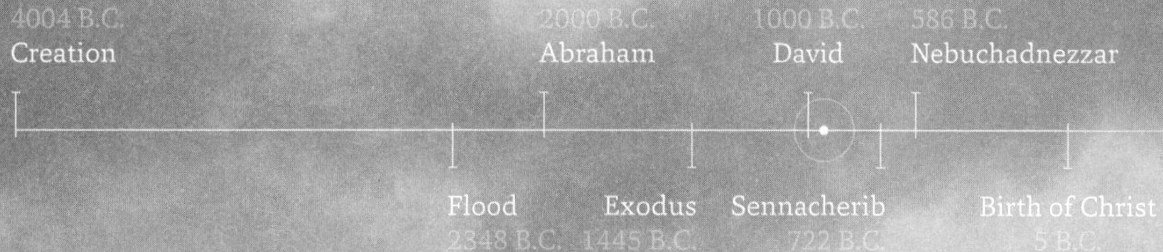

Journey through

Ecclesiastes

THEME	AUTHOR	TIME OF WRITING
Life Apart from God	Solomon	940–931 B.C.

MEMORY VERSE

*13 Let us hear the conclusion of the whole matter: fear God
and keep His commandments, for this is man's all. 14 For
God will bring every work into judgment, including every
secret thing, whether good or evil.*

Ecclesiastes 12:13–14

OVERVIEW

The book of Ecclesiastes communicates the truth that the source of true joy and satisfaction is in God alone. Solomon was on a search for his ultimate purpose in life. Ecclesiastes describes what a life lived apart from God looks like by examining "life under the sun." This is life without considering God.

Solomon explains his journey through life and the relative value of pleasure, work, wisdom, intellect, activity, and wealth. In short, the book of Ecclesiastes records Solomon's search for meaning and significance.

Top 5 Facts to Remember

1. Authentic joy and satisfaction are found in God alone.
2. There is a season and a time for everything (Eccl. 3:1–8).
3. God has set eternity in the heart of every person (Eccl. 3:11).
4. God made man upright, but they have sought out many schemes (Eccl. 7:29).
5. It will be well with those who fear God (Eccl. 8:12).

Theme: Life Apart from God

In Ecclesiastes, God is glorifying Himself through disclosing what it means to live life apart from God, so that He might demonstrate His superior goodness in the salvation sinners, the damnation of the wicked, and for the preservation of His people for His eternal glory, and their eternal joy.

Author: Solomon

Solomon is the author of Ecclesiastes. Although the name, "Solomon" never appears in the book, the author refers to himself as "the son of David" (Eccl. 1:1) and asserts that he "was king over Israel in Jerusalem" (Eccl. 1:12). Since Solomon was the only son of David to become king, and the last king to reign over both Israel and Jerusalem, this description could only be true of him.

Time of Writing: 940–931 B.C.

Solomon wrote Ecclesiastes sometime during his reign (971–931 B.C.).[1] Since Solomon seems to be looking back on his life, a date closer to 931 B.C. is probable.

Key Verses

"A good name is better than precious ointment,
And the day of death than the day of one's birth;
Better to go to the house of mourning
Than to go to the house of feasting,
For that is the end of all men;
And the living will take it to heart."

Ecclesiastes 7:1–2

"Truly, this only I have found:
That God made man upright,
But they have sought out many schemes."

Ecclesiastes 7:29

"Remember now your Creator in the days of your youth,
Before the difficult days come,
And the years draw near when you say,
'I have no pleasure in them.'"

Ecclesiastes 12:1

1. For more on how these dates are calculated, see "Time of Events" at the back of this book.

Lessons

1. There is a time and season for everything.
2. God has set eternity in the human heart.
3. It is better to go to the house of mourning than to the house of feasting.
4. Remember your Creator in the days of your youth.
5. We ought to fear God and keep His commandments.

Christ in Ecclesiastes

I. Solomon

Solomon is a type of Christ. Like Solomon, Christ was a preacher, one who demonstrated the vanity of living without God.

II. Deliverance from Vanity

Our deliverance from vanity was manifested in the person and work of Jesus Christ, who is the Wisdom of God (1 Cor. 1:22–24, 30). Without Christ, our lives would have remained vain and meaningless.

Outline

I. **Enjoying Life as a Gift from God (Eccl. 1–2)**

II. **Understanding God's Plan for Your Life (Eccl. 3–7)**

III. **Removing Discouragements and Applying God's Plan (Eccl. 8–12)**

Study Questions

CHAPTERS 1–5

When was the book of Ecclesiastes written?

Sometime between 971 and 931 B.C.

Who wrote the book of Ecclesiastes?

Solomon, "the Preacher" (Eccl. 1:1).

How does Solomon contrast the earth with the generations of men?

Generations come and go, but the earth remains (Eccl. 1:4).

What does the author conclude after seeing "all the works that are done under the sun"?

All of them are vanity and grasping for the wind (Eccl. 1:14).

What comes with an increase of wisdom and knowledge?

An increase of grief and sorrow (Eccl. 1:18).

What does the preacher say about pleasure?

It also is vanity (Eccl. 2:1).

What does the preacher say about all his works and labor?

All of it was vanity and grasping for the wind, and there was no profit under the sun (Eccl. 2:11).

What does God give to the man who is good in His sight?

Wisdom, knowledge, and joy (Eccl. 2:26).

What does God give to the wicked?

The work of gathering and collecting things that the righteous will ultimately receive (Eccl. 2:26).

What has God put in the heart of every man?

Eternity (Eccl. 3:11).

What does the preacher say about God's work?

It lasts forever and cannot be changed (Eccl. 3:14).

Where do all men come from and return to?

Dust (Eccl. 3:20).

What does the preacher say about companions?

They are needed in times of trouble (Eccl. 4:9–12).

How should we walk when we go to the house of God?

Prudently (Eccl. 5:1).

What warning does Solomon give us about our speech in God's house?

Do not be rash with your mouth (Eccl. 5:2).

What does God require of those who make a vow?

That they pay it without delay (Eccl. 5:4).

What is the difference between the sleep of the laboring man and that of the rich man?

The sleep of a laboring man is sweet, but the rich man cannot sleep (Eccl. 5:12).

Who gives men the gift of wealth?

God (Eccl. 5:19).

CHAPTERS 6–12

Why is it better to go to the house of mourning than the house of feasting?

Because death is the end of all men (Eccl. 7:2).

Where is the heart of the wise, compared with the heart of fools?

The heart of the wise is in the house of mourning, but the heart of fools is in the house of mirth (Eccl. 7:4).

In what condition did God make mankind?

Upright (Eccl. 7:29).

What have men done since creation?

They have sought out many schemes (Eccl. 7:29).

What should our response be to the king's commandment?

Obedience (Eccl. 8:2).

Why will it be well with the righteous, but not with the wicked?

Because the righteous fear God, but the wicked do not (Eccl. 8:12–13).

What should a husband's attitude be towards his wife?

He should live joyfully with her all the days of his life (Eccl. 9:9).

What should our attitude be towards the work that God has given us?

We should do it with all our might (Eccl. 9:10).

How does wisdom compare to strength?

Wisdom is better than strength (Eccl. 9:13–18).

What does the fool show everyone?

That he is a fool (Eccl. 10:3).

What is the difference between the mouth of the wise man and the mouth of the foolish man?

The words of a wise man's mouth are gracious, but the lips of a fool shall swallow him up (Eccl. 10:12).

What is the preacher's charge to young men?

To remove sorrow from their hearts, and to put away evil from their flesh (Eccl. 11:9–10).

What is the preacher's conclusion at the end of the book of Ecclesiastes?

Fear God and keep His commandments (Eccl. 12:13–14).

Oh, How I Love Jesus

WORDS: Frederick Whitfield, 1855. MUSIC: American melody. Public Domain.

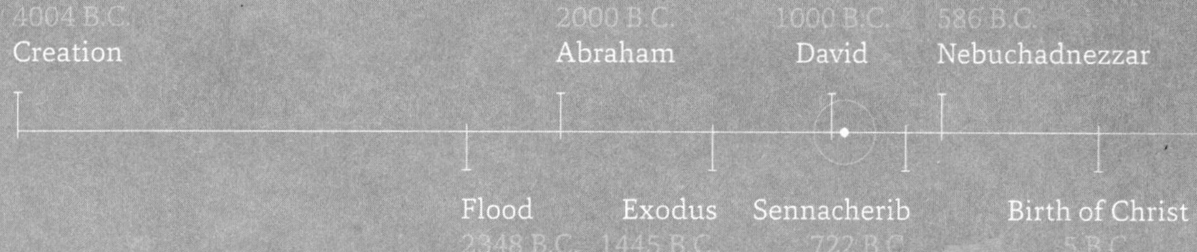

Journey through

Song *of* Solomon

THEME

Marriage

AUTHOR

Solomon

TIME OF WRITING

971–965 B.C.

MEMORY VERSE

"My beloved is mine, and I am his. He feeds his flock among the lilies."

Song of Solomon 2:16

OVERVIEW

This is a parable of marital love which is also a picture of Christ's love for His church. Solomon has given us one of the truly great and inspiring songs in the Bible. While the interpretation of this song is hotly contested, my understanding is that there are two aspects of the song: it is a parable of marital love between two real people, and it is also a picture of Christ's love for His church.

Top 5 Facts to Remember

1. The characters in this song are: Solomon (the "Beloved"), the Shulamite, the daughters of Jerusalem, Solomon's friends, and the Shulamite's brothers.
2. Marriage is honorable among all, and the bed undefiled (Heb. 13:4).
3. A husband's love for his wife is a picture of Christ's love for His church (Eph. 5:22–33).
4. Love is as strong as death (Song 8:6).
5. At three points in the song, the Shulamite charges the daughters of Jerusalem: "Do not stir up nor awaken love until it pleases" (Song 2:7; 3:5; 8:4).

Theme: Marriage

In Song of Solomon, God is glorifying Himself through marriage, so that He might demonstrate His superior goodness in the salvation sinners, the damnation of the wicked, and for the preservation of His people for His eternal glory, and their eternal joy.

Author: Solomon

The book names Solomon as its author.[1]

Time of Writing: 971–965 B.C.

The Song of Solomon was written sometime during Solomon's reign as king[2] (971–931 B.C.).[3]

Key Verses

"Let him kiss me with the kisses of his mouth—
For your love is better than wine.
Because of the fragrance of your good ointments,
Your name is ointment poured forth;
Therefore the virgins love you.
Draw me away!"

Song of Solomon 1:2–4a

1. Song 1:1.
2. See Song 3:9, 11.
3. For more on how these dates are calculated, see "Time of Events" at the back of this book.

"I charge you, O daughters of Jerusalem,
By the gazelles or by the does of the field,
Do not stir up nor awaken love
Until it pleases."

Song of Solomon 3:5

"I have come to my garden, my sister, my spouse;
I have gathered my myrrh with my spice;
I have eaten my honeycomb with my honey;
I have drunk my wine with my milk."

Song of Solomon 5:1a

Lessons

1. Husbands ought to be captivated with their wives, and wives ought to be captivated with their husbands.
2. True love between a husband and wife is a glorious thing.
3. True love seeks reconciliation after an offense.
4. To young men who are not yet married: Be men of character.
5. To young women who are not yet married: Do not awaken love before its time.

Christ in Song of Solomon

In this song, the husband's love for his wife is a picture of Christ's love for His bride, the Church (see Eph. 5:22–33).

Outline

I. **The Awakening of Love (Song 1:1–3:5)**

  A. Mutual Desire (Song 1:1–2:7)

  B. A Visit from the Beloved (Song 2:8–17)

  C. A Dream of Separation (Song 3:1–5)

II. **United in Love: The Wedding (Song 3:6–5:1)**

  A. The Wedding Procession (Song 3:6–11)

  B. Praise of the Shulamite (Song 4:1–5:1)

III. **Struggling in Love: The Problems (Song 5:2–8:4)**

  A. Anxiety of Love (Song 5:2–6:3)

  B. Praise of the Shulamite (Song 6:4–10)

  C. Marital Union (Song 6:11–8:4)

IV. **Conclusion (Song 8:5–14)**

Study Questions

What is the theme of the Song of Solomon?

The marital love between a husband and his wife.

What is the marriage relationship a picture of?

Christ's love for the church (Eph. 5:22–33).

Why was the Shulamite attracted to Solomon?

Because he was a man of good reputation (Song 1:2–4).

What was the Shulamite's first dream about?

Searching for the one she loved (Song 3:1–5).

How does Solomon describe the beauty of his wife?

He uses a wide range of imagery: goats, sheep, pomegranates, towers, honeycombs, gardens, and many other things (Song 4:1–15).

What was the Shulamite's response when Solomon knocked on her door?

She was hesitant to get up and open the door (Song 5:2–3).

What does the Shulamite say about awakening love?

"Do not stir up nor awaken love until it pleases" (Song 2:7; 3:5; 8:4).

Immortal, Invisible, God Only Wise

WORDS: Walter C. Smith, *pub.* 1876; *alt.*
MUSIC: "St. Denio"; Welsh melody, *pub.* 1839. Public Domain.

for more resources go to ***jttb.co/isaiah***

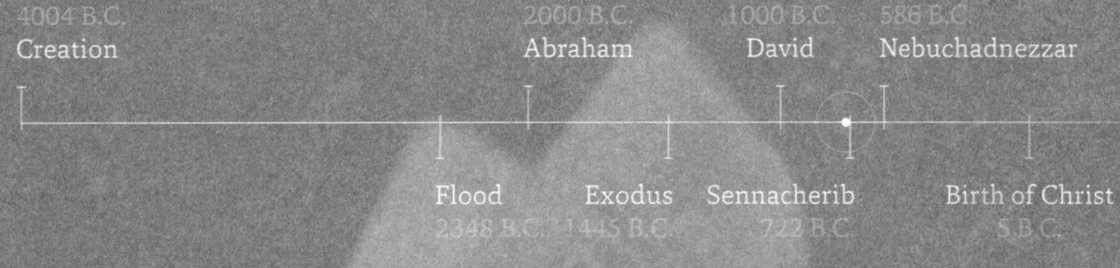

Journey through

Isaiah

THEME	AUTHOR	TIME OF WRITING
Salvation	Isaiah	700–681 B.C.

MEMORY VERSE

"O Zion, you who bring good tidings, get up into the high mountain; o Jerusalem, you who bring good tidings, lift up your voice with strength, lift it up, be not afraid; say to the cities of Judah, 'Behold your God!' "

Isaiah 40:9

OVERVIEW

The book of Isaiah is the Romans of the Old Testament and what some have called the fifth Gospel. It is the third-longest book in the Bible. Isaiah is the first of the Major Prophets in the sequence of the canon of Scripture. More is revealed about Christ in Isaiah than any other Old Testament prophetic book.

Isaiah is the Bible in miniature. There are 66 books in the Bible and 66 chapters of Isaiah. There are 39 books of the Old Testament, and 39 chapters in the first section of Isaiah. There are 27 books in the New Testament and 27 chapters in the second half of Isaiah. Similarly, Isaiah 40 begins with a voice crying in the wilderness and the New Testament begins with John the Baptist, the voice of one crying in the wilderness. Further, Isaiah 1 is equivalent to the first book of the Bible, Genesis. Isaiah 40 is equivalent to Matthew. Isaiah 66 is equivalent to Revelation; and Isaiah and Revelation contain the seven verses where God reveals Himself as the first and the last.

Top 5 Facts to Remember

1. Isaiah became a prophet in the same year that King Uzziah died (Isa. 6:1, 8).
2. God judges nations for their sin.
3. Idolatry is utterly foolish and futile.
4. Hezekiah recognized that the gods of the surrounding nations were not gods at all, but only the work of men's hands (Isa. 37:18–19).
5. Isaiah 52:13–53:12 predicts the suffering of Christ for our sins.

Theme: Salvation

In Isaiah, God is glorifying Himself through the salvation of a wayward people so that He might demonstrate His superior goodness in the salvation sinners, the damnation of the wicked, and for the preservation of His people for His eternal glory, and their eternal joy.

Author: Isaiah

The author identifies himself as Isaiah, the son of Amoz,[1] and many biblical writers confirm this.[2] The book also includes a song authored by King Hezekiah (Isa. 38:9–20).

1. Isa. 1:1; 2:1; 13:1.
2. 2 Chron. 32:32; Matt. 3:3; 4:14–16; 8:17; 12:17–21; 13:14–15; 15:7–9; Mark 7:6–7; Luke 3:4–6; 4:17–19; John 1:23; 12:37–41; Acts 8:27–35; 28:25–27; Rom. 9:27–29; 10:16, 20–21; 15:12.

Time of Writing: 700–681 B.C.

Isaiah was called to be a prophet in the same year that King Uzziah died[3] (740 B.C.).[4] The last event recorded in the book is the death of Sennacherib (681 B.C.), which means Isaiah most likely finished it during the reign of Manasseh (687–643 B.C.).

Key Verses

"So I said:
'Woe is me, for I am undone!
Because I am a man of unclean lips,
And I dwell in the midst of a people of unclean lips;
For my eyes have seen the King,
The Lord of hosts.' "

Isaiah 6:5

"Nevertheless the gloom will not be upon her who is distressed,
As when at first He lightly esteemed
The land of Zebulun and the land of Naphtali,
And afterward more heavily oppressed her,
By the way of the sea, beyond the Jordan,
In Galilee of the Gentiles.
The people who walked in darkness
Have seen a great light;
Those who dwelt in the land of the shadow of death,
Upon them a light has shined."

Isaiah 9:1–2

3. Isa. 6:1, 8.
4. For more on how these dates are calculated, see "Time of Events" at the back of this book.

"Surely He has borne our griefs
And carried our sorrows;
Yet we esteemed Him stricken,
Smitten by God, and afflicted.
But He was wounded for our transgressions,
He was bruised for our iniquities;
The chastisement for our peace was upon Him,
And by His stripes we are healed.
All we like sheep have gone astray;
We have turned, every one, to his own way;
And the Lord has laid on Him the iniquity of us all."

Isaiah 53:4–6

Lessons

1. Search out and destroy your idols, they are worthless and dangerous.
2. God does and will judge sinful nations.
3. Christ is the perfect substitute who died to redeem a chosen people.
4. Repent and believe on the Lord Jesus Christ!
5. Judgment begins in the house of God.

Christ in Isaiah

I. **The "Branch of the Lord" (Isa. 4:2)**

II. **Immanuel (Isa. 7:14; Matt. 1:22–23)**

III. **The Light (Isa. 9:1; Matt. 4:13–16)**

IV. **"Wonderful, Counselor, Mighty God, Everlasting Father, Prince of Peace" (Isa. 9:6–7)**

V. **A Rod from the Stem of Jesse (Isa. 11)**

VI. **A Stone Laid in Zion (Isa. 28:16; Rom. 9:33; 10:11)**

VII. **The Blind, Deaf, Lame, and Dumb Healed (Isa. 35:5–6)**

VIII. **Israel's Redeemer (Isa. 41:14; Gal. 4:4–5; Tit. 2:13–14)**

IX. **A Light to the Gentiles (Isa. 42:1–9; 49:6; Luke 2:32; Acts 13:47; 26:22–23)**

X. **The Beating of the Messiah (Isa. 50:6)**

XI. **The Suffering Servant (Isa. 52:13–53:12; Acts 8:32–35)**

Outline

I. **Judgment on the Nations (Isa. 1–39)**

- A. The Vision Concerning Judah and Jerusalem (Isa. 1–12)
- B. The Vision Concerning the Nations (Isa. 13–27)
- C. The Deliverer (Isa. 28–35)
- D. Historical Interlude (Isa. 36–39)

II. **The Comfort of the Suffering Servant (Isa. 40–66)**

A. The One True God and the Idols (Isa. 40–48)

B. Contrasts the Idols with the One True God and the Suffering Servant (Isa. 49–57)

C. Proclaims the End of the Babylonian Captivity, and Casts a Vision of Future Glory (Isa. 58–66)

Study Questions

What is the theme of chapters 1–39?

Judgment.

What is the theme of chapters 40–66?

Salvation.

What is the name of Christ found in Isaiah 4:2?

The Branch of the Lord.

What chapter speaks about the holiness of God, and Isaiah's response to it?

Chapter 6.

What chapter speaks of the government of our Lord Jesus Christ?

Chapter 9.

How is Christ described in Isaiah 11:1?

As a Rod that comes from the stem of Jesse, and a Branch that grows out of his roots.

What chapter speaks of the fall of Lucifer?

Chapter 14.

What is the theme of chapter 40?

"Comfort, yes, comfort my people" (Isa. 40:1).

Where are the four servant songs located in Isaiah?

1. Isaiah 42:1–9
2. Isaiah 49:1–13
3. Isaiah 50:4–11
4. Isaiah 52:13–53:12

What is the theme of Isaiah 53?

The suffering and exaltation of the Lord Jesus Christ.

When I Survey the Wondrous Cross

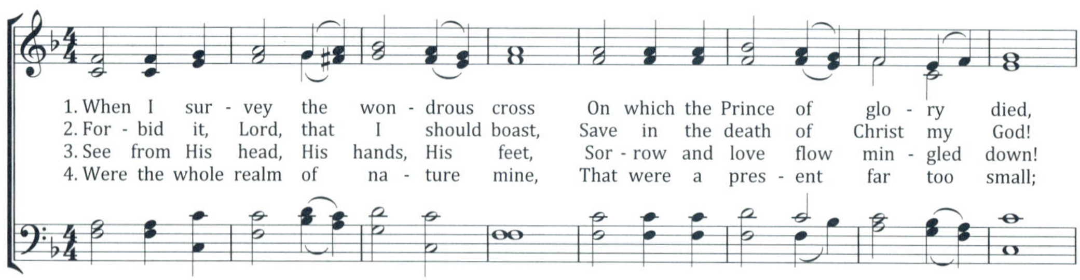

WORDS: Isaac Watts, *pub.* 1707. MUSIC: "Hamburg"; Lowell Mason, 1824. Public Domain.

for more resources go to ***jttb.co/jeremiah***

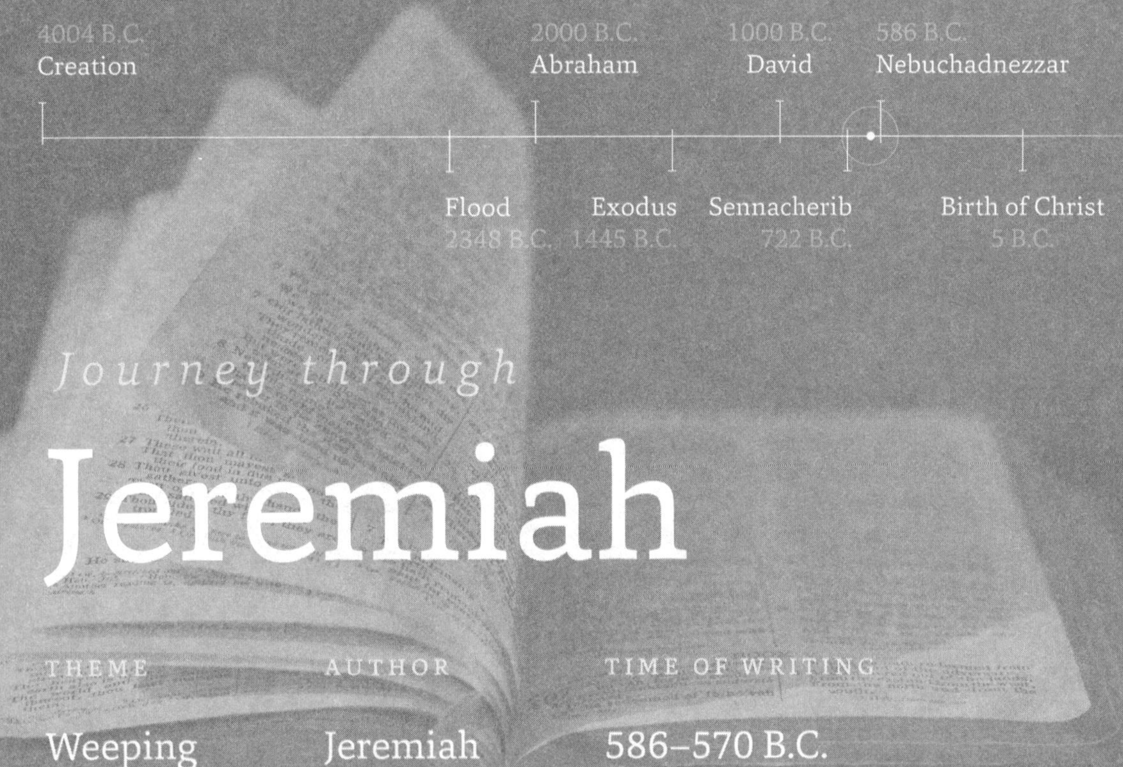

MEMORY VERSE

33 "But this is the covenant that I will make with the house of Israel after those days, says the Lord: I will put My law in their minds, and write it on their hearts; and I will be their God, and they shall be My people.

34 "No more shall every man teach his neighbor, and every man his brother, saying, 'Know the Lord,' for they all shall know Me, from the least of them to the greatest of them, says the Lord. For I will forgive their iniquity, and their sin I will remember no more."

Jeremiah 31:33–34

OVERVIEW

Jeremiah, "the weeping prophet," was one of the greatest (and most "unsuccessful") prophets who crossed the pages of Scripture. He was arrested, thrown into prison, slapped in public, his writings were burned, and he almost drowned in muck and mud at the bottom of a well. No one listened to him. God commanded him to stay unmarried (16:2). He was alone in life without a companion, he was despised, and was seemingly friendless. Jeremiah sees Nebuchadnezzar's army at the gates of Jerusalem as God's vengeance comes down. Jeremiah weeps. He was despised and yet he did not take back one word or compromise his message.

Top 5 Facts to Remember

1. Jeremiah was called to be a prophet when he was still a young man (Jer. 1:6–7).
2. Jeremiah prophesied of a New Covenant that would be established (Jer. 31:31–34; 32:36–41; 50:4–5).
3. When the king of Judah burned the scroll that contained Jeremiah's prophecies, Jeremiah (with the scribal assistance of Baruch) supernaturally wrote the same words on a different scroll (Jer. 36).
4. Out of hatred for Jeremiah's message, four of Judah's princes had Jeremiah cast into a miry dungeon, from which he was soon rescued by Ebed-Melech the Ethiopian (Jer. 38:1–13).
5. Jeremiah also prophesied Babylon's destruction (Jer. 50–51).

Theme: Weeping

In Jeremiah, God is glorifying Himself through the weeping of the "weeping prophet" so that He might demonstrate His superior goodness in the salvation sinners, the damnation of the wicked, and for the preservation of His people, for His eternal glory, and their eternal joy.

Author: Jeremiah

The author identifies himself as Jeremiah the son of Hilkiah (Jer. 1:1), and both Daniel and Matthew confirm this (Dan. 9:2; Matt. 2:17–18).

Time of Writing: 586–570 B.C.

Jeremiah began his prophetic ministry in the 13th year of Josiah's reign (629 B.C.), and wrote down his prophecies sometime after the destruction of Jerusalem (586 B.C.).

Key Verses

" 'For behold, I have made you this day
A fortified city and an iron pillar,
And bronze walls against the whole land—
Against the kings of Judah,
Against its princes,
Against its priests,
And against the people of the land.
They will fight against you,
But they shall not prevail against you.
For I am with you,' says the Lord, 'to deliver you.' "

Jeremiah 1:18–19

" 'Behold, the days are coming,' says the Lord,
'That I will raise to David a Branch of righteousness;
A King shall reign and prosper,
And execute judgment and righteousness in the earth.
In His days Judah will be saved,
And Israel will dwell safely;
Now this is His name by which He will be called:
THE Lord OUR RIGHTEOUSNESS.' "

Jeremiah 23:5–6

Lessons

1. Repent, and turn to the Lord Jesus Christ! He is your only hope.

2. Sin is a downward spiral, and it will only make you miserable. The claim that sin will make you happy is a lie.

3. Unbelievers hate the truth, and they hate those who proclaim it.

Christ in Jeremiah

I. Jeremiah

Jeremiah is a type of Christ. Like Jeremiah, Christ wept over Jerusalem.[1] Like Jeremiah, Christ had enemies who were seeking to trap Him in His words[2] or murder Him secretly.[3]

II. The "Branch of Righteousness"

In Jeremiah 23:5–6, we see Christ portrayed as Son of David ("I will raise to David a Branch of righteousness"), King ("A King shall reign and prosper"), Savior ("In His days Judah will be saved"), and the source of righteousness for His people ("The Lord Our Righteousness").[4]

1. Jer. 13:17; Luke 19:41.
2. Jer. 20:10; Luke 11:53–54.
3. Jer. 18:23; John 11:53.
4. See also Jer. 33:14–16.

Outline

I. **Jeremiah's Call to be a Prophet (Jer. 1)**

II. **Judgment on Judah Foretold (Jer. 2–19)**

III. **Jeremiah's Interaction With the Kings of Judah (Jer. 20–38)**

- A. Jehoiakim (Jer. 25–26, 35–36)
- B. Jehoiachin (Jer. 22–23)
- C. Zedekiah (Jer. 20–21, 24, 27–34, 37–38)

IV. **Nebuchadnezzer Destroys Jerusalem (Jer. 39)**

V. **Jeremiah's Ministry After the Destruction (Jer. 40–44)**

- A. Jeremiah's Ministry in Judah (Jer. 40:1–43:7)
- B. Jeremiah's Ministry in Egypt (Jer. 43:8–44:30)

VI. **The Lord's Promise to Baruch (Jer. 45)**

VII. **Judgment on the Nations Foretold (Jer. 46–49)**

VIII. **Judgment on Babylon Foretold (Jer. 50–51)**

IX. **Conclusion (Jer. 52)**

- A. The Destruction of Jerusalem Reiterated (Jer. 52:1–30)
- B. Jehoiachin's Release from Prison (Jer. 52:31–34)

Study Questions

What title is Jeremiah often given?

"The Weeping Prophet."

What does Jeremiah's name mean?

"Yah is my appointer."

Who were the other prophets that prophesied in Jeremiah's day?

Zephaniah, Habakkuk, Daniel, and Ezekiel.

When did the Lord ordain Jeremiah to be a prophet?

Before he was born (Jer. 1:5).

Why did God tell Jeremiah not to be dismayed?

Because He would deliver him from his enemies (Jer. 1:17–19).

What name is used to describe Christ in Jeremiah 23:6?

"The Lord Our Righteousness."

Which section of Jeremiah explains the New Covenant?

Jeremiah 31:31–34.

Where in Jeremiah does it say that God divorced Israel?

Jeremiah 3:8.

What a Friend We Have in Jesus

WORDS: Joseph M. Scriven, 1855. MUSIC: "Erie"; Charles C. Converse, 1868. Public Domain.

for more resources go to ***jttb.co/lamentations***

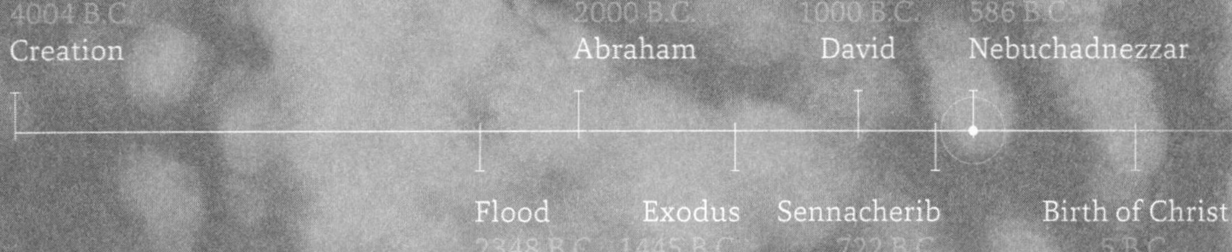

Journey through

Lamentations

THEME	AUTHOR	TIME OF WRITING
Grief	Jeremiah	586 B.C.

MEMORY VERSE

"Jerusalem has sinned gravely, therefore she has become vile. All who honored her despise her because they have seen her nakedness; yes, she sighs and turns away."

Lamentations 1:8

OVERVIEW

Lamentations is a poem expressing personal and national grief for the ravages that disobedience brings. The title of this book is the short Hebrew word, "eka," or "how." It indicates a loud cry. Jeremiah is appealing to a nation under judgment to help them to examine how they came to be under judgment, the results of their disobedience, and how they were to move forward. Lamentations answers all three of these questions.

Top 5 Facts to Remember

1. The destruction of Jerusalem was part of God's sovereign plan (Lam. 2:17).
2. God's compassions are new every morning (Lam. 3:22–23).
3. The Lord is good to those who wait for Him (Lam. 3:25).
4. Jeremiah emphasized the Lord's sovereignty when he asked rhetorically, "Who is he who speaks and it comes to pass, when the Lord has not commanded it?" (Lam. 3:37).
5. During the siege of Jerusalem, food became so scarce that women were cooking their own children (Lam. 4:10).

Theme: Grief

In Lamentations, God is glorifying Himself through grief, so that He might demonstrate His superior goodness in the salvation sinners, the damnation of the wicked, and for the preservation of His people for His eternal glory, and their eternal joy.

Author: Jeremiah

While Lamentations makes no claim about its authorship, both the Septuagint[1] and Jewish tradition[2] attribute the book to Jeremiah.

Time of Writing: 586 B.C.

Lamentations provides eyewitness testimony of Jerusalem's destruction by the Chaldeans (586 B.C.).[3] Lamentations was probably written before Cyrus' decree to return and build the temple (538 B.C.), since this event is not mentioned or alluded to in the text.

1. The following words are included in the Septuagint (an ancient Greek translation of the Old Testament), before the book of Lamentations: "And it came to pass, after Israel was taken captive, and Jerusalem made desolate, that Jeremias sat weeping, and lamented with this lamentation over Jerusalem, and said..." See Lancelot C.L. Brenton, The Septuagint with Apocrypha: Greek and English (United States: Hendrickson Publishers, 2011), 972.
2. According to the Babylonian Talmud (a written collection of Jewish rabbinic tradition), "Jeremiah wrote his book, Kings, and Lamentations." See Michael Levi Rodkinson, The Babylonian Talmud: Book 7 (Vols. XIII. and XIV.): Tract Baba Bathra (Last Gate) (Seattle, W.A.: Amazon Digital Services LLC, 2012), 45.
3. For more on how these dates are calculated, see "Time of Events" at the back of this book.

Key Verses

"How lonely sits the city
That was full of people!
How like a widow is she,
Who was great among the nations!
The princess among the provinces
Has become a slave!
"She weeps bitterly in the night,
Her tears are on her cheeks;
Among all her lovers
She has none to comfort her.
All her friends have dealt treacherously with her;
They have become her enemies."

Lamentations 1:1–2

"Through the Lord's mercies we are not consumed,
Because His compassions fail not.
They are new every morning;
Great is Your faithfulness."

Lamentations 3:22–23

"You, O Lord, remain forever;
Your throne from generation to generation.
Why do You forget us forever,
And forsake us for so long a time?
Turn us back to You, O Lord, and we will be restored;
Renew our days as of old,
Unless You have utterly rejected us,
And are very angry with us!"

Lamentations 5:19–22

Lessons

1. Calamities sometimes come as a result of national sin.
2. If a nation refuses to listen to God's prophets, they are heading for judgment.
3. In times of calamity, pour out your heart to the Lord.

Christ in Lamentations

Jeremiah is a type of Christ. Throughout the book of Lamentations, we see Jeremiah interceding on behalf of a sinful people. That is what Christ does for us.

Outline

I. **A Broken City (Lam. 1)**

II. **A Broken People (Lam. 2)**

III. **A Suffering Prophet (Lam. 3)**

IV. **A Broken Kingdom (Lam. 4)**

V. **A Praying/Repentant Nation (Lam. 5)**

Study Questions

What does the word, "Lamentations" mean?

"Loud Cries."

When was the book of Lamentations written?

After the destruction of Jerusalem (586–537 B.C.).

What is the book of Lamentations about?

It laments the destruction of Jerusalem.

Why did God destroy the city of Jerusalem?

So that people would pass by and see that God judges His people.

What kind of animal does Jeremiah compare the princes of Judah to?

Deer (Lam. 1:6).

Why did Jerusalem become vile?

Because she had sinned gravely (Lam. 1:8).

What was the Lord's attitude toward Judah's sin?

He was angry (Lam. 2:1).

What was Jeremiah's response to the destruction of Jerusalem?

Sorrow (Lam. 2:11).

Was God's judgment on Judah a rash judgment?

No, the Lord fulfilled the word that He had commanded long before (Lam. 2:17).

What does Jeremiah say about the mercies and compassions of God?

They are new every morning (Lam. 3:22–24).

What does Jeremiah say the people should do?

Examine their ways and turn back to the Lord (Lam. 3:40–41).

Was God's punishment upon Judah completed?

Yes (Lam. 4:22).

What is the last request that Jeremiah makes in his prayer?

That God would restore the people of Judah (Lam. 5:19–22).

Glorious Things of Thee Are Spoken

WORDS: John Newton, *pub.* 1779. MUSIC: "Austrian Hymn"; *attr. to* Croatian melody; *alt. by* Franz J. Hadyn, 1797. Public Domain.

*assuage: relieve

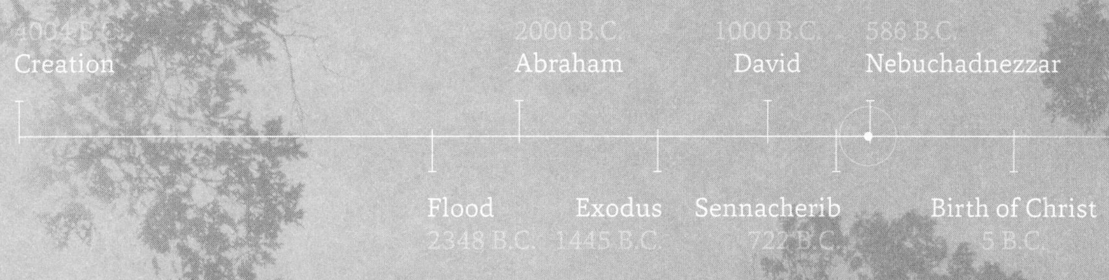

Journey through

Ezekiel

THEME	AUTHOR	TIME OF WRITING
Glory	Ezekiel	590–570 B.C.

MEMORY VERSE

26 "I will give you a new heart and put a new spirit within
you; I will take the heart of stone out of your flesh and give
you a heart of flesh.

27 "I will put My Spirit within you and cause you to walk in
My statutes, and you will keep My judgments and do them.

Ezekiel 36:26–27

OVERVIEW

The book of Ezekiel takes place in Babylon during the Babylonian captivity. Therefore, Ezekiel is one of the "exilic" prophets. He encouraged the exiles to be faithful during the seventy-year exile. It is a story of glory departed and glory restored. God exiled His people to punish them, but that was not His only objective. He chastised them in order to restore them. Ezekiel's wife dies in 587 at the beginning of the siege of Jerusalem.

Top 5 Facts to Remember

1. Ezekiel was called into ministry while in Babylon - "the land of the Chaldeans," (Ezek. 1:1–3).

2. Ezekiel was unable to speak, except when he spoke the word of the Lord (Ezek. 3:26–27). After receiving the news of Jerusalem's destruction, Ezekiel's mouth was "opened," and he was able to speak freely (Ezek. 33:21–22).

3. The Lord told Ezekiel that even if Noah, Daniel, and Job lived in Judah, they would not be able to deliver anyone by their righteousness, except themselves (Ezek. 14:12–20).

4. God's shows His compassion in Ezekiel 18:23: " 'Do I have any pleasure at all that the wicked should die?' says the Lord GOD, 'and not that he should turn from his ways and live?' "

5. When Israel rejected God's statues, He "gave them up to statutes that were not good, and judgments by which they could not live" (Ezek. 20:25).

Theme: The Glory of God

In Ezekiel, God is glorifying Himself through His glory, so that He might demonstrate His superior goodness in the salvation sinners, the damnation of the wicked, and for the preservation of His people for His eternal glory, and their eternal joy.

Author: Ezekiel

The author identifies himself as Ezekiel the priest, the son of Buzi (Ezek. 1:1–3). He was a contemporary of Jeremiah and Daniel.

Time of Writing: 590–570 B.C.

Ezekiel prophesied from the 5th year of King Jehoiachin's captivity[1] (590 B.C.)[2] to the 27th year[3] (570 B.C.). Ezekiel does not record Jehoiachin's release from prison (561 B.C.), making it likely that his book was completed before this event.

Key Verses

"And above the firmament over their heads was the likeness of a throne, in appearance like a sapphire stone; on the likeness of the throne was a likeness with the appearance of a man high above it. Also from the appearance of His waist and upward I saw, as it were, the color of amber with the appearance of fire all around within it; and from the appearance of His waist and downward I saw, as it were, the appearance of fire with brightness all around. Like the appearance of a rainbow in a cloud on a rainy day, so was the appearance of the brightness all around it. This was the appearance of the likeness of the glory of the Lord.

"So when I saw it, I fell on my face, and I heard a voice of One speaking."

Ezekiel 1:26–28

"Again He said to me, 'Prophesy to these bones, and say to them, "O dry bones, hear the word of the Lord! Thus says the Lord GOD to these bones: 'Surely I will cause breath to enter into you, and you shall live. I will put sinews on you and bring flesh upon you, cover you with skin and put breath in you; and you shall live. Then you shall know that I am the Lord.' "' "

Ezekiel 37:4–6

1. Ezek. 1:1–3.
2. For more on how these dates are calculated, see "Time of Events" at the back of this book.
3. Ezek. 29:17.

Lessons

1. God always protects His people.
2. There is a future glory that the people of God can look forward to.
3. For a person to be saved, they must be regenerated. Their heart of stone must be torn out and replaced with a heart of flesh.
4. Beware of idolatry and repent of it.

Christ in Ezekiel

I. **The "Son of Man"—Ezekiel**

II. **David (Ezek. 34:23–24)**

Outline

I. **Prophecies Before the Siege (Ezek. 1–24)**

II. **Prophecies During the Siege (Ezek. 25–32)**

III. **Prophecies After the Siege (Ezek. 33–48)**

Study Questions

When did Ezekiel prophesy?

During the Babylonian Captivity.

When was Ezekiel deported?

Probably during the first deportation in 605 B.C.

How old was Ezekiel when he started prophesying?

30 years old (Ezek. 1:1).

Where did he begin his prophetic ministry?

In the land of the Chaldeans, by the River Chebar (Ezek. 1:1, 3).

What title do Ezekiel and Jesus have in common?

Son of Man.

What kind of visions did Ezekiel see?

Visions of God (Ezek. 1:1).

Who did God send Ezekiel to?

The children of Israel (Ezek. 2:3).

What happens to those who do not warn the wicked to turn from their wickedness?

The blood of the wicked is required at their hand (Ezek. 3:18).

What were the sins of Sodom?

Pride, fullness of food, idleness, refusal to help the poor, haughtiness, and committing an abomination (Ezek. 16:49–50).

All the Way My Savior Leads Me

WORDS: Frances J. Crosby, *pub.*1875. MUSIC: Robert Lowry, *pub.*1875. Public Domain.

for more resources go to ***jttb.co/daniel***

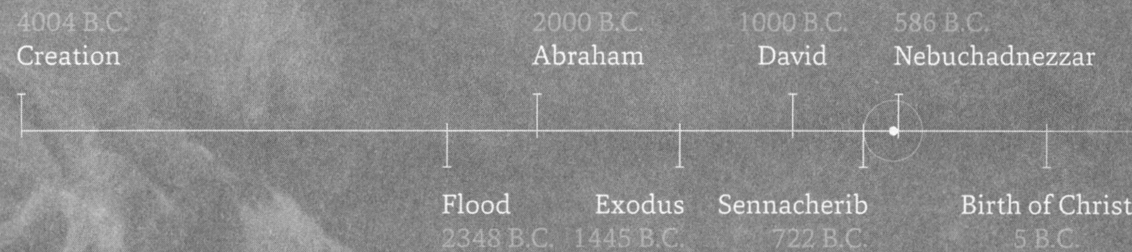

Journey through

Daniel

THEME	AUTHOR	TIME OF WRITING
Sovereignty	Daniel	536–530 B.C.

MEMORY VERSE

20 Daniel answered and said: "Blessed be the name of God
forever and ever, for wisdom and might are His. 21 And He
changes the times and the seasons; he removes kings and
raises up kings; he gives wisdom to the wise and knowledge
to those who have understanding. 22 He reveals deep and
secret things; he knows what is in the darkness, and light
dwells with Him.

Daniel 2:20–22

OVERVIEW

God is in control, despite appearances. Daniel declares the sovereignty of God over the shifting political, social and moral scenes of life on earth. He protects, prospers, promotes and preserves His people. Daniel is a mixture of prophesy and narrative.

The first section contains some of the most inspiring stories in the Bible. It has been called the "Book of Revelation" of the Old Testament. Daniel documents the years surrounding the Babylonian captivity. He was a prophet during the years of Nebuchadnezzar, Belshazzar, Darius, and Cyrus.

Top 5 Facts to Remember

1. Notwithstanding the threats of King Nebuchadnezzar; Shadrach, Meshach, and Abed-Nego refused to worship his gold image (Dan. 3:16–18).
2. The fiery furnace was so hot, that it killed the men who cast Shadrach, Meshach, and Abed-Nego into it (Dan. 3:22).
3. The Lord caused Nebuchadnezzar's kingdom to depart from him, until he recognized that God is the Supreme Ruler (Dan. 4).
4. When a man's hand appeared and wrote on the wall of King Belshazzar's palace, only Daniel was able to interpret the message (Dan. 5).
5. Not only did Daniel disobey King Darius by praying to God, but he did so with his windows open (Dan. 6:10).

Theme: Sovereignty

In Daniel, God is glorifying Himself through His sovereignty over history, so that He might demonstrate His superior goodness in the salvation sinners, the damnation of the wicked, and for the preservation of His people for His eternal glory, and their eternal joy.

Author: Daniel

The author identifies himself as Daniel throughout the book,[1] which Christ also confirms.[2] The book also includes a chapter written by King Nebuchadnezzar (Dan. 4).

1. Dan. 7:1–2, 15, 28; 8:1, 15, 27; 9:2, 22; 10:2, 7, 11–12; 12:4–5, 9.
2. Matt. 24:15.

Time of Writing: 536–530 B.C.

Daniel delivered his last prophecy in the 3rd year of Cyrus's reign (536 B.C.). He wrote down his prophecies sometime after this date.

Key Verses

"Therefore Daniel went to Arioch, whom the king had appointed to destroy the wise men of Babylon. He went and said thus to him: 'Do not destroy the wise men of Babylon; take me before the king, and I will tell the king the interpretation.'

Then Arioch quickly brought Daniel before the king, and said thus to him, 'I have found a man of the captives of Judah, who will make known to the king the interpretation.' "

Daniel 2:24–25

"Shadrach, Meshach, and Abed-Nego answered and said to the king, 'O Nebuchadnezzar, we have no need to answer you in this matter. If that is the case, our God whom we serve is able to deliver us from the burning fiery furnace, and He will deliver us from your hand, O king. But if not, let it be known to you, O king, that we do not serve your gods, nor will we worship the gold image which you have set up.' "

Daniel 3:16–18

"And at the end of the time I, Nebuchadnezzar, lifted my eyes to heaven, and my understanding returned to me; and I blessed the Most High and praised and honored Him who lives forever:

"For His dominion is an everlasting dominion,
And His kingdom is from generation to generation.
All the inhabitants of the earth are reputed as nothing;
He does according to His will in the army of heaven
And among the inhabitants of the earth.

No one can restrain His hand
Or say to Him, 'What have You done?' "

Daniel 4:34–35

Lessons

1. God is sovereign over all things.
2. God protects and preserves His people.
3. God has the power to humble and convert wicked rulers.
4. When the civil authorities command us to go against the will of God, we ought to obey God rather than men.

Christ in Daniel

I. **The Stone Cut Without Hands (Dan. 2:34–35, 44)**

II. **The Son of God (Dan. 3:24–25)**

III. **The Son of Man (Dan. 7:13–14)**

IV. **Messiah the Prince (Dan. 9:25–26)**

Outline

I. **Moral and Spiritual Instruction (Dan. 1–6)**

  A. Faithful Under Pressure (Dan. 1)

  B. Nebuchadnezzar's Troubling Dream (Dan. 2)

  C. Tested by Fire (Dan. 3)

- D. The Vision of the Tree (Dan. 4:1–27)
- E. The Conversion of Nebuchadnezzar (Dan. 4:28–37)
- F. Handwriting on the Wall (Dan. 5)
- G. Daniel and the Lions' Den (Dan. 6)

II. Prophecies of the Future (Dan. 7–12)

- A. Daniel Dreams of Four Beasts (Dan. 7)
- B. Daniel's Dream in Shushan (Dan. 8)
- C. The Seventy Weeks (Dan. 9)
- D. Introduction to the Vision (Dan. 10)
- E. More Details Given (Dan. 11)
- F. An Overview of Daniel's Prophecies (Dan. 12)

Study Questions

CHAPTERS 1–5

When did Daniel prophesy?

During the 70-year Babylonian captivity.

How old was Daniel when he was taken captive?

16 years old.

What time period does the book of Daniel cover?

605–536 B.C.

After Nebuchadnezzar had a dream, what did he command his servants to do?

He demanded that they tell him what his dream was, along with its interpretation (Dan. 2:2).

What did Nebuchadnezzar say he would do to his servants if they could not tell him his dream?

Cut them in pieces and make their houses an ash heap (Dan. 2:5).

When Nebuchadnezzar made an image of gold, what did he command all the people to do?

He told them to fall down and worship it (Dan. 3:4–5).

What would be done to the person who refused to worship Nebuchadnezzar's image?

They would be cast immediately into a burning fiery furnace (Dan. 3:6).

What did Shadrach, Meshach, and Abed-Nego do while everyone else bowed down to the image?

They refused to worship it (Dan. 3:12).

What did Nebuchadnezzar do to them when they refused?

He had them cast into the burning fiery furnace (Dan. 3:20).

What happened while they were in the fiery furnace?

The fire did not consume them (Dan. 3:24–27).

What was Nebuchadnezzar's response when Shadrach, Meshach, and Abed-Nego came out alive and untouched by the flames?

He blessed God (Dan. 3:28–29).

What was Nebuchadnezzar's second dream about?

A giant tree, which "a holy one" said would be cut down (Dan. 4:10–16).

What was Daniel's interpretation of the dream?

Nebuchadnezzar would be driven from his kingdom and left to graze in a field, until he recognized that God rules in the kingdom of men (Dan. 4:19–27).

What did Nebuchadnezzar say that brought down the judgment of God?

"Is not this great Babylon, that I have built for a royal dwelling by my mighty power and for the honor of my majesty?" (Dan. 4:30–33).

What was the judgment that God brought down on Nebuchadnezzar?

He was driven from his kingdom and left to eat grass like an ox (Dan. 4:31–33).

What happened to Nebuchadnezzar after the judgment?

He blessed the Most High, and his kingdom was restored (Dan. 4:34–36).

Which section of Daniel contains Nebuchadnezzar's testimony of the sovereignty of God?

Daniel 4:34–35.

Who was Belshazzar?

He was the king of Babylon, the son of Nebuchadnezzar (Dan. 5:1, 2, 11,18).

What happened at Belshazzar's feast?

A man's hand appeared and wrote a message on the palace wall (Dan. 5:5).

Who did the queen recommend to Belshazzar as one who could interpret the writing?

Daniel (Dan. 5:10–12).

What did the inscription on the wall mean?

Because of his wickedness, Belshazzar's kingdom would come to an end, and instead be given to the Medes and the Persians (Dan. 5:25–28).

CHAPTERS 6–12

What was the law that went out under King Darius's reign, and what was the punishment for breaking it?

No one was allowed to pray to any god or man except Darius for 30 days. Anyone who disobeyed would be cast into the den of lions (Dan. 6:7–8).

What was Daniel's response to King Darius's law?

He prayed and gave thanks to God, as he had before (Dan. 6:10).

What did the governors and satraps do when they found out Daniel was praying to God?

They went to King Darius and demanded that he punish Daniel (Dan. 6:13–15).

What did God do to the lions while Daniel was in the lions' den?

He shut the lions' mouths (Dan. 6:22).

What decree did King Darius issue after Daniel came out of the lions' den?

He commanded that everyone tremble and fear before the God of Daniel (Dan. 6:25–28).

What did Daniel dream about during the first year of Belshazzar's reign?

Four great beasts (Dan. 7:2–14).

What was the interpretation of Daniel's dream?

The four beasts represented four kingdoms. The fourth kingdom would be divided between 10 kings. One king would be different than the others, and subdue three kings. This king would speak pompous words and persecute the saints but eventually, his dominion would be taken away, and the saints would receive an everlasting kingdom (Dan. 7:15–28).

What animal defeated the ram in Daniel's vision?

A male goat (Dan. 8:5–7).

Who interpreted Daniel's vision of the ram and goat?

The angel Gabriel (Dan. 8:16).

When did Daniel have the vision of the glorious man?

In the third year of Cyrus king of Persia (Dan. 10:1).

How does Daniel describe the glorious man in his vision?

He was clothed in linen, girded with gold of Uphaz. He had a body like beryl, a face like the appearance of lightning, eyes like torches of fire, arms and feet like burnished bronze, and spoke words like the voice of a multitude (Dan. 10:5–6).

What did Daniel prophesy regarding Greece and Persia?

Three more kings would arise in Persia. The fourth and richest king of Persia (Xerxes) would war against Greece. Afterwards, a mighty king (Alexander the Great) would arise, but his kingdom would be divided among those who were not his family (Dan. 11:2–4).

O the Deep, Deep Love of Jesus

WORDS: Samuel T. Francis, 1875.
MUSIC: "Ebenezer [Tôn-y-Botel]"; Thomas J. Williams, *pub.* 1890. Public Domain.

for more resources go to ***jttb.co/hosea***

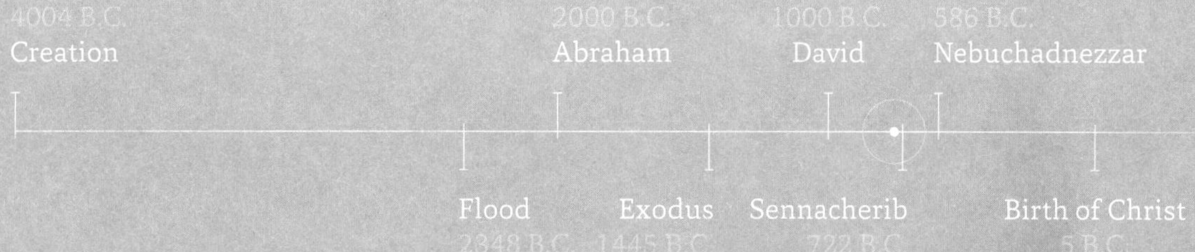

Journey through

Hosea

THEME

Mercy for Harlots

AUTHOR

Hosea

TIME OF WRITING

750–710 B.C.

MEMORY VERSE

"Come, and let us return to the Lord; for He has torn, but He will heal us; he has stricken, but He will bind us up."

Hosea 6:1

OVERVIEW

The book of Hosea is one of the great love stories in the Bible – a drama of persistent love in the face of rejection. The focus of Hosea is a people that love the world through their misplaced affections.

Hosea was commanded to do the unthinkable – marry a harlot. His home would be a picture of spiritual harlotry, to declare Israel's spiritual condition. Astonishingly, this situation is meant to describe the magnificence of the love of God. It is a story of betrayal and despising the marriage covenant contrasted with salvation and God's faithfulness, patience, and mercy. In short, Hosea shows us just how faithful God is to the unfaithful. God chose us when we were dead in our sins and loved us to the end.

Top 5 Facts to Remember

1. The unfaithful nation of Israel is pictured by Hosea's unfaithful wife, Gomer (Hos. 1:2).
2. Hosea had three children with symbolic names: Jezreel - "a city in Israel", Lo-Ruhamah - "No Mercy", and Lo-Ammi - "Not My People" (Hos. 1:3–9).
3. God desires mercy and not sacrifice (Hos. 6:6).
4. God wrote the great things of His law for Ephraim, "But they were considered a strange thing" (Hos. 8:12).
5. According to Hosea, the Israelites had "eaten the fruit of lies" by trusting in their own way (Hos. 10:13).

Theme: Mercy for Harlots

In Hosea, God is glorifying Himself through harlotry, so that He might demonstrate His superior goodness in the salvation sinners, the damnation of the wicked, and for the preservation of His people for His eternal glory, and their eternal joy.

Author: Hosea

The author identifies himself as Hosea the son of Beeri,[1] which is also confirmed by the Apostle Paul.[2]

1. Hos. 1:1.
2. Rom. 9:25–26.

Time of Writing: 750–710 B.C.

Hosea prophesied from the reign of Uzziah[3] (792–740 B.C.)[4] to that of Hezekiah (716–687 B.C.). He probably finished his book during Hezekiah's reign.

Key Verses

"When the Lord began to speak by Hosea, the Lord said to Hosea:
'Go, take yourself a wife of harlotry
And children of harlotry,
For the land has committed great harlotry
By departing from the Lord.' "

Hosea 1:2

"I will betroth you to Me forever;
Yes, I will betroth you to Me
In righteousness and justice,
In lovingkindness and mercy;
I will betroth you to Me in faithfulness,
And you shall know the Lord."

Hosea 2:19–20

"I will heal their backsliding,
I will love them freely,
For My anger has turned away from him.
I will be like the dew to Israel;
He shall grow like the lily,
And lengthen his roots like Lebanon.
His branches shall spread;

3. Hos. 1:1.

4. For more on how these dates are calculated, see "Time of Events" at the back of this book.

His beauty shall be like an olive tree,
And his fragrance like Lebanon.
Those who dwell under his shadow shall return;
They shall be revived like grain,
And grow like a vine.
Their scent shall be like the wine of Lebanon."

Hosea 14:4–7

Lessons

1. Idolatry is spiritual unfaithfulness towards God.
2. The Lord is in the business of redeeming idolaters.
3. God's love towards His elect is unconditional.

Christ in Hosea

I. Hosea

Hosea is a type of Christ. Like Hosea, Christ came to redeem a bride who had not been faithful to Him.

II. Other Types of Christ

1. The Son called out of Egypt (Hos. 11:1; Matt. 2:15)
2. The only Savior (Hos. 13:4; Acts 4:12)

Outline

I. **The Tragedy in Hosea's Home (Hos. 1–3)**

II. **The Tragedy in Hosea's Homeland (Hos. 4–14)**

Study Questions

When was Hosea written?

792–686 B.C.

What prophet was Hosea's contemporary?

Isaiah

What kings reigned during Hosea's ministry?

Uzziah, Jotham, Ahaz, and Hezekiah, kings of Judah; and Jeroboam, the son of Joash, king of Israel (Hos. 1:1).

Whom did Hosea marry?

A harlot named Gomer (Hos. 1:2–3).

How many children did Hosea have, and what were their names?

He had three children, whose names were Jezreel, Lo-Ruhamah, and Lo-Ammi (Hos. 1:3–9).

Who is Hosea referring to when he speaks of "Israel"?

Either the northern kingdom, the descendants of Jacob, or the true people of God.

What three themes are found in the book of Hosea?

Spiritual adultery, love, and judgment.

How much did Hosea pay to buy Gomer back?

Fifteen shekels of silver, and one and one-half homers of barley (Hos. 3:2).

How did Hosea treat Gomer after he bought her back?

He showed her much love and kindness (Hos. 3:3).

Breathe on Me, Breath of God

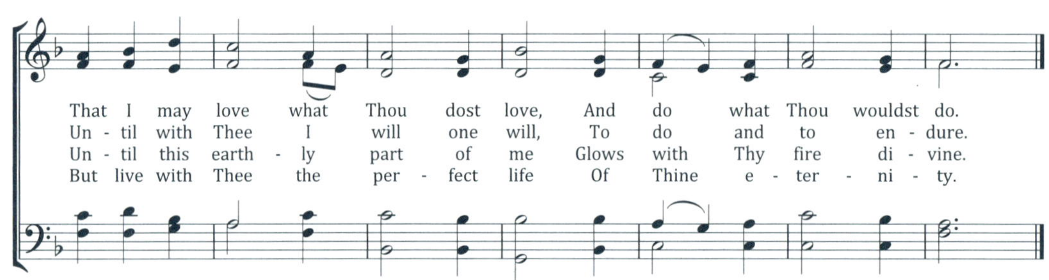

WORDS: Edwin Hatch, 1878.
MUSIC: "Trentham"; Robert Jackson, pub.1888. Public Domain.

for more resources go to ***jttb.co/joel***

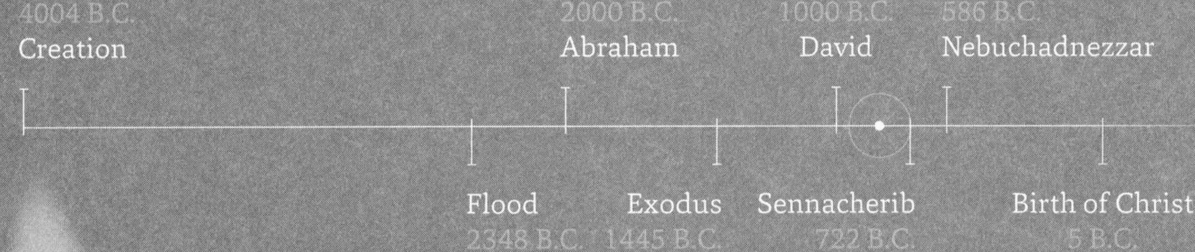

Journey through

Joel

THEME

The Day of the Lord

AUTHOR

Joel

TIME OF WRITING

835–796 B.C.

MEMORY VERSE

"And it shall come to pass afterward that I will pour out My Spirit on all flesh; your sons and your daughters shall prophesy, your old men shall dream dreams, your young men shall see visions."

Joel 2:28

OVERVIEW

Joel's message is this: the day of the Lord is coming, so we must warn people and call them to repentance and faith before it is too late! He uses a past incident of judgment and a locust infestation to cast a vision for future judgment. He issues a call to hear the word of the Lord and tell the next generation.

The theme of Joel is, "The Day of the Lord." The phrase occurs 12 times total throughout the books of the minor prophets and five times in the book of Joel alone. Joel prophesies the day of Pentecost, when the Holy Spirit would be poured out on the new converts in the early church.

Top 5 Facts to Remember

1. Joel lists four kinds of locusts that had consumed the crops: the chewing locust, the swarming locust, the crawling locust, and the consuming locust (Joel 1:4).

2. In the midst of famine, Joel saw that crying out to the Lord was the people's only hope (Joel 1:14).

3. The Lord "is gracious and merciful, slow to anger, and of great kindness" (Joel 2:13).

4. In Joel 2:28–32, the Lord promises to pour out His Spirit. Peter later quotes this prophecy as being fulfilled in Acts 2:16–21.

5. If His people repented, the Lord promised to restore to them the years that the locusts had eaten (Joel 2:25).

Theme: The Day of the Lord

In Joel, God is glorifying Himself through the day of the Lord, so that He might demonstrate His superior goodness in the salvation sinners, the damnation of the wicked, and for the preservation of His people for His eternal glory, and their eternal joy.

Author: Joel

The author identifies himself as Joel, the son of Pethuel,[1] which the Apostle Peter confirms.[2]

1. Joel 1:1.
2. Acts 2:16–21.

Time of Writing: 835–796 B.C.

Joel's prophetic ministry (and hence the writing of his book) probably took place when Joash was reigning over Judah (835–796 B.C.),[3] but this timeframe is not certain.

Key Verses

"Consecrate a fast,
Call a sacred assembly;
Gather the elders
And all the inhabitants of the land
Into the house of the Lord your God,
And cry out to the Lord."

Joel 1:14

"Blow the trumpet in Zion,
And sound an alarm in My holy mountain!
Let all the inhabitants of the land tremble;
For the day of the Lord is coming,
For it is at hand:
A day of darkness and gloominess,
A day of clouds and thick darkness,
Like the morning clouds spread over the mountains.
A people come, great and strong,
The like of whom has never been;
Nor will there ever be any such after them,
Even for many successive generations."

Joel 2:1–2

3. For more on how these dates are calculated, see "Time of Events" at the back of this book.

" 'Now, therefore,' says the Lord,
'Turn to Me with all your heart,
With fasting, with weeping, and with mourning.'
So rend your heart, and not your garments;
Return to the Lord your God,
For He is gracious and merciful,
Slow to anger, and of great kindness;
And He relents from doing harm.
Who knows if He will turn and relent,
And leave a blessing behind Him—
A grain offering and a drink offering
For the Lord your God?"

Joel 2:12–14

Lessons

1. We should tell the next generation the words of the Lord.
2. The Day of the Lord is coming, so we must warn people and call them to repentance and faith before it's too late.

Christ in Joel

I. **The Judge in the Day of the Lord**[4]

II. **Salvation for Whoever Calls on the Name of the Lord (Joel 2:32)**

4. Joel 1:15; 2:1, 11, 31; 3:14.

Outline

I. **The Past Day of the Lord: Locusts and Drought (Joel 1)**

A. Locusts (Joel 1:1–12)

B. Drought (Joel 1:13–20)

II. **The Future Day of the Lord (Joel 2–3)**

Study Questions

What is the theme of Joel's prophecy?

The Day of the Lord, in which He will set everything right and judge all wrongs.

To whom is Joel's prophecy addressed?

The elders and inhabitants of Judah (Joel 1:2).

Why are the drunkards told to wake up and weep?

Because there would be no more wine to drink (Joel 1:5–7).

How are the people supposed to lament?

Like a virgin girded with sackcloth, for the husband of her youth (Joel 1:8).

Why are the farmers told to be ashamed and wail?

Because the harvest of the field had perished (Joel 1:11–12).

Why are the priests told to lament?

Because the offerings had been withheld from the house of God (Joel 1:13).

What are the priests commanded to do?

Gather the people and cry out to the Lord (Joel 1:14).

Why did Joel cry out to the Lord?

Because the trees and open pastures had been burned up (Joel 1:19).

Who was crying out to the Lord with Joel?

The beasts of the field (Joel 1:20).

Why is there a call to blow the trumpet in Zion?

Because the day of the Lord is coming (Joel 2:1–2).

How does Joel describe the land?

Like the Garden of Eden before the locusts, and like a desolate wilderness behind them (Joel 2:3).

What does the Lord call His people to "rend" instead of their garments?

Their hearts (Joel 2:12–17).

What does the Lord promise to His people if they obey His call?

He will be zealous for His land and pity His people (Joel 2:18).

What does God promise He will pour out "on all flesh"?

His Spirit (Joel 2:28–29).

What does God say will happen to the land when He brings back the captives?

He will judge all nations (Joel 3:1–3).

What will happen to Jerusalem after the judgment of the Lord?

Jerusalem shall be holy, no alien shall pass through her again, and God will dwell there (Joel 3:17).

Why will Egypt and Edom be made desolate?

Because they shed innocent blood (Joel 3:19).

Why will Judah and Jerusalem abide forever?

Because God will acquit them of the guilt of bloodshed (Joel 3:20–21).

I Sing the Mighty Power of God

WORDS: Isaac Watts, *pub.*1715. MUSIC: "Ellacombe"; Gesangbuch der H. W. K. Hofkapelle, 1784; *arr., har. by* William H. Monk, 1868. Public Domain.

for more resources go to **jttb.co/amos**

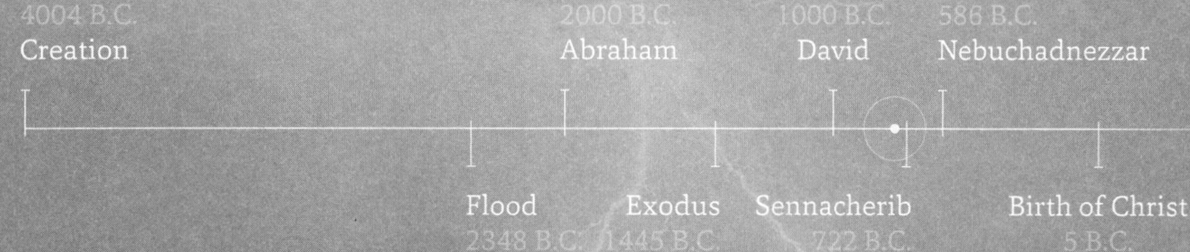

Journey through

Amos

THEME

Prepare to Meet Your God

AUTHOR

Amos

TIME OF WRITING

750 B.C.

MEMORY VERSE

"For thus says the Lord to the house of Israel:
'Seek Me and live.' "

Amos 5:4

OVERVIEW

Outwardly, everything was working well in Israel at the time that the book of Amos was written. The economy was booming, religion was growing, and their borders were expanding. It was a time of optimism. Then, the skunk at the garden party showed up – Amos. He looked at the outward success, but could see the dark underbelly of injustice, greed, hypocrisy, and oppression. He declares the coming judgment of God.

Top 5 Facts to Remember

1. God is patient, but there is coming a time when He will judge the world.
2. God judged His people for their treatment of the poor.
3. Judah was punished for despising the law of the Lord (Amos 2:4).
4. The Israelites commanded the Lord's prophets not to prophesy (Amos 2:11–12).
5. One grievance that the Lord had against Israel was their turning of justice into "wormwood" (Amos 5:7).

Theme: Prepare to Meet Your God

In Amos, God is glorifying Himself through the necessity to prepare to meet your God, so that He might demonstrate His superior goodness in the salvation sinners, the damnation of the wicked, and for the preservation of His people for His eternal glory, and their eternal joy.

Author: Amos

The author identifies himself as Amos.[1]

Time of Writing: 750 B.C.

Amos prophesied shortly before the death of Jeroboam II of Israel (750 B.C.).

Key Verses

"You only have I known of all the families of the earth;
Therefore I will punish you for all your iniquities."

Amos 3:2

"Therefore thus says the Lord GOD:
'An adversary shall be all around the land;
He shall sap your strength from you,
And your palaces shall be plundered.' "

Amos 3:11

1. Amos 1:1.

"Therefore thus will I do to you, O Israel;
Because I will do this to you,
Prepare to meet your God, O Israel!"

Amos 4:12

" 'Behold, the days are coming,' says the Lord,
'When the plowman shall overtake the reaper,
And the treader of grapes him who sows seed;
The mountains shall drip with sweet wine,
And all the hills shall flow with it.
I will bring back the captives of My people Israel;
They shall build the waste cities and inhabit them;
They shall plant vineyards and drink wine from them;
They shall also make gardens and eat fruit from them.
I will plant them in their land,
And no longer shall they be pulled up
From the land I have given them,'
Says the Lord your God."

Amos 9:13–15

Lessons

1. God is patient with the wicked, but one day He will judge the world.

2. The church has a duty to love and care for the poor.

3. If you do not repent, you will be counted among the wicked on the Day of Judgment.

4. Seek the Lord and live (Amos 5:6).

Christ in Amos

I. The Nazirites (Amos 2:11–12)

Christ kept the Nazirite vow. He humbled Himself and took on the form of a bondservant. He set Himself apart to do the will of His Father. That was the heart of what it meant to be a Nazirite. In a way that the best Nazirite could never compare to, Jesus Christ set Himself aside in perfect holiness to God. He was perfectly holy and did all things well.

II. Amos

Like all the prophets, Amos was a type of Christ. Like Amos, Christ spoke the words of God to a rebellious people. In Hebrews 1:1–2, we read that while God spoke "at various times and in various ways" by the prophets, He "has in these last days spoken to us by His Son." Christ is the final and greatest Prophet, the pinnacle of God's revelation, and the eternal Son of God.

III. The Poor

Unlike Judah and Israel in Amos' time, Christ loved and had compassion on the poor. He was never brutal towards the poor, He did not oppress or exploit them for His own gain, and He was always full of grace and truth.

IV. Other Types of Christ:

1. The Lion (Amos 3:4, 8)
2. The Trumpet (Amos 3:6)

Outline

I. Eight Prophecies Directed to the Nations (Amos 1–2)

II. Three Sermons Directed to the Northern Kingdom (Amos 3–6)

A. First Sermon – Can Two Walk Together (Amos 3)

B. Second Sermon – The Luxury Will End (Amos 4)

C. Third Sermon – Lamentation and a Call to Return (Amos 5–6)

III. Five Visions Directed to the Northern Kingdom (Amos 7:1–9:10)

A. First Vision – Locust (Amos 7:1–3)

B. Second Vision – Fire (Amos 7:4–6)

C. Third Vision – Plumb Line (Amos 7:7–9)

D. Fourth Vision – Amaziah (Amos 7:10–17)

E. Fifth Vision – Basket of Rotten Fruit (Amos 8)

F. The Destruction of the House of Israel (Amos 9:1–10)

IV. Five Promises Directed to the Northern Kingdom (Amos 9:11–15)

A. First Promise – Tabernacle of David Repaired (Amos 9:11)

B. Second Promise – Expansion Among the Foreigners (Amos 9:12)

C. Third Promise – Astonishing Fruitfulness (Amos 9:13)

D. Fourth Promise: The Captives Will Return (Amos 9:14)

E. Fifth Promise – Security in their Land (Amos 9:15)

Study Questions

What is the main message of Amos' prophecy?

Justice should run down like water and righteousness like a mighty stream (Amos 5:24).

What was Amos' occupation?

He was a "sheepbreeder" (Amos 1:1).

What does the name, "Amos" mean?

"Burden."

What was Israel's problem in Amos' time?

They did not know to do right (Amos 3:10).

What did the Lord say He would do to the people of Samaria?

All but a few would be destroyed (Amos 3:12).

What kind of famine did the Lord promise to bring on Israel?

A famine of hearing the words of the Lord (Amos 8:11).

I Sing the Mighty Power of God

WORDS: *attr. to* Charles Wesley, *pub.*1757.
MUSIC: "Italian Hymn"; Felice de Giardini, *pub.*1769. Public Domain.

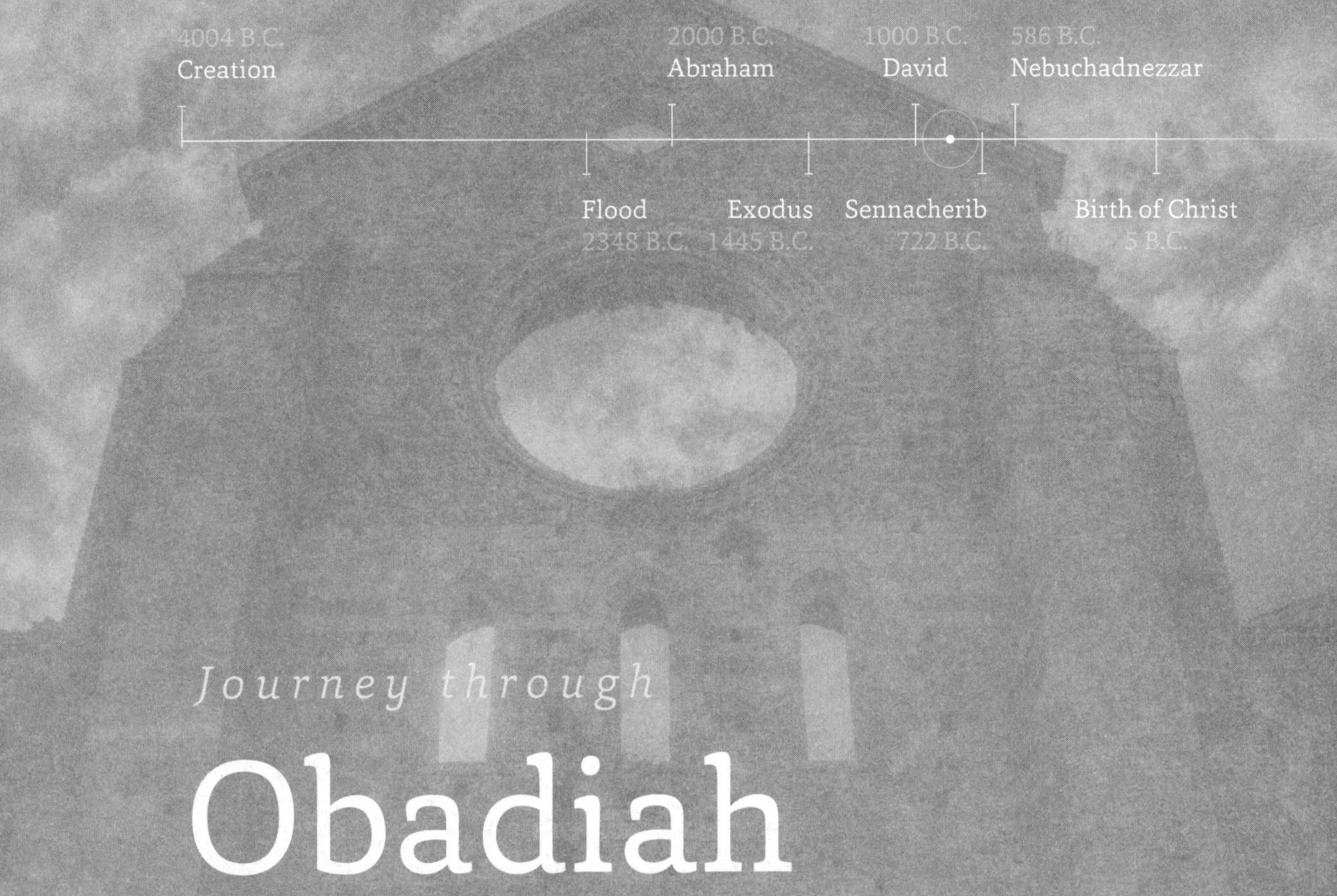

Journey through

Obadiah

THEME	AUTHOR	TIME OF WRITING
The Church's Enemies Destroyed	Obadiah	850–840 B.C.

MEMORY VERSE

"Then saviors shall come to Mount Zion to judge the mountains of Esau, and the kingdom shall be the Lord's."

Obadiah 1:21

OVERVIEW

The book of Obadiah communicates the message that the people of God should not fret when the wicked prosper, because they will be cut down in due time. In like manner, God will silence and destroy the enemies of the church. Obadiah is a word of encouragement to the church. Obadiah is one of the pre-exilic, minor prophets, who writes the shortest book in the Old Testament.

Top 5 Facts to Remember

1. The primary focus of Obadiah's vision is God's judgment on the nation of Edom.
2. The Edomites were the descendants of Esau, Jacob's brother.
3. The Edomites had deceived themselves by their own pride (Obad. 1:3).
4. God promised to turn Edom's allies against them (Obad. 1:7).
5. Edom incurred God's wrath by assisting Judah's enemies (Obad. 1:10–14).

Theme: The Church's Enemies Destroyed

In Obadiah, God glorifies Himself through the destruction of the enemies of the Church, so that He might demonstrate His superior goodness in the salvation sinners, the damnation of the wicked, and for the preservation of His people for His eternal glory, and their eternal joy.

Author: Obadiah

The author identifies himself as Obadiah.[1]

Time of Writing: 850–840 B.C.

Obadiah was probably written during Jehoram's reign over Israel (850–840 B.C.),[2] though some think a 586 B.C. date is more likely.

Key Verses

" 'Behold, I will make you small among the nations;
You shall be greatly despised.
The pride of your heart has deceived you,
You who dwell in the clefts of the rock,
Whose habitation is high;
You who say in your heart, "Who will bring me down to the ground?"
Though you ascend as high as the eagle,

1. Obad. 1:1.
2. For more on how these dates are calculated, see "Time of Events" at the back of this book.

And though you set your nest among the stars,
From there I will bring you down,' says the Lord."

Obadiah 1:2–4

" 'But on Mount Zion there shall be deliverance,
And there shall be holiness;
The house of Jacob shall possess their possessions.
The house of Jacob shall be a fire,
And the house of Joseph a flame;
But the house of Esau shall be stubble;
They shall kindle them and devour them,
And no survivor shall remain of the house of Esau,'
For the Lord has spoken."

Obadiah 1:17–18

Lessons

1. God will destroy His enemies.
2. God's enemies hate the church.
3. God judges the sin of pride.
4. God preserves His people.

Christ in Obadiah

Obadiah's prophecy is fulfilled in the book of Acts. Every chapter in the book of Acts shows the victory of the gospel over the enemies of God, and this is the primary message of Obadiah. The prophecies of Obadiah are fulfilled in the resurrection of our Lord Jesus Christ, His salvation of the Gentiles, and the final judgment at the end of the age. Obadiah's prophecy was given to tell us that the handwriting is on the wall for the enemies of God.

Outline

I. **God's Punishment on Edom (Obad. 1:1–14)**

- A. Edom's Punishment (Obad. 1:1–9)
- B. Edom's Rebellion (Obad. 1:10–14)

II. **God's Judgment on the Nations (Obad. 1:15–16)**

III. **God's Restoration of Israel (Obad. 1:17–21)**

Study Questions

What two prophets prophesied at the same time as Obadiah?

Jeremiah and Ezekiel.

What is the main message of Obadiah's prophecy?

Judgment against Edom (Obad. 1:1).

Why did God judge Edom?

For rejoicing in Judah's destruction (Obad. 1:12).

What was the judgment that God declared against Edom?

He would make them small and greatly despised (Obad. 1:2–5).

Why will Edom be covered with shame?

For violence against Jacob (Obad. 1:10).

What will be on Mount Zion?

Deliverance and holiness (Obad. 1:17–18).

Grace Greater than Our Sin

WORDS: Julia H. Johnston, *pub.*1910. MUSIC: "Moody"; Daniel B. Towner, 1910. Public Domain.

for more resources go to ***jttb.co/jonah***

Journey through

Jonah

THEME

God of Compassion

AUTHOR

Probably Jonah

TIME OF WRITING

775 B.C.

MEMORY VERSE

"But I will sacrifice to You with the voice of thanksgiving; I will pay what I have vowed. Salvation is of the Lord."

Jonah 2:9

OVERVIEW

There are two main messages found in the book of Jonah: First, it shows what God is like in His love toward pagan nations. Second, it displays God's grace, truth, and mercy towards Jonah even though he tried to run from God. God's grace is greater than Jonah's and is sufficient to save even the most grievous sinners of the Ninevites. Throughout the entire book, we see God teaching Jonah that He is a God of compassion.

Top 5 Facts to Remember

1. Jonah tried to flee from the presence of the Lord, but he soon found this to be impossible (Jon. 1:3–4).
2. After the storm was calmed, the mariners who had been with Jonah feared the Lord (Jon. 1:16).
3. When the Ninevites heard the preaching of Jonah, they repented of their sin and threw themselves on the mercy of God (Jon. 3:5–9).
4. Jonah himself gives us his reason for refusing to go to Nineveh—he did not want the Ninevites to receive any mercy (Jon. 4:2).
5. The Lord exposed Jonah's inconsistency in having more pity for a withered plant than for the entire city of Nineveh (Jon. 4:10–11).

Theme: God of Compassion

In Jonah, God is glorifying Himself through His compassion, so that He might demonstrate His superior goodness in the salvation sinners, the damnation of the wicked, and for the preservation of His people for His eternal glory, and their eternal joy.

Author: Probably Jonah

It is not clear who wrote the book of Jonah. However, the author clearly knew a lot about Jonah, even down to the very words that he prayed while he was in the great fish,[1] making it probable that the author was Jonah himself.

Time of Writing: 775 B.C.

Jonah most likely prophesied during the reign of Jeroboam II over Israel[2] (793–753 B.C.).[3]

Key Verses

"Now the word of the Lord came to Jonah the son of Amittai, saying, 'Arise, go to Nineveh, that great city, and cry out against it; for their wickedness has come up before Me.' But Jonah arose to flee to Tarshish from the presence of the Lord.

1. Jon. 2:1–9.
2. See the reference to Jonah in 2 Kings 14:25.
3. For more on how these dates are calculated, see "Time of Events" at the back of this book.

He went down to Joppa, and found a ship going to Tarshish; so he paid the fare, and went down into it, to go with them to Tarshish from the presence of the Lord."

Jonah 1:1–3

"Let neither man nor beast, herd nor flock, taste anything; do not let them eat, or drink water. But let man and beast be covered with sackcloth, and cry mightily to God; yes, let every one turn from his evil way and from the violence that is in his hands. Who can tell if God will turn and relent, and turn away from His fierce anger, so that we may not perish?"

Jonah 3:7b-9

"So he prayed to the Lord, and said, 'Ah, Lord, was not this what I said when I was still in my country? Therefore I fled previously to Tarshish; for I know that You are a gracious and merciful God, slow to anger and abundant in lovingkindness, One who relents from doing harm. Therefore now, O Lord, please take my life from me, for it is better for me to die than to live!' "

Jonah 4:2–3

Lessons

1. God is merciful to those who repent and believe on Him.
2. God always chastens His children when they run from Him.
3. God is sovereign over all creation, including the animals.
4. No one can escape God's presence.

Christ in Jonah

Jonah is a type of Christ. The three days and three nights that Jonah spent in the belly of the fish are given to us as a picture of the three days and three nights that Christ spent in the tomb before His resurrection (Jonah 1:17; Matt. 12:39–40).

Outline

I. **Jonah's Call and Rebellion (Jon. 1)**

   A. Jonah's First Call (Jon. 1:1–2)

   B. Jonah's Rebellion Against the Call (Jon. 1:3)

   C. God's Judgment Against Jonah (Jon. 1:4–17)

II. **Prayer of Desperation (Jon. 2)**

III. **Begrudging Obedience (Jon. 3)**

   A. Jonah's Second Call (Jon. 3:1–2)

   B. Jonah's Obedience (Jon. 3:3–4)

   C. The People of Nineveh Repent and Believe (Jon. 3:5–10)

IV. **Jonah's Displeasure (Jon. 4)**

   A. Jonah's Disposition (Jon. 4:1)

   B. Jonah's Prayer – The Reason He Fled is Revealed (Jon. 4:2–3)

   C. The Lord Rebukes Jonah (Jon. 4:4–11)

Study Questions

Who was Jonah?

He was one of the earlier prophets, living in the northern kingdom in a small town near Nazareth, in Galilee.

What do we learn from the book of Jonah?

It declares to us what God is like and what happens when we run away from Him. God is full of grace and truth and His grace is greater than all our sin.

When was Jonah's prophecy written?

793–753 B.C. – During the reign of Jeroboam II.

What city was Jonah commanded to go to?

Nineveh (Jon. 1:2).

Where did Jonah go instead of Nineveh?

Tarshish (Jon. 1:3).

What happened while Jonah was at sea?

The Lord sent a great wind, which caused a mighty tempest (Jon. 1:4).

What did the mariners ask Jonah to do when the storm was raging?

They asked him to call on his God (Jon. 1:6).

How did the mariners determine who caused the storm to come upon them?

They cast lots (Jon. 1:7).

What did Jonah tell the mariners to do to him?

He told them to throw him into the sea (Jon. 1:12).

What did the Lord prepare to swallow Jonah?

A great fish (Jon. 1:17).

How long was Jonah in the belly of the fish?

Three days and three nights (Jon. 1:17).

What did Jonah do while he was in the belly of the fish?

He prayed to the Lord his God (Jon. 2:1).

What happened after Jonah was in the belly of the fish for three days and three nights?

The Lord spoke to the fish and it vomited Jonah onto dry land (Jon. 2:10).

What did Christ say the account of Jonah in the belly of the fish is a picture of?

His own death and resurrection (Matt. 12:40).

What did God command Jonah to do after the fish vomited him onto dry land?

To go preach to the people of Nineveh (Jon. 3:1–2).

What did Jonah do after God commanded him to go to Nineveh the second time?

He arose and went to Nineveh (Jon. 3:3).

What was Jonah's message to the people of Nineveh?

He said Nineveh would be overthrown in 40 days (Jon. 3:4).

What was the response of the people of Nineveh to Jonah's message?

They repented (Jon. 3:5–9).

What did God do after He saw the people of Nineveh repent?

He relented and did not bring disaster upon them (Jon. 3:10).

What was Jonah's response when God had mercy on Nineveh?

He became angry (Jon. 4:1–3).

How did the Lord teach Jonah through the death of the plant?

He exposed Jonah's hypocrisy in having pity on the plant but not on the people and cattle that lived in Nineveh (Jon. 4:10–11).

O God, Our Help in Ages Past

WORDS: Isaac Watts, *pub.* 1719.
MUSIC: "St. Anne"; William Croft, 1708. Public Domain.

4004 B.C. Creation
2000 B.C. Abraham
1000 B.C. David
586 B.C. Nebuchadnezzar
Flood 2348 B.C.
Exodus 1445 B.C.
Sennacherib 722 B.C.
Birth of Christ 5 B.C.

Journey through

Micah

THEME	AUTHOR	TIME OF WRITING
Who Is Like God?	Micah	735–710 B.C.

MEMORY VERSE

"He has shown you, O man, what is good; and what does the Lord require of you but to do justly, to love mercy, and to walk humbly with your God?"

Micah 6:8

OVERVIEW

The prophet Micah's name means, "Who is like God"? Micah's ministry was closely linked to answering that question. What does God love? What does He hate? What does He require? How does He evaluate culture? What is it that draws His wrath? How do you understand His mercy? What words are used to describe Him? In short, "Who is like God"? The answer is that no one is like God. He is holy and in every way different from us.

Top 5 Facts to Remember

1. Micah spoke out against oppressive rulers and self-seeking prophets, and promised judgment for both (Micah 3).

2. In almost identical language, both Micah 4:1–3 and Isaiah 2:2–4 speak of the gospel going forth to all the nations.

3. Man's duty to God is summed up in Micah 6:8—to do justly, to love mercy, and to walk humbly with God.

4. At the time of Micah's prophecy, faithful men were virtually nonexistent (Mic. 7:2).

5. In Micah 7:18–19, we see the mercy of God in both pardoning and subduing the iniquity of His people (i.e. both justifying and sanctifying them).

Theme: Who is Like God?

In Micah, God is glorifying Himself through His uniqueness, so that He might demonstrate His superior goodness in the salvation sinners, the damnation of the wicked, and for the preservation of His people for His eternal glory, and their eternal joy.

Author: Micah

The author identifies himself as Micah of Moresheth (Mic. 1:1; cf. Jer. 26:18). He was a contemporary of Isaiah, Amos, and Hosea.

Time of Writing: 735–710 B.C.

Micah prophesied from the reign of Jotham (750–732 B.C.)[1] to that of Hezekiah[2] (716–687 B.C.).

1. For more on how these dates are calculated, see "Time of Events" at the back of this book.
2. Mic. 1:1.

Key Verses

"Hear, all you peoples!
Listen, O earth, and all that is in it!
Let the Lord GOD be a witness against you,
The Lord from His holy temple."

Micah 1:2

"I will surely assemble all of you, O Jacob,
I will surely gather the remnant of Israel;
I will put them together like sheep of the fold,
Like a flock in the midst of their pasture;
They shall make a loud noise because of so many people.
The one who breaks open will come up before them;
They will break out,
Pass through the gate,
And go out by it;
Their king will pass before them,
With the Lord at their head."

Micah 2:12–13

"Who is a God like You,
Pardoning iniquity
And passing over the transgression of the remnant of His heritage?
"He does not retain His anger forever,
Because He delights in mercy.
He will again have compassion on us,
And will subdue our iniquities."

Micah 7:18–19

Lessons

1. God is both perfectly just and perfectly merciful.
2. When God redeems a people, He casts their sins into the depths of the sea.

3. The God of the Bible is like no other god.

4. Someday, God will come and judge the nations.

5. God requires men to do justly, love mercy, and walk humbly with Him.

Christ in Micah

I. The One who Breaks Open (Mic. 2:12–13)

Some commentators interpret "the one who breaks open" as a ram with big horns that crashes through the gate and lets the sheep go free. This is symbolic of Jesus Christ. He is the one who breaks through the barrier and triumphantly leads His flock into the open pastures. Slaves of sin are set free (Rom. 6:7–18), and the devil's works are destroyed (1 John 3:8).

II. The Ruler from Bethlehem (Mic. 5:2)

The prophet Micah predicted that Christ would come out of Bethlehem (even the Jews recognized this in Jesus' day, see Matt. 2:1–6; John 7:42). This Man, according to Micah, would be no ordinary man, but one "whose goings forth are from of old, from everlasting," that is, God Himself.

Outline

I. Failure of Judah and Samaria (Mic. 1–3)

II. Restoration: The Future Glory and What God is Like (Mic. 4–5)

III. Micah's Calls for Repentance (Mic. 6:1–7:6)

- A. His First Call to Repentance and His Reply (Mic. 6)
- B. His Second Call for Repentance and His Reply (Mic. 7:1–6)

IV. The Promise of Restoration (Mic. 7:7–20)

Study Questions

What was the historical setting that prompted Micah's prophesy?

Micah prophesied during a period of intense social injustice in Judah. Prophets preached for riches. Princes thrived on cruelty, violence, and corruption. Priests ministered out of greed. Landlords stole from the poor and evicted widows. Judges lusted after bribes. Businessmen used deceitful scales and weights.

What is the central message of Micah's prophecy?

God judges those who practice injustice.

What was the state of families at this time?

They were divided (Mic. 7:6).

What was Samaria?

Samaria was the capital city of Israel (the northern kingdom).

What was Jerusalem?

Jerusalem was the capital city of Judah (the southern kingdom).

What does God say He will do to Samaria in chapter 1?

He promised to make Samaria a heap of ruins (Mic. 1:6–7).

What sin did God judge Israel for?

Idolatry (Mic. 1:7).

What did the Lord promise to gather?

A remnant (Mic. 2:12; 4:6–7).

What were the sins of Israel's civil leaders?

They were devouring the people (Mic. 3:1–3).

What were the sins of the false prophets?

They made the people go astray (Mic. 3:5).

What was the judgment that the Lord said He would bring upon the false prophets?

They would receive no revelation from God (Mic. 3:6–7).

What did God say would happen in the latter days?

People would flow to the house of the Lord (Mic. 4:1).

What kind of people did God say He would gather to make a strong nation?

The lame, outcast, and afflicted (Mic. 4:6–7).

Where did Micah say the Christ would come from?

Bethlehem (Mic. 5:2).

What does the Lord require of all men?

To do justly, to love mercy, and to walk humbly with their God (Mic. 6:8).

To whom does Micah look for salvation?

The Lord (Mic. 7:7).

Where does God cast the sins of His people?

Into the depths of the sea (Mic. 7:19).

Lead On, O King Eternal

WORDS: Ernest W. Shurtleff, 1888. MUSIC: “Lancashire”; Henry T. Smart, 1836. Public Domain.

for more resources go to ***jttb.co/nahum***

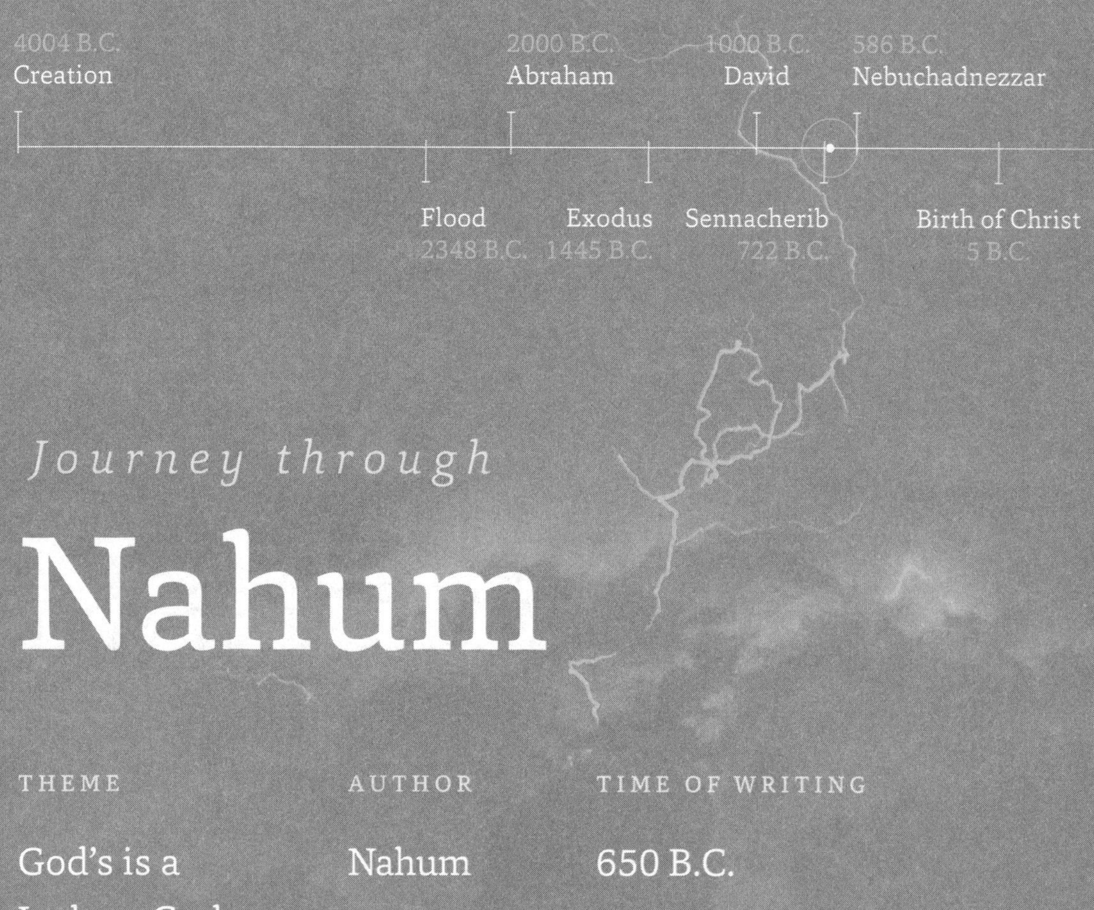

Journey through

Nahum

THEME

God's is a Jealous God

AUTHOR

Nahum

TIME OF WRITING

650 B.C.

MEMORY VERSE

2 God is jealous, and the Lord avenges; the Lord avenges and
is furious. The Lord will take vengeance on His adversaries,
and He reserves wrath for His enemies; 3 the Lord is slow
to anger and great in power, and will not at all acquit the
wicked. the Lord has His way in the whirlwind and in the
storm, and the clouds are the dust of His feet.

Nahum 1:2–3

OVERVIEW

God spared Nineveh through the reluctant ministry of Jonah. It took Jonah three days to walk across the city and they repented. Now 150 years later, they have reverted to their old ways of ungodliness and brutality. What is the central message of Nahum? God is a jealous God! Nineveh is an example that explains the doctrine of God's jealousy.

Top 5 Facts to Remember

1. Nahum prophesied to the Ninevites roughly 150 years after Jonah.
2. The Lord is slow to anger and great in power and will not at all acquit the wicked (Nah. 1:3).
3. The terrifying statement, "Behold, I am against you," occurs twice in the book (Nah. 2:13; 3:5).
4. Nineveh is called "the bloody city" in Nah. 3:1.
5. The book ends with the assertion that all who would hear of Nineveh's destruction would clap their hands, "For upon whom has not your wickedness passed continually?" (Nah. 3:19).

Theme: God is a Jealous God

In Nahum, God is glorifying Himself through jealousy, so that He might demonstrate His superior goodness in the salvation sinners, the damnation of the wicked, and for the preservation of His people for His eternal glory, and their eternal joy.

Author: Nahum

The author identifies himself as Nahum the Elkoshite (Nah. 1:1).

Time of Writing: 650 B.C.

Nahum wrote after the fall of Thebes[1] in 663 B.C.,[2] but before Nineveh's fall in 612 B.C.

Key Verses

"The Lord is good,
A stronghold in the day of trouble;
And He knows those who trust in Him.
But with an overflowing flood
He will make an utter end of its place,
And darkness will pursue His enemies."

Nahum 1:7–8

1. The fall of No Amon (aka Thebes) is mentioned in Nah. 3:8–10.
2. For more on how these dates are calculated, see "Time of Events" at the back of this book.

" 'Behold, I am against you,' says the Lord of hosts;
'I will lift your skirts over your face,
I will show the nations your nakedness,
And the kingdoms your shame.
I will cast abominable filth upon you,
Make you vile,
And make you a spectacle.
It shall come to pass that all who look upon you
Will flee from you, and say,
"Nineveh is laid waste!
Who will bemoan her?"
Where shall I seek comforters for you?' "

Nahum 3:5–7

Lessons

1. God is a jealous God and cannot tolerate the worship of false gods in His place.
2. The Lord is slow to anger.
3. God will pour out His wrath on His enemies.
4. The Lord will preserve those who take refuge in Him.

Christ in Nahum

In Nahum 1:15, the prophet speaks about those who bring good tidings and proclaim peace. The Apostle Paul quotes this verse in Romans 10:15 and applies it to those who proclaim the gospel of Jesus Christ.

Outline

I. **Nineveh's Destruction Announced (Nah. 1)**

II. **Nineveh's Destruction Described (Nah. 2)**

III. **Nineveh's Destruction Explained (Nah. 3)**

Study Questions

Who was the audience of Nahum's prophecy?

Nineveh (Nah. 1:1).

When did Nahum prophesy?

150 years after Jonah and the repentance of Nineveh, but before Jeremiah and Ezekiel.

What had happened to Nineveh since the time of Jonah's prophecy?

They had returned to their violence (Jon. 3:8; Nah. 3:1–3).

What is the key verse in Nahum?

"God is jealous, and the Lord avenges; the Lord avenges and is furious. The Lord will take vengeance on His adversaries, and He reserves wrath for His enemies" Nahum 1:2.

Rock of Ages

WORDS: Augustus M. Toplady, 1776.
MUSIC: "Toplady"; Thomas Hastings, 1830. Public Domain.

for more resources go to ***jttb.co/habakkuk***

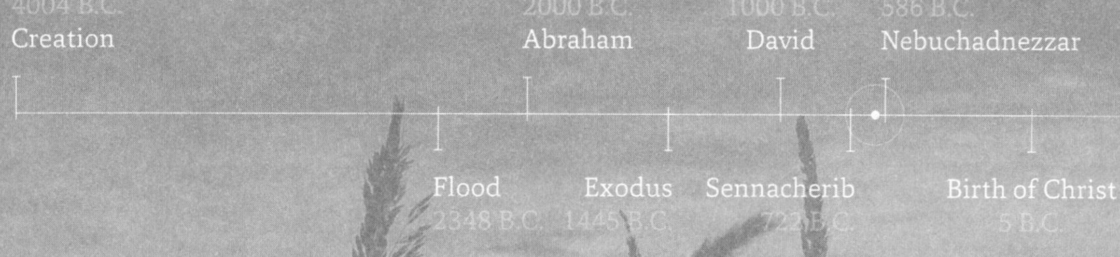

Journey through

Habakkuk

THEME	AUTHOR	TIME OF WRITING
Rejoice in the Lord	Habakkuk	615–605 B.C.

MEMORY VERSE

"Behold the proud, his soul is not upright in him; but the just shall live by his faith."

Habakkuk 2:4

OVERVIEW

In this book, the prophet Habakkuk sees the advancing of evil and darkness and cries out to God for understanding. It is often difficult for Christians to reconcile tragic events or the rise of evil with the sovereign, perfect plan of God. We hear about or experience the dominating power of the wicked and wonder if God is looking, working to defeat the wicked, or if He is even there at all. Accordingly, we often struggle to reconcile God's omnipotence and His sovereignty with our experiences. While we know God is good and sovereign, that He hates the works of darkness, and that He is omnipotent, we often wonder why He does not spring to action. Habakkuk teaches us that we can "rejoice in the Lord," for He will deal with the wicked in His own way in His own time.

Top 5 Facts to Remember

1. Habakkuk's prophecy addresses the question that Christians have struggled with to this day—Why does God permit evil?

2. Habakkuk 2:4, "The just shall live by his faith," is quoted three times in the New Testament.[1]

3. In the midst of pronouncements of woe upon evildoers, the Lord promises to fill the earth with the knowledge of His glory, "as the waters cover the sea" (Hab. 2:14).

4. The prophet points out the futility of idolatry in Habakkuk 2:18–19: "What profit is the image, that its maker should carve it?"

5. At the conclusion of his prophecy, Habakkuk purposes to "rejoice in the Lord," no matter the circumstances (Heb. 3:17–18).

Theme: Rejoice in the Lord

In Habakkuk, God is glorifying Himself through justification by faith alone, so that He might demonstrate His superior goodness in the salvation sinners, the damnation of the wicked, and for the preservation of His people for His eternal glory, and their eternal joy.

Author: Habakkuk

The author identifies himself as Habakkuk the prophet.[2]

1. Rom. 1:17; Gal. 3:11; Heb. 10:38.
2. Hab. 1:1; 3:1.

Time of Writing: 615–605 B.C.

Habakkuk prophesied as God was "raising up the Chaldeans,"[3] which fits best with the period between Nabopolassar's ascension to power over Babylon (626 B.C.)[4] and Judah's subjugation to the Neo-Babylonian Empire (605 B.C.).

Key Verses

"Look among the nations and watch—
Be utterly astounded!
For I will work a work in your days
Which you would not believe, though it were told you."

Habakkuk 1:5

"You are of purer eyes than to behold evil,
And cannot look on wickedness.
Why do You look on those who deal treacherously,
And hold Your tongue when the wicked devours
A person more righteous than he?"

Habakkuk 1:13

"What profit is the image, that its maker should carve it,
The molded image, a teacher of lies,
That the maker of its mold should trust in it,
To make mute idols?
Woe to him who says to wood, 'Awake!'
To silent stone, 'Arise! It shall teach!'

3. Hab. 1:6.
4. For more on how these dates are calculated, see "Time of Events" at the back of this book.

Behold, it is overlaid with gold and silver,
Yet in it there is no breath at all."

Habakkuk 2:18–19

Lessons

1. Answers to hard questions about God come from reading and meditating on His Word.
2. Notwithstanding the apparent success of the wicked at times, God will punish them one day.
3. God works out all things—even the evil actions of men—for His glory and the good of His people.
4. We should trust that God's ways are perfect and just, even when we don't understand them.
5. Sinners can receive righteousness apart from the law through faith in Jesus Christ.[5] This is what Habakkuk was referring to when he said, "The just shall live by his faith."[6]

Christ in Habakkuk

The prophet refers to Christ as God's "Anointed"—the agent of salvation for God's people (Hab. 3:13).

5. See Rom. 3:21–22.
6. Hab. 2:4; cf. Rom. 1:17; Gal. 3:11.

Outline

I. **Habakkuk's Burden and Two Burning Questions (Hab. 1–2)**

  A. The First Question (Hab. 1:1–11)

    1. How Can a Good God Permit Evil? (Hab. 1:1–4)

    2. The Lord Responds (Hab. 1:5–11)

  B. The Second Question (Hab. 1:12–2:5)

    1. How Can God Use Evil for Good? (Hab. 1:12–17)

    2. The Lord Responds (Hab. 2:1–5)

  C. Five Woes (Hab. 2:6–20)

    1. Greed (Hab. 2:6–8)

    2. Exploitation of Others (Hab. 2:9–11)

    3. Builds a Town with Bloodshed (Hab. 2:12–14)

    4. Exploiting People Through Drunkenness (Hab. 2:15–17)

    5. Idolatry (Hab. 2:18–20)

II. **Habakkuk's Prayer of Trust (Hab. 3)**

Study Questions

What was the state of the people when Habakkuk delivered his prophecy?

The righteous were in the minority (Hab. 1:4).

What nation did the Lord promise to bring against Israel?

The Chaldeans (Hab. 1:6).

What does Habakkuk say about God's moral perfection when he cries out to Him the second time?

"You are of purer eyes than to behold evil,
And cannot look on wickedness" (Hab. 1:13).

What is the central verse in Habakkuk's prophecy?

"But the just shall live by his faith" (Hab. 2:4).

Who is the first woe against?

Thieves (Hab. 2:6–8).

Who is the second woe against?

Those who are covetous (Hab. 2:9–11).

Who is the third woe against?

Murderers (Hab. 2:12–13).

Who is the fourth woe against?

Those who encourage drunkenness (Hab. 2:15–17).

Who is the fifth and final woe against?

Idolaters (Hab. 2:18–19).

In what way does Habakkuk ask the Lord for mercy?

"In wrath remember mercy" (Hab. 3:2).

What happened to Habakkuk when he heard the Lord?

He trembled (Hab. 3:16).

What does Habakkuk resolve to do at the end of his prophecy?

To rejoice in the Lord, no matter the circumstance (Hab. 3:17–19).

Rejoice, the Lord Is King

WORDS: Charles Wesley, *pub.*1744.
MUSIC: "Darwall's 148th"; John Darwall, *pub.*1770. Public Domain.

for more resources go to **jttb.co/zephaniah**

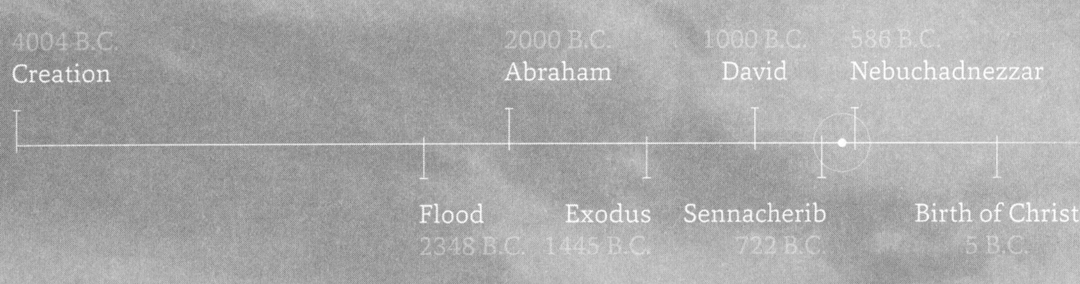

Journey through

Zephaniah

THEME

God's Judgment on All Nations

AUTHOR

Zephaniah

TIME OF WRITING

635–625 B.C.

MEMORY VERSE

*1 Gather yourselves together, yes, gather together, o undesir-
able nation, 2 before the decree is issued, or the day passes
like chaff, before the Lord's fierce anger comes upon you,
before the day of the Lord's anger comes upon you! 3 Seek
the Lord, all you meek of the earth, who have upheld His
justice. Seek righteousness, seek humility. It may be that
you will be hidden in the day of the Lord's anger.*

Zephaniah 2:1–3

OVERVIEW

The cry of the book of Zephaniah is to seek the Lord while He may be found, for judgment is coming.

The prophet Zephaniah affirms that God will gather all people for judgment if they do not repent. The striking ferocity and comprehensive judgment of God is illustrated in this book, which takes place on the heels of a revival. The revival produced external changes, but in many of the people, it did not reach their hearts and transform their lives.

Top 5 Facts to Remember

1. According to Zephaniah, the only way to escape God's wrath is to "Seek the Lord" (Zeph. 2:3).
2. The Lord promised to destroy Nineveh, a city so secure that she could say of herself, "I am it, and there is none besides me" (Zeph. 2:15).
3. Jerusalem's rulers are described as "roaring lions" and "evening wolves" (Zeph. 3:3).
4. Unlike Jerusalem's wicked leaders, the Lord brings His justice to light every morning (Zeph. 3:3–5).
5. The Lord promises to remove the proud from His holy mountain so that only the meek and humble remain (Zeph. 3:11–12).

Theme: God's Judgment on All Nations

In Zephaniah, God is glorifying Himself through His judgment on all nations, so that He might demonstrate His superior goodness in the salvation sinners, the damnation of the wicked, and for the preservation of His people for His eternal glory, and their eternal joy.

Author: Zephaniah

The author identifies himself as Zephaniah, Hezekiah's great-great-grandson (Zeph. 1:1).

Time of Writing: 635–625 B.C.

Zephaniah prophesied during the reign of Josiah (Zeph. 1:1), who ruled Judah from 641 to 609 B.C.[1] Since Zephaniah's prophecy appears to precede the fall of Nineveh (Zeph. 2:13–15)—which took place in 612 B.C.—the most probable time of writing for Zephaniah would be 641–612 B.C.

Key Verse

"And it shall come to pass at that time
That I will search Jerusalem with lamps,
And punish the men
Who are settled in complacency,
Who say in their heart,
'The Lord will not do good,
Nor will He do evil.'

1. For more on how these dates are calculated, see "Time of Events" at the back of this book.

Therefore their goods shall become booty,
And their houses a desolation;
They shall build houses, but not inhabit them;
They shall plant vineyards, but not drink their wine.
"The great day of the Lord is near;
It is near and hastens quickly.
The noise of the day of the Lord is bitter;
There the mighty men shall cry out.
That day is a day of wrath,
A day of trouble and distress,
A day of devastation and desolation,
A day of darkness and gloominess,
A day of clouds and thick darkness,
A day of trumpet and alarm
Against the fortified cities
And against the high towers."

Zephaniah 1:12–16

Lessons

1. God punishes those who syncretize His worship with the worship of idols.
2. The temporal judgments on this earth are types of the final judgment to come.
3. The Lord will punish and destroy the wicked.
4. Repent and seek the Lord, or His wrath will be poured out upon you on Judgment Day.
5. The Lord will preserve His people.
6. The people of God are meant to be a holy people.

Christ in Zephaniah

I. **The King of Israel (Zeph. 3:15)**

II. **The Mighty One (Zeph. 3:17)**

Outline

I. **Look Inward: Judgment Against Judah (Zeph. 1:1–2:2)**

II. **Look Outward: Judgment Against All the Nations (Zeph. 2:3–3:8)**

III. **Look Forward: Restoration of Jews and Gentiles (Zeph. 3:9–3:20)**

Study Questions

Who was Zephaniah's great, great grandfather?

Hezekiah (Zeph. 1:1).

When did Zephaniah prophesy?

In the days of Josiah the son of Amon, king of Judah (Zeph. 1:1).

What did the Lord say He would consume?

Everything in the land (Zeph. 1:2–3).

What is the call that Zephaniah makes to the nations?

He tells them to seek the Lord (Zeph. 2:1–3).

What city would Moab become like?

Sodom (Zeph. 2:9).

What were the sins of Jerusalem?

She was rebellious and polluted (Zeph. 3:1–2).

What qualities does Zephaniah ascribe to the remnant?

Meekness, humbleness, righteousness, and truthfulness (Zeph. 3:12–13).

Why are the people of God called to rejoice?

Because the Lord is in their midst (Zeph. 3:14–15).

My Jesus, I Love Thee

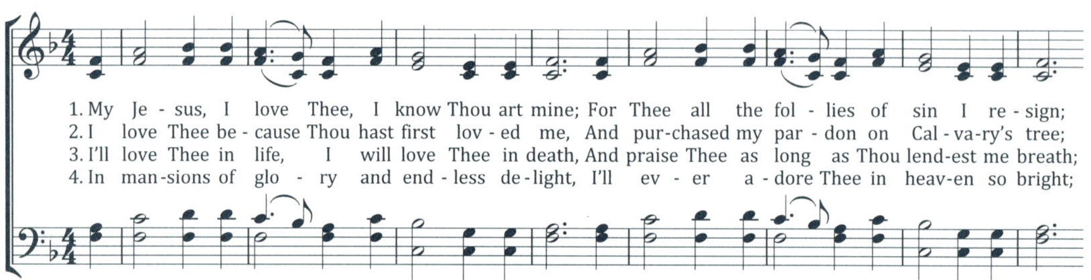

WORDS: William R. Featherston, 1864.
MUSIC: "Gordon"; Adoniram J. Gordon, 1876. Public Domain.

4004 B.C. Creation
2348 B.C. Flood
2000 B.C. Abraham
1445 B.C. Exodus
1000 B.C. David
722 B.C. Sennacherib
586 B.C. Nebuchadnezzar
5 B.C. Birth of Christ

Journey through

Haggai

THEME

Neglecting the Temple

AUTHOR

Haggai

TIME OF WRITING

520 B.C.

MEMORY VERSE

6 "For thus says the Lord of hosts: 'Once more (it is a little
while) I will shake heaven and earth, the sea and dry land;
7 'and I will shake all nations, and they shall come to the
Desire of All Nations, and I will fill this temple with glory,'
says the Lord of hosts. 8 'The silver is Mine, and the gold is
Mine,' says the Lord of hosts. 9 'The glory of this latter tem-
ple shall be greater than the former,' says the Lord of hosts.
'And in this place I will give peace,' says the Lord of hosts."

Haggai 2:6–9

OVERVIEW

The prophet Haggai delivers a sharp rebuke for the people who have returned from captivity. They started out with zeal for God and His ways but now have fallen into sinful patterns. It has been sixteen years since they returned and now their personal goals are hindering how God commanded them to worship Him. They were neglecting the temple and gratifying themselves.

The people who returned from captivity were distracted. They had little zeal to establish worship in the way that God had commanded. They were sluggish about rebuilding the temple and overly focused on their possessions and homes. Accordingly, Haggai preached sermons to shake the returnees out of their neglect. His message was that their priorities were off. He made it clear that neglecting the house of God always has consequences.

Top 5 Facts to Remember

1. Haggai prophesied to both the civil and religious leaders of his day (Hag. 1:1; 2:2).
2. God punished His people economically for neglecting His temple (Hag. 1:3–11; 2:15–19).
3. It was God Himself who stirred up the people to build His temple (Hag. 1:14).
4. The restored temple was nothing compared to the one originally built by Solomon, but God promised that it would be greater (Hag. 2:1–9).
5. Zerubbabel is in the family line of Christ (Matt. 1:1–17).

Theme: Neglecting the Temple

In Haggai, God is glorifying Himself through confronting the neglect of the temple, so that He might demonstrate His superior goodness in the salvation sinners, the damnation of the wicked, and for the preservation of His people for His eternal glory, and their eternal joy.

Author: Haggai

The author identifies himself as Haggai the prophet (Hag. 1:1).

Time of Writing: 520 B.C.

Haggai preached his four sermons over the course of a four-month period, in the second year of Darius the Great's reign[1] (520 B.C.).[2] He was a contemporary of Zechariah, Zerubbabel, and Jeshua.[3]

Key Verses

"Thus says the Lord of hosts: 'Consider your ways! Go up to the mountains and bring wood and build the temple, that I may take pleasure in it and be glorified,' says the Lord. 'You looked for much, but indeed it came to little; and when you brought it home, I blew it away. Why?' says the Lord of hosts. 'Because of My house that is in ruins, while every one of you runs to his own house. Therefore the heavens above you withhold the dew, and the earth withholds its fruit. For I called for a drought on the land and the mountains, on the grain and the new wine and the oil, on whatever the ground brings forth, on men and livestock, and on all the labor of your hands.' "

Haggai 1:7–11

" 'Who is left among you who saw this temple in its former glory? And how do you see it now? In comparison with it, is this not in your eyes as nothing? Yet now be strong, Zerubbabel,' says the Lord; 'and be strong, Joshua, son of Jehozadak, the high priest; and be strong, all you people of the land,' says the Lord, 'and work; for I am with you,' says the Lord of hosts."

Haggai 2:3–4

1. Hag. 1:1; 2:1; 2:10; 2:20.
2. For more on how these dates are calculated, see "Time of Events" at the back of this book.
3. Hag. 1:1; Ezra 5:1–2; 6:14.

Lessons

1. The Lord cares how you spend your money.
2. Our nation desperately needs to be brought back to the true worship of God.

Christ in Haggai

I. Zerubbabel

The Lord's promise to make Zerubbabel like a signet ring is typological of Jesus Christ's authority as King.

II. Other Types of Christ

1. The "Desire of All Nations" (Hag. 2:7)
2. The New Temple (Hag. 2:9)

Outline

III. The Command to Complete the Temple (Hag. 1)

IV. The Glory of the Temple (Hag. 2:1–9)

V. The Blessings of Obedience (Hag. 2:10–19)

VI. Promised Blessing (Hag. 2:20–23)

Study Questions

When did Haggai prophesy?

In the second year of King Darius.[4]

What was distracting the people from rebuilding the house of the Lord?

Their own houses (Hag. 1:4, 9).

Why was God punishing the people economically?

Because no one was rebuilding the house of God (Hag. 1:6, 9).

How did the Lord awaken the people from their slumber?

Haggai preached a series of fiery sermons.

What did the Lord command the people of Israel to do?

To go up to the mountains, bring wood, and build the temple (Hag. 1:7–8).

Why did God bring a drought on the land?

Because no one was building God's house (Hag. 1:9–11).

Whose hearts did the Lord stir up to resume rebuilding the temple?

Zerubbabel the son of Shealtiel, Joshua the son of Jehozadak, and all the remnant of the people (Hag. 1:14).

4. Hag. 1:1; 2:1; 2:10; 2:20.

What did the Lord say about the glory of the latter temple?

"The glory of this latter temple shall be greater than the former" (Hag. 2:9).

Who did the Lord promise to make like a signet ring?

Zerubbabel (Hag. 2:23).

Abide with Me

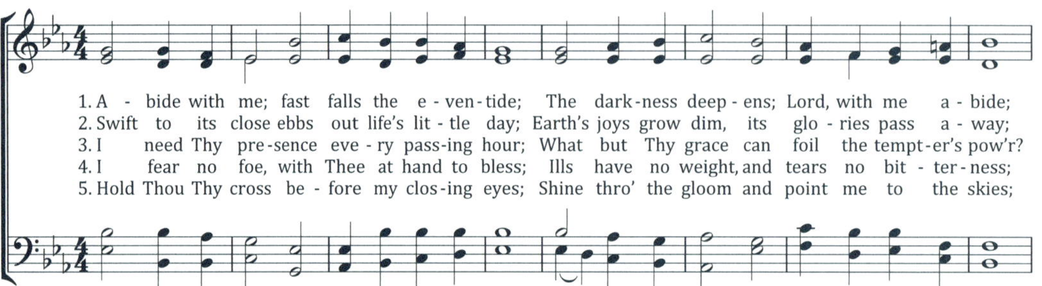

WORDS: Henry F. Lyte, 1847. MUSIC: "Eventide"; William H. Monk, 1861. Public Domain.

for more resources go to ***jttb.co/zechariah***

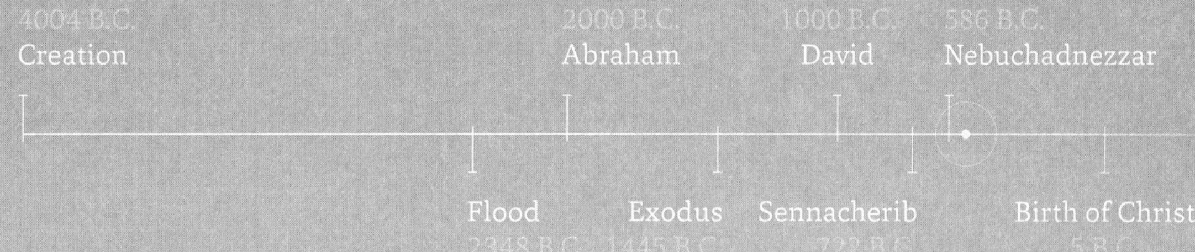

Journey through

Zechariah

THEME	AUTHOR	TIME OF WRITING
Visions of the Future	Zechariah	480–470 B.C.

MEMORY VERSE

"Rejoice greatly, O daughter of Zion! Shout, O daughter of Jerusalem! Behold, your King is coming to you; He is just and having salvation, lowly and riding on a donkey, a colt, the foal of a donkey."

Zechariah 9:9

OVERVIEW

The prophet Zechariah prophesies to the beleaguered returnees from Babylon. Zechariah's message is, "My house shall be built" for the temple that God dwells in is not made with hands. He uses dozens of images that display the beauty of God's kingdom as reasons for the people to finish rebuilding the temple in Jerusalem, which they have neglected for the past sixteen years.

The book of Zechariah is a beautifully-crafted poem that graphically illustrates the love of God for His people. Zechariah's name means, "the Lord remembers." Though the people sinned greatly, God preserved a remnant. The Old Testament does not end in captivity but in the restoration of His people and the providing of a vision for future glory.

Top 5 Facts to Remember

1. The book of Zechariah opens with the Lord's offer of pardon to those who repent: " 'Return to Me,' says the Lord of hosts, 'and I will return to you,' says the Lord of hosts" (Zech. 1:3).

2. In Zechariah 3, Zechariah sees a vision of Joshua the high priest standing in filthy garments before the Angel of the Lord, with Satan standing to accuse him. The Lord rebukes Satan and replaces Joshua's filthy garments with rich robes.

3. In Zechariah 7:4–7, the Lord asks the Jews to consider whether they are fasting for Him or themselves.

4. The Lord's anger was kindled against the shepherds because they had caused the sheep to go astray (Zech. 10:2–3).

5. Zechariah's book foretells many details of Christ's life, most notably His entry into Jerusalem on the back of a donkey, His betrayal for thirty pieces of silver, and the piercing of His side (see Christ in Zechariah).

Theme: Visions of the Future

In Zechariah, God is glorifying Himself through visions of the future as reasons to quit neglecting the house of God so that He might demonstrate His superior goodness in the salvation sinners, the damnation of the wicked, and for the preservation of His people for His eternal glory, and their eternal joy.

Author: Zechariah

The author identifies himself as Zechariah, the son of Berechiah, the son of Iddo the prophet (Zech. 1:1). He was a young man, for Zechariah 2:4 notes that the angel said "run to this young man."

Time of Writing: 480–470 B.C.

Zechariah prophesied from 520 to 518 B.C.[1] during Darius the Great's reign.[2] He was a contemporary of Haggai and Zerubbabel.[3] It is possible that the oracles contained in chapters 9–14 were delivered at a later point in Zechariah's life since they do not provide any clear time markers.

Key Verses

"Therefore say to them, 'Thus says the Lord of hosts: "Return to Me," says the Lord of hosts, "and I will return to you," says the Lord of hosts. "Do not be like your fathers, to whom the former prophets preached, saying, 'Thus says the Lord of hosts: "Turn now from your evil ways and your evil deeds." ' But they did not hear nor heed Me," says the Lord.' "

Zechariah 1:3–4

"Therefore thus says the Lord:
'I am returning to Jerusalem with mercy;
My house shall be built in it,' says the Lord of hosts,
'And a surveyor's line shall be stretched out over Jerusalem.' "

Zechariah 1:16

"And I will pour on the house of David and on the inhabitants of Jerusalem the Spirit of grace and supplication; then they will look on Me whom they pierced. Yes, they will mourn for Him as one mourns for his only son, and grieve for Him as one grieves for a firstborn. In that day there shall be a great mourning in Jerusalem, like the mourning at Hadad Rimmon in the plain of Megiddo. And the land shall mourn, every family by itself: the family of the house of David by itself, and

1. For more on how these dates are calculated, see "Time of Events" at the back of this book.
2. Zech. 1:1, 7; 7:1.
3. Ezra 5:1–2; 6:14.

their wives by themselves; the family of the house of Nathan by itself, and their wives by themselves; the family of the house of Levi by itself, and their wives by themselves; the family of Shimei by itself, and their wives by themselves; all the families that remain, every family by itself, and their wives by themselves."

Zechariah 12:10–14

Lessons

1. God is always calling His people to repent of their sins and return to Him.
2. The Lord will destroy the enemies of the church.
3. God desires obedience more than fasting.
4. God will build His church.

Christ in Zechariah

I. A King Riding on a Donkey (Zech. 9:9–11; Matt. 21:1–7; John 12:14–15)

In Zechariah 9:9, Christ's coming to Jerusalem on the back of a donkey is foretold. Matthew and John directly cite this passage in both of their Gospels and the parallels between Zechariah's prophecy and Christ's fulfillment are not hard to see. The prophet accurately portrays Christ's moral character as "just" and His mission as "having salvation"—both of them critical themes in the Gospel accounts.

The central element of the prophecy is Christ's lowly means of arrival: "riding on a donkey." Zechariah also alludes to the bringing in of the Gentiles, "He shall speak peace to the nations" and the all-encompassing nature of Christ's Kingdom, "His dominion shall be from sea to sea, and from the river to the ends of the earth."

II. "Thirty Pieces of Silver" (Zech. 11:12–13; Matt. 26:14–16; 27:3–10)

Zechariah 11:12–13 serves as a foreshadowing of Christ's betrayal for thirty pieces of silver. Zechariah is paid thirty pieces of silver as his wages, but is then commanded by the Lord to "Throw it to the potter—that princely price they set on me." Zechariah writes, "So I took the thirty pieces of silver and threw them into the house of the Lord for the potter." No explanation is given as to who the potter was, or what significance there would be in throwing the silver to him. However, Matthew quotes this Scripture as being fulfilled in Judas' betrayal of Christ, and there are indeed many correlations. We see Judas receiving thirty pieces of silver in exchange for betraying Christ (Matt. 26:15), the same amount that Zechariah received. We later see a remorseful Judas throw down the thirty pieces of silver in the temple (Matt. 27:5), the same action that Zechariah took. We see Judas' discarded funds being used by the chief priests to buy the potter's field, corresponding to Zechariah's wages being thrown "to the potter."

III. "They Will Look on Me Whom They Pierced" (Zech. 12:10; John 19:34–37; 20:27; Rev. 1:7)

Another Messianic prophecy is located in Zechariah 12:10, which predicts the piercing of Christ's side. In Zechariah's prophecy, the Lord promises to "pour on the house of David and on the inhabitants of Jerusalem the Spirit of grace and supplication" which in turn would cause them to "look on Me whom they pierced." In his Gospel, the Apostle John saw the fulfillment of this prophecy in the Roman solider who, finding Jesus already dead, pierced His side with a spear. It is important to note that the person speaking in Zechariah's prophecy is the Lord Himself, and that He is speaking of His own piercing: "they will look on Me whom they pierced." This is yet another attestation of Christ's divinity, for how could His piercing fulfill this prophecy if He were something less than God?

IV. Other Types of Christ

1. A Living Cornerstone (Zech. 3:9; 1 Pet. 2:4–8)
2. God's Servant the Branch (Zech. 3:8)
3. The Stricken Shepherd (Zech. 13:7; Matt. 26:31; Mark 14:27; John 10:11)
4. Living Waters (Zech. 14:8; John 4:10–15; 7:37–39; Rev. 7:17)

Outline

I. **Eight Symbolic Visions (Zech. 1–6)**

A. Introduction (Zech. 1:1–6)

B. The Eight Visions (Zech. 1:7–6:8)

1. The Vision of the Red-Horse Rider Among the Myrtles (Zech. 1:7–17)
2. The Vision of the Four Horns and the Four Craftsman (Zech. 1:18–21)
3. The Vision of the Surveyor with the Measuring Line (Zech. 2)
4. The Vision of the Cleansing and Crowning of Joshua (Zech. 3)
5. The Vision of the Gold Lampstand and the Two Olive Trees (Zech. 4)
6. The Vision of the Flying Scroll (Zech. 5:1–4)
7. The Vision of the Woman in the Basket (Zech. 5:5–11)
8. The Vision of the Four Chariots (Zech. 6:1–8)

C. Conclusion (Zech. 6:9–15)

II. **Four Explanatory Messages (Zech. 7–8)**

A. A Question about Fasting (Zech. 7:1–3)

B. The Four Messages (Zech. 7:4–8:23)

1. A Message of Rebuke (Zech. 7:4–7)
2. A Message of Repentance (Zech. 7:8–14)
3. A Message of Restoration (Zech. 8:1–17)
4. A Message of Rejoicing (Zech. 8:18–23)

III. **Two Revelatory Oracles (Zech. 9–14)**

A. The Anointed King Rejected (Zech. 9–11)

B. The Rejected King Enthroned (Zech. 12–14)

Study Questions

What was Zechariah's message?

"My house shall be built" (Zech. 1:16).

What did the Lord promise to do if the people returned to Him?

He would return to them (Zech. 1:3).

What was the vision of the horses?

Zechariah saw horses who had been sent out to walk to and fro throughout the earth, who reported that all the earth was resting quietly (Zech. 1:7–11).

What was the vision of the horns?

Zechariah saw four horns which represented those responsible for scattering Israel. Four craftsmen came to terrify and cast out the horns (Zech. 1:18–21).

What was the vision of the measuring line?

Zechariah saw a man with a measuring line who was going to measure Jerusalem. An angel then told Zechariah that Jerusalem would "be inhabited as towns without walls" (Zech. 2:1–5).

Who opposed Joshua the high priest before the Angel of the Lord?

Satan (Zech. 3:1).

Who does the Lord promise to bring forth?

His Servant the Branch (Zech. 3:8).

What is the vision of the lampstand and olive trees?

Zechariah saw a lampstand of solid gold with seven lamps on it and two olive trees replenishing its oil (Zech. 4:1–14).

What did Zechariah see in the vision of the flying scroll?

He saw a flying scroll, twenty cubits long and ten cubits wide, going out as a curse over the whole earth. He was then told that the scroll would enter and consume the house of every thief and perjurer (Zech. 5:1–4).

What did Zechariah see in the vision of the woman in a basket?

He saw a basket with a woman called Wickedness sitting in it. The basket was carried to the land of Shinar (Zech. 5:5–11).

What was the vision of the four chariots?

Zechariah saw four chariots, representing the four spirits of heaven, coming from between two mountains. The horses for each chariot were either red, black, white, or dappled (Zech. 6:1–8).

Who did the Lord command Zechariah to crown?

Joshua the son of Jehozadak, the high priest (Zech. 6:11).

What did the Lord say to the people about their fasting?

He questioned whether they had really been fasting for Him (Zech. 7:5–7).

What did the Lord say He would do to Tyre?

He promised to cast her out, destroy her power in the sea, and cause her to be devoured by fire (Zech. 9:4).

Where in Zechariah's prophecy does he speak of Christ's triumphal entry into Jerusalem?

Zechariah 9:9.

What was the sin of the worthless shepherd?

Devouring the sheep instead of caring for them (Zech. 11:16–17).

What will the Lord do to the families that refuse to worship Him?

On them there will be no rain (Zech. 14:17).

The Love of God

WORDS: Frederick M. Lehman, 1917; *v. 3 by* Meir Ben Isaac Nehorai, 1050; *v. 3 tr.*
MUSIC: F. M. L., 1917; *arr. by* Claudia L. Mays. Public Domain.

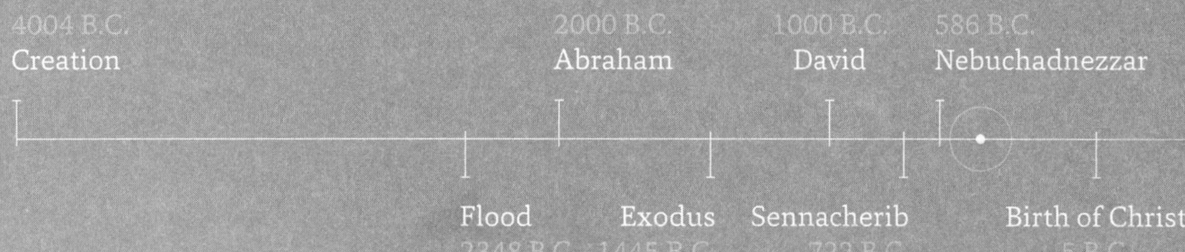

Journey through

Malachi

THEME	AUTHOR	TIME OF WRITING
Love	Malachi	433–424 B.C.

MEMORY VERSE

4 *"Remember the Law of Moses, My servant, which I com-*
manded him in Horeb for all Israel, with the statutes and
judgments. 5 *Behold, I will send you Elijah the prophet before*
the coming of the great and dreadful day of the Lord. 6 *And*
he will turn the hearts of the fathers to the children, and the
hearts of the children to their fathers, lest I come and strike
the earth with a curse."

Malachi 4:4–6

OVERVIEW

The theme of the book of Malachi is love. This is illustrated in the very first verse when God declares, "I have loved you." Immediately, the people retort, "How have you loved us?" Through the entire book, God's love for His people Israel is proved repeatedly while Israel questions His love for them.

What is love? How does God demonstrate His love toward His people? God answers this question very specifically. His answer may sound surprising.

Top 5 Facts to Remember

1. After Malachi delivered his prophecy, 400 years followed in which no more revelation was received from God. The silence was finally broken by the prophetic ministry of John the Baptist. Malachi even prophesied of John the Baptist's coming (Mal. 3:1; 4:5–6).

2. Paul quotes Malachi 1:2–3 as Scriptural evidence for the doctrine of election (Rom. 9:13).

3. The Jews were dishonoring God by offering blind, lame, sick, and even stolen animals as sacrifices (Mal. 1:6–14).

4. The Lord refused to receive the offerings of those who had divorced their wives (Mal. 2:13–16).

5. The Lord promises to take those who fear Him and make them His jewels (Mal. 3:16–17).

Theme: I Have Loved You

In Malachi, God is glorifying Himself through His love, so that He might demonstrate His superior goodness in the salvation sinners, the damnation of the wicked, and for the preservation of His people for His eternal glory, and their eternal joy.

Author: Malachi

The author identifies himself as Malachi (Mal. 1:1).

Time of Writing: 433–424 B.C.

While we don't know the exact year in which Malachi prophesied, we do know it was after the rebuilding of the temple[1] (516 B.C.)[2] and probably before the fall of the Persian Empire[3] (330 B.C.). It should also be noted that the sins condemned by Malachi are very similar to those addressed by Nehemiah (such as marrying pagan wives).[4]

1. Mal. 3:10.

2. For more on how these dates are calculated, see "Time of Events" at the back of this book.

3. The reference to Judah's "governor" in Mal. 1:8 would seem to indicate that Judah was still under Persian control at the time Malachi was written.

4. Mal. 2:11–12; Neh. 13:23–27.

Key Verses

" 'I have loved you,' says the Lord.
Yet you say, "In what way have You loved us?"
Was not Esau Jacob's brother?'
Says the Lord.
'Yet Jacob I have loved;
But Esau I have hated,
And laid waste his mountains and his heritage
For the jackals of the wilderness.' "

Malachi 1:2–3

"A son honors his father,
And a servant his master.
If then I am the Father,
Where is My honor?
And if I am a Master,
Where is My reverence?
Says the Lord of hosts
To you priests who despise My name.
Yet you say, 'In what way have we despised Your name?'
"You offer defiled food on My altar,
But say,
'In what way have we defiled You?'
By saying,
'The table of the Lord is contemptible.' "

Malachi 1:6–7

" 'Behold, I send My messenger,
And he will prepare the way before Me.
And the Lord, whom you seek,
Will suddenly come to His temple,
Even the Messenger of the covenant,
In whom you delight.
Behold, He is coming,'
Says the Lord of hosts.
" 'But who can endure the day of His coming?
And who can stand when He appears?

For He is like a refiner's fire
And like launderers' soap.
He will sit as a refiner and a purifier of silver;
He will purify the sons of Levi,
And purge them as gold and silver,
That they may offer to the Lord
An offering in righteousness.' "

Malachi 3:1–3

Lessons

1. You rob God when you withhold tithes and offerings.
2. We should never grow weary of worshipping God.
3. God hates divorce.

Christ in Malachi

I. **"The Messenger of the Covenant"**

Malachi predicted that a messenger would come and prepare the way for a greater Messenger, "the Messenger of the covenant" (Mal. 3:1–3). The first messenger is revealed in the New Testament to be John the Baptist (Matt. 11:10; Mark 1:2, 4; Luke 7:27), while "the Messenger of the covenant" is clearly a title for Christ Himself.

II. **"The Sun of Righteousness"**

Malachi prophesied that "The Sun of Righteousness" would arise "with healing in His wings" (Mal. 4:2). This is a picture of what Christ does for the elect. He brings light into their dark lives and heals their wounded souls.

Outline

I. **God Declares His Love to a Doubting People (Mal. 1:1–5)**

II. **How Israel Has Not Loved God (Mal. 1:6–2:16)**

III. **The Reason God Is Wearied (Mal. 2:17)**

IV. **Another Messenger Is Coming (Mal. 3:1–7)**

V. **How to Return to the Lord: Do Not Rob God (Mal. 3:8–12)**

VI. **The People Complain Harshly (Mal. 3:13–15)**

VII. **A Book of Remembrance Is Written By Those Who Fear God (Mal. 3:16–18)**

VIII. **Four Ways God Will Express His Love Toward His People in the Future (Mal. 4)**

Study Questions

When did Malachi prophesy?

Sometime between 516 and 330 B.C.

What were some of the major sins of the Israelites that Malachi addressed?

1. Robbing God by bringing their worst sacrifices (Mal. 1:8, 3:8).
2. Growing weary of worshipping God (Mal. 1:13).
3. Dealing treacherously with their wives (Mal. 2:10–16).
4. Condoning evil (Mal. 2:17).

What was Israel's response when God said He loved them?

"In what way have You loved us?" (Mal. 1:2).

Where is Malachi 1:2–3, "Jacob I have loved; But Esau I have hated," quoted in the New Testament?

Romans 9:13.

What did the Lord say He would do if Edom tried to "build the desolate places" (Mal. 1:4)?

He would throw it down.

In what ways were the people despising the name of the Lord?

By offering defiled food on His altar (Mal. 1:6–7).

In what way were the people of Israel profaning the offering of the Lord?

By offering stolen, lame, and sick animals (Mal. 1:12–14).

What were the sins of the priests at the time?

They had departed from the way, caused many to stumble at the law, and corrupted the covenant of Levi (Mal. 2:8).

What punishment did the Lord place on the priests?

He made them contemptible and base before all the people (Mal. 2:9).

What abomination did the people of Judah commit?

Intermarriage with idolaters (Mal. 2:11).

What was the second abomination that the people of Judah committed?

Dealing treacherously with their wives (Mal. 2:13–15).

What does the Lord seek?

Godly offspring (Mal. 2:15).

Who does the Lord promise to send to prepare the way before Him?

His messenger (Mal. 3:1).

Who will purify and purge the sons of Levi, like gold and silver?

The Lord, the Messenger of the covenant (Mal. 3:3).

How will the Lord view the people's offering after the sons of Levi are purified?

It will be pleasant to Him (Mal. 3:4).

In what ways were the people robbing God?

In tithes and offerings (Mal. 3:8).

What will the Lord do to the wicked one day?

He will burn them up (Mal. 4:1).

What does the Lord say will happen to those who fear Him?

They will go out, grow fat like stall-fed calves, and trample the wicked (Mal. 4:2–3).

What is the last prophesy in the Old Testament?

The coming of "Elijah the prophet" (Mal. 4:5–6).

The New Testament

5 B.C.
Birth of Christ

Christ's Baptism & Ministry Start
26 A.D.

30 A.D.
Crucifixion & Resurrection

Paul's First Missionary Journey
48 A.D.

95 A.D.
John Writes Revelation

When I Survey the Wondrous Cross

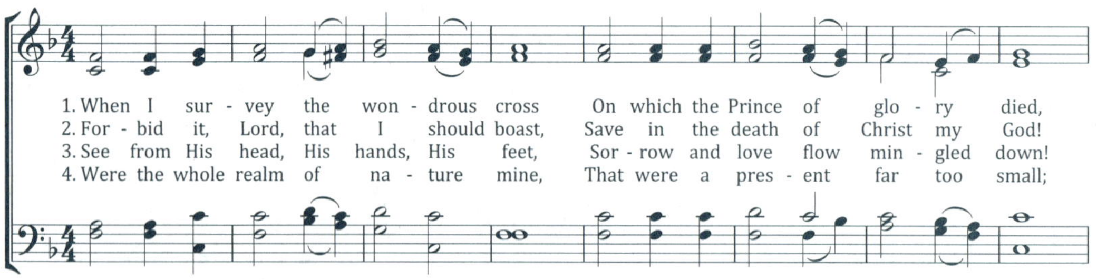

WORDS: Isaac Watts, pub. 1707. MUSIC: “Hamburg”; Lowell Mason, 1824. Public Domain

5 B.C.
Birth of Christ

30 A.D.
Crucifixion & Resurrection

95 A.D.
John Writes Revelation

Christ's Baptism & Ministry Start
26 A.D.

Paul's First Missionary Journey
48 A.D.

Journey through

Matthew

THEME	AUTHOR	TIME OF WRITING
The Promised Messiah	Matthew	50–60 A.D.

MEMORY VERSE

"And Jesus came and spoke to them, saying, 'All authority has been given to Me in heaven and on earth. Go therefore and make disciples of all the nations, baptizing them in the name of the Father and of the Son and of the Holy Spirit, teaching them to observe all things that I have commanded you; and lo, I am with you always, even to the end of the age.' Amen."

Matthew 28:18–20

OVERVIEW

As you read the Gospel of Matthew, you will see how God keeps His promises. Jesus is the promised Messiah of the Old Testament. Over and over again, Matthew refers to the ministry of Jesus to show how the Old Testament was fulfilled.

Top 5 Facts to Remember

1. Of the four Gospels, it was very likely the first account to be written.
2. Matthew uses the Jewish phrase "kingdom of heaven" rather than "kingdom of God."
3. Matthew quotes the Old Testament 62 times, more than any of the other Gospel writers.
4. Matthew is addressing a primarily Jewish audience to prove that Jesus Christ was the Messiah prophesied throughout the Old Testament.
5. Matthew's Gospel account breaks the 400-year silence, transitioning from the Old Covenant to the New Covenant.

Theme: The Promised Messiah

In Matthew, God is glorifying Himself by sending the promised Messiah, so that He might demonstrate His superior goodness in the salvation sinners, the damnation of the wicked, and for the preservation of His people, for His eternal glory, and their eternal joy.

Author: Matthew

Matthew was a tax collector who encountered Jesus on an ordinary day: "As Jesus passed on from there, He saw a man named Matthew sitting at the tax office. And He said to him, 'Follow Me.' So he arose and followed Him" (Matt. 9:9).

Audience: Jewish Christians

Matthew directs his Gospel to a Jewish audience to demonstrate how Christ is the long-awaited Messiah and the fulfillment of Old Testament prophesies. (Matthew 5:38–40).

Key Verses

" 'Behold, the virgin shall be with child, and bear a Son, and they shall call His name Immanuel,' which is translated, 'God with us.' "

Matthew 1:23

"For this is he who was spoken of by the prophet Isaiah, saying: 'The voice of one crying in the wilderness: "Prepare the way of the Lord; Make His paths straight." ' "

Matthew 3:3

"And He answered and said to them, 'Have you not read that He who made them at the beginning "made them male and female," and said, "For this reason a man

shall leave his father and mother and be joined to his wife, and the two shall become one flesh?" ' "

Matthew 19:4–5

Lessons

1. "Repent, for the kingdom of heaven is at hand."
2. Christ is the promised Messiah.
3. The Old Testament points to Christ.
4. Christ was crucified, died, was buried, and rose again.
5. Go out and make disciples of all nations.
6. All authority has been given to Christ.

Outline

I. **Christ Incarnated (Matt. 1:1–4:11)**

II. **Christ Declared (Matt. 4:12–7:29)**

III. **Christ's Messengers Commissioned (Matt. 8:1–11:1)**

IV. **Christ Opposed (Matt. 11:2–13:53)**

V. **Christ's Reaction (Matt. 13:54–19:2)**

VI. **Christ Rejected (Matt. 19:3–26:1)**

VII. **Christ Crucified and Resurrected (Matt. 26:2–28:20)**

Study Questions

CHAPTERS 1–7

Who was Jesus' mother?

Mary (Matt. 1:18).

Where was Jesus born?

Bethlehem (Matt. 2:1).

Of whom was Isaiah prophesying when he said "Prepare the way of the Lord"?

John the Baptist (Matt. 3:1–3).

What message did Jesus preach in Capernaum?

"Repent, for the kingdom of heaven is at hand" (Matt. 4:17).

List the Beatitudes.

1. Blessed are the poor in spirit, for theirs is the kingdom of heaven.
2. Blessed are those who mourn, for they shall be comforted.
3. Blessed are the meek, for they shall inherit the earth.
4. Blessed are those who hunger and thirst for righteousness, for they shall be filled.
5. Blessed are the merciful, for they shall obtain mercy.
6. Blessed are the pure in heart, for they shall see God.
7. Blessed are the peacemakers, for they shall be called sons of God.
8. Blessed are those who are persecuted for righteousness' sake, for theirs is the kingdom of heaven.

9. Blessed are you when they revile and persecute you, and say all kinds of evil against you falsely for My sake. Rejoice and be exceedingly glad, for great is your reward in heaven, for so they persecuted the prophets who were before you (Matt. 5:3–12).

Where should we be laying up our treasures?

In heaven (Matt. 6:20).

What will God say to hypocrites when they stand before Him?

"Depart from Me, you who practice lawlessness" (Matt. 7:23).

CHAPTERS 8–14

What happened to the wind and the waves when Christ rebuked them?

There "was a great calm" (Matt. 8:26).

Who did Christ come to call?

He came to call "sinners to repentance" (Matt. 9:13).

Who does Christ say we should fear?

"Fear Him who is able to destroy both soul and body in hell" (Matt. 10:28).

What does Jesus say to those who "labor and are heavy laden"?

"Come to Me" (Matt. 11:28).

Who is the Lord of the Sabbath?

Christ (Matt. 12:8).

Why did Jesus speak in parables?

"Because it has been given to you to know the mysteries of the kingdom of heaven, but to them it has not been given" (Matt. 13:11).

How did Jesus feed the five thousand?

"He took the five loaves and the two fish, and looking up to heaven, He blessed and broke and gave the loaves to the disciples; and the disciples gave to the multitudes" (Matt. 14:19).

CHAPTERS 15–21

What defiles a man?

The things that proceed out of the mouth that come from the heart (Matt. 15:18).

What is required of those who desire to come to Christ?

They must deny themselves, take up their cross and follow Him (Matt. 16:24).

What happened to Jesus when He was on a high mountain with Peter, James, and John?

He was transfigured before them (Matt. 17:2).

What must happen before someone can enter the kingdom of heaven?

They must be "converted and become as little children" (Matt. 18:3).

What was Jesus' response to the disciples when they prevented children from coming to Him?

"Let the little children come to Me, and do not forbid them; for of such is the kingdom of heaven" (Matt. 19:14).

What did Jesus come to do?

He came "to serve, and to give His life as a ransom for many" (Matt. 20:28).

Why did Jesus overturn the tables in the temple?

Because it had been made into a "den of thieves" (Matt. 21:13).

CHAPTERS 22–28

What did Jesus compare the kingdom of heaven to in Matthew 22?

A wedding (Matt. 22:2).

What did Jesus desire for Jerusalem?

To gather its children together as a hen gathers her chicks under its wings (Matt. 23:37).

What does Christ say about the Word of God in Matthew 24?

It "will by no means pass away" (Matt. 24:35).

What will the Lord do when He comes again?

He will divide His sheep from the goats, and the goats "will go away into everlasting punishment, but the righteous into eternal life" (Matt. 25:46).

What did Christ say when He prayed to His Father in the garden?

"O My Father, if it is possible, let this cup pass from Me; nevertheless, not as I will, but as You will" (Matt. 26:39).

What did Jesus say during the ninth hour on the cross?

"My God, My God, why have You forsaken Me?" (Matt. 27:46).

What is Christ's final command in the book of Matthew?

The Great Commission (Matt. 28:19–20).

Jesus Paid It All

WORDS: Elvina M. Hall, 1865. MUSIC: "All to Christ"; John T. Grape, 1868. Public Domain

for more resources go to ***jttb.co/mark***

5 B.C.
Birth of Christ

30 A.D.
Crucifixion & Resurrection

95 A.D.
John Writes Revelation

Christ's Baptism & Ministry Start
26 A.D.

Paul's First Missionary Journey
48 A.D.

Journey through

Mark

THEME

The Mission of Jesus Christ

AUTHOR

Mark

TIME OF WRITING

50–60 A.D.

MEMORY VERSE

"The time is fulfilled, and the kingdom of God is at hand. Repent, and believe in the gospel."

Mark 1:15

OVERVIEW

The Gospel of Mark focuses on stories which reveal the life and the perspectives of Jesus. In Mark, Christ is the Servant King. Ray Stedman summarizes it this way: Christ is the servant who rules and the ruler who serves. He serves and rules by preaching, teaching, and healing. The book is fast-paced and full of action. Mark allocates much of his Gospel to the last weeks of Jesus' life, particularly the last seven days in Jerusalem.

Top 5 Facts to Remember

1. The Gospel of Mark is the shortest of the four Gospel accounts.
2. It was written primarily towards a Gentile audience.
3. Mark primarily focuses on narratives and what Christ did during His earthly ministry.
4. Mark portrays Christ as the Servant King, a king who rules and serves.
5. A lot of Mark's Gospel account records the events during the final weeks of Jesus' life.

Theme: The Mission of Jesus Christ

In Mark, God is glorifying Himself through the mission of Jesus Christ, so that He might demonstrate His superior goodness in the salvation sinners, the damnation of the wicked, and for the preservation of His people, for His eternal glory, and their eternal joy.

Author: Mark

This is the same "John Mark" who did not go with Paul and Barnabas on a missionary journey (Acts 15:37–39).

Audience: The Gentiles

Mark uses less Hebrew terminology than Matthew, making it likely that his Gospel was aimed at a Gentile audience.

Key Verses

"Then He arose and rebuked the wind, and said to the sea, 'Peace, be still!' And the wind ceased and there was a great calm. But He said to them, 'Why are you so fearful? How is it that you have no faith?' And they feared exceedingly, and said to one another, 'Who can this be, that even the wind and the sea obey Him!' "

Mark 4:39–41

"When He had called the people to Himself, with His disciples also, He said to them, 'Whoever desires to come after Me, let him deny himself, and take up his cross, and follow Me. For whoever desires to save his life will lose it, but whoever loses his life for My sake and the Gospel's will save it. For what will it profit a

man if he gains the whole world, and loses his own soul? Or what will a man give in exchange for his soul?' "

Mark 8:34–37

"But Jesus called them to Himself and said to them, 'You know that those who are considered rulers over the Gentiles lord it over them, and their great ones exercise authority over them. Yet it shall not be so among you; but whoever desires to become great among you shall be your servant. And whoever of you desires to be first shall be slave of all. For even the Son of Man did not come to be served, but to serve, and to give His life a ransom for many.' "

Mark 10:42–45

Lessons

1. Repent and believe in the gospel (Mark 1:15).
2. Christ is Lord of the Sabbath (Mark 2:28).
3. Parables involving physical things are meant to teach us truths about spiritual things (Mark 4:11–12).
4. Take up your cross and follow Christ (Mark 8:34).
5. It is hard for a rich man to enter the kingdom of heaven (Mark 10:25).
6. All things are possible with God (Mark 10:27).

Outline

I. **Jesus Begins His Ministry (Mark 1:1–13)**

II. **Jesus Ministers in Galilee (Mark 1:14–6:6a)**

III. **Jesus Withdraws from Galilee (Mark 6:6b-8:21)**

IV. **Jesus Predicts His Own Suffering (Mark 8:22–38)**

V. **Jesus Journeys to Jerusalem (Mark 9–10)**

VI. **Jesus Ministers in Jerusalem (Mark 11–13)**

VII. **Jesus' Death and Resurrection (Mark 14–16)**

Study Questions

CHAPTERS 1–8

What was Christ's call to the disciples?

"Follow Me, and I will make you fishers of men" (Mark 1:17).

What did Christ do to show He had "power on earth to forgive sins"?

He healed the paralytic (Mark 2:11).

What is the unpardonable sin?

Blasphemy against the Holy Spirit (Mark 3:29).

What does the seed that fell on the good ground resemble?

"Those who hear the word, accept it, and bear fruit" (Mark 4:20).

How did Christ heal the demon-possessed man?

He commanded the demons to come out of the man and sent them into a herd of swine (Mark 5:8–13).

How did Jesus get to the disciples' boat while they were out at sea?

He walked on the water (Mark 6:48).

What are the sins that Christ lists that come from within?

The sins are: "evil thoughts, adulteries, fornications, murders, thefts, covetousness, wickedness, deceit, lewdness, an evil eye, blasphemy, pride, [and] foolishness" (Mark 7:21–22).

What did Christ say to Peter when Peter rebuked Him?

"Get behind Me, Satan! For you are not mindful of the things of God, but the things of men" (Mark 8:33).

CHAPTERS 9–16

What was Christ's response to the question "who would be the greatest" (Mark 9:34)?

"If anyone desired to be first, he shall be last of all and servant of all" (Mark 9:35).

What was required of the rich young ruler before he could follow the Lord?

To sell all he had and give it to the poor (Mark 10:21).

What will happen to those who do not forgive?

God will not forgive them (Mark 11:26).

What did Christ say to the Pharisees when they asked Him about paying taxes to Caesar?

"Render to Caesar the things that are Caesar's, and to God the things that are God's" (Mark 12:17).

Why did Christ command His disciples to "watch" (v. 35)?

Because they "do not know when the master of the house is coming" (Mark 13:35).

What does Christ say of Judas, the man who betrayed Him?

"It would have been good for that man if he had never been born" (Mark 14:21).

What happened to the veil of the temple when Christ died?

It was "torn in two from top to bottom" (Mark 15:38).

What happened to Christ at the very end of the book of Mark?

He ascended into heaven (Mark 16:19).

O The Deep, Deep Love of Jesus

WORDS: Samuel T. Francis, 1875.
MUSIC: “Ebenezer [Ton-y-Botel]”; Thomas J. Williams, pub. 1890. Public Domain

for more resources go to ***jttb.co/luke***

5 B.C.
Birth of Christ

30 A.D.
Crucifixion & Resurrection

95 A.D.
John Writes Revelation

Christ's Baptism & Ministry Start
26 A.D.

Paul's First Missionary Journey
48 A.D.

Journey through

Luke

THEME

The Son of Man

AUTHOR

Luke

TIME OF WRITING

60–61 A.D.

MEMORY VERSE

"Then He lifted up His eyes toward His disciples, and said: 'Blessed are you poor, for yours is the kingdom of God. Blessed are you who hunger now, for you shall be filled. Blessed are you who weep now, for you shall laugh. Blessed are you when men hate you, and when they exclude you, and revile you, and cast out your name as evil, for the Son of Man's sake. Rejoice in that day and leap for joy! For indeed your reward is great in heaven, for in like manner their fathers did to the prophets.' "

Luke 6:20–23

OVERVIEW

The Gospel of Luke presents Jesus in His humanity as "the Son of Man." He illustrates Christ's compassion for the broken by recording more miracles than any other Gospel writer. Luke sees Jesus as the one who came to "seek and save the lost" and the one who came to minister to the sick and poor while resisting the proud and the self-sufficient. Christ's tenderheartedness is displayed by Luke demonstrating how He healed the brokenhearted and saved the outcast. Luke was a historian and as such he provides a more sequential account of the life of Jesus than any of the other Gospel writers.

Top 5 Facts to Remember

1. Luke gives the most complete account of Jesus' birth and the historical events surrounding it.
2. Luke is the longest book of the entire New Testament, comprising 14% of it.
3. Luke portrays Jesus as a compassionate Savior who came "to seek and to save that which was lost" (Luke 19:10).
4. Luke is the only Gentile author out of the four Gospel accounts.
5. He was not a first-hand eyewitness; rather, he was an educated historian who drew from the accounts of many eyewitnesses (Luke 1:1–4).

Theme: The Son of Man

In Luke, God is glorifying Himself as "The Son of Man," so that He might demonstrate His superior goodness in the salvation sinners, the damnation of the wicked, and for the preservation of His people, for His eternal glory, and their eternal joy.

Author: Luke

He was a physician and companion of Paul.

Audience: Theophilus

Luke is writing to Theophilus and is addressing Hellenistic Greeks. "It seemed good to me also, having had perfect understanding of all things from the very first, to write to you an orderly account, most excellent Theophilus, that you may know the certainty of those things in which you were instructed" (Luke 1:3–4).

Key Verses

"And He was handed the book of the prophet Isaiah. And when He had opened the book, He found the place where it was written:

'The Spirit of the Lord is upon Me,
Because He has anointed Me
To preach the Gospel to the poor;
He has sent Me to heal the brokenhearted,
To proclaim liberty to the captives
And recovery of sight to the blind,
To set at liberty those who are oppressed;
To proclaim the acceptable year of the Lord.'

Then He closed the book, and gave it back to the attendant and sat down. And the eyes of all who were in the synagogue were fixed on Him. And He began to say to them, 'Today this Scripture is fulfilled in your hearing.' "

Luke 4:17–21

"And He strictly warned and commanded them to tell this to no one, saying, 'The Son of Man must suffer many things, and be rejected by the elders and chief priests and scribes, and be killed, and be raised the third day.' "

Luke 9:21–22

"And they were all amazed at the majesty of God.

"But while everyone marveled at all the things which Jesus did, He said to His disciples,' Let these words sink down into your ears, for the Son of Man is about to be betrayed into the hands of men.' But they did not understand this saying, and it was hidden from them so that they did not perceive it; and they were afraid to ask Him about this saying."

Luke 9:43–45

Lessons

1. Christ has come to glorify God by seeking and saving the lost.
2. God is sovereign over salvation.
3. Repent and believe on the Lord Jesus Christ!

Outline

I. **Prologue (Luke 1:1–4)**

II. **Christ's Infancy (Luke 1:5–2:52)**

III. **Christ's Preparation (Luke 3:1–4:13)**

IV. **Christ's Ministry in Galilee (Luke 4:14–9:50)**

V. **Christ's Journey to Jerusalem (Luke 9:51–19:27)**

VI. **Christ's Ministry in Jerusalem (Luke 19:28–21:38)**

VII. **Christ's Death and Resurrection (Luke 22:1–24:53)**

Study Questions

CHAPTERS 1–6

What did Elizabeth's baby do when Mary came to her?

It leaped for joy in her womb (Luke 1:41).

What was Jesus doing in the temple when His parents found Him?

He was listening to the teachers and asking questions (Luke 2:46).

What was the message that John the Baptist preached?

A message of "a baptism of repentance for the remission of sins" (Luke 3:3).

How did Christ answer Satan when he tempted Him in the wilderness?

He answered him with the Word of God (Luke 4:1–13).

What was Christ's response to the faith of the paralytic and his friends?

He healed him and declared his sins forgiven (Luke 5:20–24).

Who were the twelve apostles?

The twelve apostles were Peter (also called, Simon), Andrew, James, John, Philip, Bartholomew, Matthew, Thomas, James, Simon, Judas, and Judas Iscariot (Luke 6:14–16).

CHAPTERS 7–12

How did Christ raise the son of the widow of Nain?

He "touched the open coffin" and said, "Young man, I say to you arise" (Luke 7:14).

Who did Jesus say His mother and brothers are?

Those "who hear the word of God and do it" (Luke 8:21).

Who did Peter say Jesus was?

"The Christ of God" (Luke 9:20).

What was Christ's response to Martha when she wanted Mary's help?

"Martha, Martha, you are worried and troubled about many things. But one thing is needed, and Mary has chosen that good part which will not be taken away from her" (Luke 10:41–42).

How did Christ say we should pray?

"When you pray, say:
Our Father in heaven,
Hallowed be Your name.
Your kingdom come.
Your will be done
On earth as it is in heaven.
Give us day by day our daily bread.
And forgive us our sins,
For we also forgive everyone who is indebted to us.
And do not lead us into temptation,
But deliver us from the evil one" (Luke 11:2–4).

What will become of the secret actions of hypocrites?

They will be revealed (Luke 12:2–3).

CHAPTERS 13–18

What gate should one strive to enter through?

The narrow gate (Luke 13:24).

What must one forsake in order to be a disciple of Christ?

Everything (Luke 14:33).

What happens in heaven when one sinner repents?

There is much joy (Luke 15:7).

Can anyone serve two masters?

No (Luke 16:13).

Where is the kingdom of God?

"For indeed, the kingdom of God is within you" (Luke 17:21).

Who is good?

God (Luke 18:19).

CHAPTERS 19–24

What did Christ say would happen if His disciples were silent?

"The stones would immediately cry out" (Luke 19:40).

Who will receive greater condemnation and why?

The scribes for their hypocrisy (Luke 20:46–47).

How did the widow put in more than everyone else?

She gave all she had (Luke 21:4).

What did Peter do after he denied Christ three times?

He "went out and wept bitterly" (Luke 22:62).

What did Christ say to the repentant thief on the cross?

"Assuredly, I say to you, today you will be with Me in Paradise" (Luke 23:43).

What happened to the disciples after Christ broke bread and gave it to them?

"Their eyes were open and they knew Him" (Luke 24:31).

Oh How I Love Jesus

WORDS: Frederick Whitfield, 1855. MUSIC: American melody. Public Domain

5 B.C.
Birth of Christ

30 A.D.
Crucifixion & Resurrection

95 A.D.
John Writes Revelation

Christ's Baptism & Ministry Start
28 A.D.

Paul's First Missionary Journey
48 A.D.

Journey through

John

THEME

The Son of God

AUTHOR

John

TIME OF WRITING

80–90 A.D.

MEMORY VERSE

"And Jesus said to them, 'I am the bread of life. He who comes to Me shall never hunger, and he who believes in Me shall never thirst.' "

John 6:35

OVERVIEW

The focus of John's Gospel is to prove the deity of Jesus Christ and to identify various facets of His glory. The beauty of the imagery describing Jesus is perhaps why so many recommend John for unbelievers to get to know Jesus. He is called "Life" thirty-two times in this Gospel. John's disclosure of Jesus hangs upon seven miracle narratives which he uses to explain the power and glory of Jesus Christ. John's purpose is clearly stated. He writes so that his readers might believe in Jesus.

Top 5 Facts to Remember

1. John focuses on the deity of Christ, proclaiming that He is the Son of God.
2. John never refers to himself by name.
3. John's Gospel account begins with Christ, who was with God in the beginning before creation (John 1:1–3).
4. The prologue of John introduces the major themes of the book.
5. John does not record any of Christ's parables.

Theme: The Son of God

In John, God is glorifying Himself through the glory of His Son so that He might demonstrate His superior goodness in the salvation sinners, the damnation of the wicked, and for the preservation of His people, for His eternal glory, and their eternal joy.

Author: John

He is the disciple whom Jesus loved, the brother of James, and one of the "Sons of Thunder." Jesus trusted John to take care of his mother (John 19:26–27). He is the author of 1st, 2nd, and 3rd John as well as the book of Revelation and was the pastor of the church in Ephesus.

Audience: Unknown

We don't know whether John wrote his Gospel with a specific audience in mind. However, we do know that he intended for it to function as a sort of apologetic for Christianity (John 19:35; 20:30–31).

Key Verses

"Then Jesus said to them again, 'Most assuredly, I say to you, I am the door of the sheep. All who ever came before Me are thieves and robbers, but the sheep did not hear them. I am the door. If anyone enters by Me, he will be saved, and will go in and out and find pasture. The thief does not come except to steal, and to kill, and to destroy. I have come that they may have life, and that they may have it more abundantly.' "

John 10:7–10

"Thomas said to Him, 'Lord, we do not know where You are going, and how can we know the way?' "Jesus said to him, 'I am the way, the truth, and the life. No one comes to the Father except through Me.' "

John 14:5–6

"And truly Jesus did many other signs in the presence of His disciples, which are not written in this book; but these are written that you may believe that Jesus is the Christ, the Son of God, and that believing you may have life in His name."

John 20:30–31

Lessons

1. Christ is the Son of God!
2. Unless you are born again, you cannot see the kingdom of heaven.
3. Christ has overcome the world.
4. Jesus died, was buried, and rose again.
5. John wrote this epistle so that people would believe that "Jesus is the Christ, the Son of God."

Outline

I. **Prologue: The Word Became Flesh (John 1:1–18)**

II. **The Son of God's Manifestation to the Jews (John 1:19–12:50)**

III. **The Son of God's Ministry to His Disciples (John 13:1–17:26)**

IV. **The Son of God's Suffering and Glory (John 18:1–20:31)**

V. **Epilogue: The Death of the Apostle Peter Foretold (John 21:1–25)**

Study Questions

CHAPTERS 1–7

Who was with God and was God?

The Word (John 1:1).

What did Christ turn to wine at the wedding feast?

Water (John 2:7–9).

What must happen for one to see the kingdom of God?

They must be born again (John 3:3).

How must we worship God?

"In spirit and truth" (John 4:24).

What did Jesus say when He healed the man at the pool of Bethesda?

"Rise, take up your bed and walk" (John 5:8).

Who is the "bread of God"?

"He who comes down from heaven and gives life to the world" (John 6:33).

What flows out of the heart of one who believes in God?

"Rivers of living water" (John 7:38).

CHAPTERS 8–14

What sets a man free?

The truth (John 8:32).

Why was the man born blind?

So that the "works of God" would "be revealed in him" (John 9:3).

What kind of a shepherd is Christ?

He is the good shepherd (John 10:11).

What did Jesus say was the reason for Lazarus' sickness?

"That the Son of God may be glorified through it" (John 11:4).

On whose authority does Christ command?

The Father (John 12:49).

How will people know who the disciples of God are?

His disciples have love for one another (John 13:35).

How do you know if you love God?

If you keep His commandments (John 14:21, 23).

Can we bear fruit apart from Christ?

No (John 15:4).

Why can we have peace during times of tribulation in the world?

Because Christ has overcome the world (John 16:33).

How does God sanctify Christians?

By the Word of God (John 17:17).

Is God's kingdom of this world?

No (John 18:36).

What were the final words spoken by Jesus on the cross?

"It is finished" (John 19:30).

Who was the first person that Christ revealed Himself to when He rose from the dead?

Mary Magdalene (John 20:14).

How many times did Christ ask Peter if he loved Him?

Three times (John 21:15–17).

The Church's One Foundation

WORDS: Samuel J. Stone, pub.1866; alt. & v. 3–5 by Charles W. Naylor, 1907.
MUSIC: Samuel Sebastian Wesley, 1864. Public Domain.

for more resources go to ***jttb.co/acts***

5 B.C.
Birth of Christ

30 A.D.
Crucifixion & Resurrection

95 A.D.
John Writes Revelation

Christ's Baptism & Ministry Start
26 A.D.

Paul's First Missionary Journey
48 A.D.

Journey through

Acts

THEME

The Power of the Holy Spirit

AUTHOR

Luke

TIME OF WRITING

62 A.D.

MEMORY VERSE

"I will deliver you from the Jewish people, as well as from the Gentiles, to whom I now send you, to open their eyes, in order to turn them from darkness to light, and from the power of Satan to God, that they may receive forgiveness of sins and an inheritance among those who are sanctified by faith in Me."

Acts 26:17–18

OVERVIEW

Acts is one of the most exciting books of the Bible - full of action, ideas, and conflict. The central concern of the book of Acts is expressed in the promise the Lord Jesus gave to His disciples at the very beginning of the book, "You shall receive power." Acts teaches us plainly that our mission is not only local but global in scope. The disciples were witnesses in Jerusalem, Judea, and the uttermost parts of the earth. All throughout the book of Acts, men boldly proclaimed the gospel by the power of the Holy Spirit.

Top 5 Facts to Remember

1. When they were commanded not to teach in the name of Jesus, Peter and John replied, "Whether it is right in the sight of God to listen to you more than to God, you judge. For we cannot but speak the things which we have seen and heard" (Acts 4:19–20).

2. Ananias and Sapphira were struck dead when they lied to the apostles (Acts 5:1–11).

3. When asked about the meaning of Isaiah 53, Philip preached Jesus to an Ethiopian eunuch (Act 8:26–40).

4. Paul preached the gospel to all audiences, even Greek philosophers (Acts 17:16–33).

5. Paul was, by occupation, a tentmaker (Acts 18:3).

Theme: The Power of the Holy Spirit

In Acts, God is glorifying Himself through the power of the Holy Spirit, so that He might demonstrate His superior goodness in the salvation sinners, the damnation of the wicked, and for the preservation of His people, for His eternal glory, and their eternal joy.

Author: Luke

Luke was a historian and physician. He was also Paul's traveling companion,[1] which explains the many references to "we" and "us" in the parts of the Book of Acts that record details of Paul's ministry.[2]

Audience: Theophilus

"The former account I made, O Theophilus, of all that Jesus began both to do and teach..."

Acts 1:1

1. Luke is named as Paul's companion in three of Paul's letters (Col. 4:14; 2 Tim. 4:11; Philemon 1:24).

2. Acts 16:10–17; 20:5–6, 13–15; 21:1–8, 10–12, 14–18; 27:1–8, 15–16, 18–20, 27, 29, 37; 28:2, 7, 10–14, 15–16.

Key Verses

"When the Day of Pentecost had fully come, they were all with one accord in one place. And suddenly there came a sound from heaven, as of a rushing mighty wind, and it filled the whole house where they were sitting. Then there appeared to them divided tongues, as of fire, and one sat upon each of them. And they were all filled with the Holy Spirit and began to speak with other tongues, as the Spirit gave them utterance."

Acts 2:1–4

"Now when they heard this, they were cut to the heart, and said to Peter and the rest of the apostles, 'Men and brethren, what shall we do?' "Then Peter said to them, 'Repent, and let every one of you be baptized in the name of Jesus Christ for the remission of sins; and you shall receive the gift of the Holy Spirit. For the promise is to you and to your children, and to all who are afar off, as many as the Lord our God will call.' "

Acts 2:37–39

"So they called them and commanded them not to speak at all nor teach in the name of Jesus. But Peter and John answered and said to them, 'Whether it is right in the sight of God to listen to you more than to God, you judge. For we cannot but speak the things which we have seen and heard.' "

Acts 4:18–20

Lessons

1. There are some who are willing to do anything to silence preachers of the gospel.
2. The gospel changes a person's entire perspective of the world.
3. Great revivals can happen when Christians preach the Word of God.

Outline

I. **Witness in Jerusalem (Acts 1–8)**

II. **Witness in Judea and Samaria (Acts 9–12)**

III. **Witness to the Ends of the Earth (Acts 13–28)**

Study Questions

CHAPTERS 1–7

What did Jesus mean when He told the disciples that they would be His witnesses?

That they would tell people about Jesus (Acts 1:8).

How did the Jews respond to Peter's preaching?

They repented and were baptized (Acts 2:41).

Why do you think Peter referred to God as "The God of Abraham, Isaac, and Jacob" (Acts 3:13)?

The audience was Jewish and they knew God by His covenant with Abraham, Isaac, and Jacob (Acts 3:1).

What is special about the name of Jesus?

It is the only name by which we can be saved (Acts 4:12).

Why was God's punishment to Ananias and Sapphira so severe?

Because they lied to the Holy Spirit (Acts 5:3).

Who were the seven men that the church selected to serve the widows and why were they needed?

Stephen, Philip, Prochorus, Nicanor, Timon, Parmenas, and Nicolas (Acts 6:5); They were given this task so that the apostles could devote themselves to prayer and to the Word (Acts 6:4).

Why was Stephen put to death?

The people were convicted through his preaching (Acts 7:54).

CHAPTERS 8–14

Why did the Holy Spirit lead Philip into the desert?

To share the gospel with the Ethiopian eunuch (Acts 8:35).

Describe Saul's encounter with Jesus.

Jesus confronted him, saying, "Saul, Saul, why are you persecuting Me" (Acts 9:4)? Saul then surrendered his life to Him (9:6).

Why did God send Peter to Cornelius's house?

To share the gospel with him and his household (Acts 10:34–43).

How did the Christians in Jerusalem respond to Peter's account of the conversion of Cornelius?

They glorified God (Acts 11:18).

How did God deal differently with Peter than with James?

He allowed James to be killed (Acts 12:2), but rescued Peter from prison (12:17).

Stephen preached in Acts 7 and Paul preached in Acts 13. How were they similar? How were they different?

Both men reminded them of Israel's history (Acts 13:17). Paul focused on the Gentiles at the end of the sermon (13:47), while Stephen had accused the Jews of being stubborn and rebellious.

Why did the Lycaonians think that Paul and Barnabas were gods? How did Paul and Barnabas respond?

God healed a crippled man through Paul (Acts 14:11). They tore their clothes and rebuked them (14:14–15).

CHAPTERS 15–21

What decision did the leaders in Jerusalem reach concerning Gentile Christians?

That they should "abstain from things polluted by idols, from sexual immorality, from things strangled, and from blood" (Acts 15:20).

How do you think the jailer knew that Paul and Silas could tell him how to be saved?

They had been singing hymns and praying (Acts 16:25).

Why were the Bereans considered more "fair-minded" than the Thessalonians?

They received the word eagerly and searched the Scriptures for themselves (Acts 17:11).

What do you think Paul meant when he told the Jews, "Your blood be on your own heads"?

Because they had rejected Paul's preaching, they were responsible for their own destruction (Acts 18:6).

What was Demetrius' livelihood?

He was a silversmith who made shrines of the goddess Diana (Acts 19:24)

Why did Demetrius want Paul to stop preaching the gospel?

Because the gospel threatened Demetrius' livelihood (Acts 19:25).

What can we learn from the account of Eutychus' death?

To pay attention when the Word is preached and not to allow ourselves to fall asleep (literally and figuratively) (Acts 20:9).

Why didn't Paul listen to those who told him not to go to Jerusalem?

He was prepared to die in Jerusalem for the name of Jesus (Acts 21:13).

CHAPTERS 22–28

What did Paul say that made the Jews stop listening to him?

That God was sending him to the Gentiles (Acts 22:21).

How did Jesus comfort Paul the night following his trial?

He stood near Paul and told him that he was going to have the opportunity to preach the gospel in Rome (Acts 23:11).

How did Felix respond to the gospel?

He was afraid but did not repent and believe (Acts 24:25).

Compare Festus' response to Felix's.

Felix was afraid but Festus could only think of how he might do the Jews a favor (Acts 25:9).

How does Agrippa's response compare to those of the other two rulers?

Agrippa seems to have been the most affected, telling Paul, "You almost persuade me to become a Christian" (Acts 26:28).

What do you think Paul was doing during the storm? How do you know?

The message the angel brought to Paul saying that God had granted him the lives of everyone on the ship implies that he had been praying (Acts 27:24).

Why did Paul quote the prophet Isaiah when he was speaking to the Jews in Rome?

The Jews rejected the Word of God as Isaiah prophesied they would (Acts 28:25).

Amazing Grace

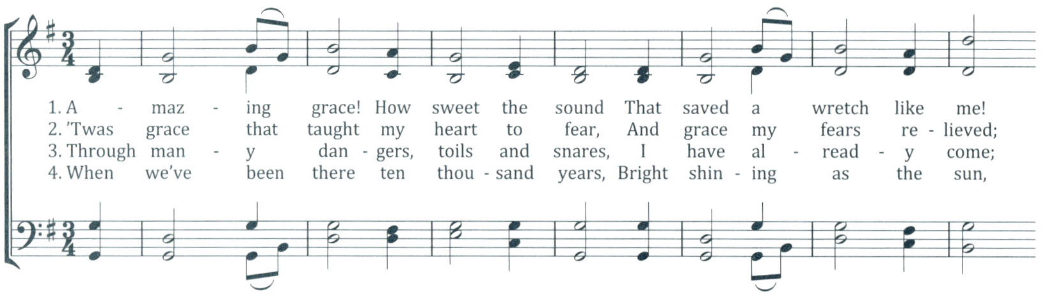

WORDS: John Newton, pub.1779; v. 4 Unknown, pub.1829.
MUSIC: "New Britain"; Unknown, pub.1829. Public Domain.

5 B.C.
Birth of Christ

30 A.D.
Crucifixion & Resurrection

95 A.D.
John Writes Revelation

Christ's Baptism & Ministry Start
26 A.D.

Paul's First Missionary Journey
48 A.D.

Journey through

Romans

THEME	AUTHOR	TIME OF WRITING
The Gospel	Paul	56 A.D.

MEMORY VERSE

"For I am not ashamed of the gospel of Christ, for it is the power of God to salvation for everyone who believes, for the Jew first and also for the Greek. For in it the righteousness of God is revealed from faith to faith; as it is written, 'The just shall live by faith.' "

Romans 1:16–17

OVERVIEW

Paul's letter to the Romans reveals God's solution for sin and sinners and what some have called "the cosmic crime." This crime is the rebellion of creatures against their Creator. Imagine for a moment the magnitude of this. The creature is turning away from the Creator saying, "I don't want You."

Top 5 Facts to Remember

1. The wrath of God is revealed from heaven against all ungodliness and unrighteousness of men who suppress the truth in unrighteousness (Rom. 1:18).
2. Every person has the law of God written on their heart (Rom. 2:14–15).
3. There is none righteous (Rom. 3:10).
4. The central message of the gospel is that we can receive righteousness apart from the law through faith in Jesus Christ (Rom. 3:21–22).
5. Many individuals were saved after reading Romans:
    - Augustine was saved when reading Romans 13:13–14.
    - Martin Luther was saved after reading Romans 1:16–17.
    - John Wesley was saved while reading Romans 8:1–4.
    - John Bunyan used Romans as a guide while writing Pilgrim's Progress.

Theme: The Gospel

In Romans, God is glorifying Himself through the gospel, so that He might demonstrate His superior goodness in the salvation sinners, the damnation of the wicked, and for the preservation of His people, for His eternal glory, and their eternal joy.

Author: Paul

"Paul, a bondservant of Jesus Christ, called to be an apostle, separated to the gospel of God... " (Rom. 1:1).

Audience: The Church at Rome

"To all who are in Rome, beloved of God, called to be saints"

Romans 1:7

"So, as much as is in me, I am ready to preach the gospel to you who are in Rome also"

Romans 1:15

Key Verses

"But now the righteousness of God apart from the law is revealed, being witnessed by the Law and the Prophets, even the righteousness of God, through faith in Jesus Christ, to all and on all who believe. For there is no difference; for all have sinned and fall short of the glory of God, being justified freely by His grace through the redemption that is in Christ Jesus, whom God set forth as a propitiation by His blood, through faith, to demonstrate His righteousness, because in His forbearance God had passed over the sins that were previously

committed, to demonstrate at the present time His righteousness, that He might be just and the justifier of the one who has faith in Jesus."

Romans 3:21–26

"For when we were still without strength, in due time Christ died for the ungodly. For scarcely for a righteous man will one die; yet perhaps for a good man someone would even dare to die. But God demonstrates His own love toward us, in that while we were still sinners, Christ died for us."

Romans 5:6–8

"Who shall separate us from the love of Christ? Shall tribulation, or distress, or persecution, or famine, or nakedness, or peril, or sword? As it is written: 'For Your sake we are killed all day long; We are accounted as sheep for the slaughter.'

Yet in all these things we are more than conquerors through Him who loved us. For I am persuaded that neither death nor life, nor angels nor principalities nor powers, nor things present nor things to come, nor height nor depth, nor any other created thing, shall be able to separate us from the love of God which is in Christ Jesus our Lord."

Romans 8:35–39

Lessons

1. Men and women are justified by faith alone, not by the works of the law.
2. All men know that God exists, but unbelievers suppress the truth in unrighteousness.
3. The Law and the Prophets are witnesses to the truth of the gospel.

Outline

I. **Introduction (Rom. 1:1–17)**

II. **Justification by Faith Alone (Rom. 1:18–11:36)**

III. **Relationships that Mark a Justified People (Rom. 12–16)**

Study Questions

CHAPTERS 1–8

Will anyone be excused from God's judgement because they didn't know about Him? How do you know?

No. They will be without excuse because He has revealed Himself to them through His creation (Rom. 1:20).

Why do you think God's judgements were on the Jews first?

They had a greater level of responsibility because they had more knowledge (Rom. 2:9).

What does it mean for a person to be justified?

To be righteous in God's sight (Rom. 3:22).

How do we know that Abraham was justified by faith and not by works?

God declared him righteous before he acted in obedience (Rom. 4:12).

How is Jesus like Adam? How is He different?

The actions of both had an impact far beyond themselves. In Adam's case, the effect was negative, while in Jesus' case, it was positive (Rom. 5:18).

What are some ways that a person's life might change when they are freed from slavery to sin and become a slave to righteousness?

They will joyfully obey God's commandments (Rom. 6:19).

How does the law cause sin to come to life in a person's heart?

Because the action is forbidden, it becomes attractive to the person (Rom. 7:7).

How do we know that no true Christian will face God's wrath in the day of judgement?

There is no condemnation for those who are in Christ (Rom. 8:1).

CHAPTERS 9–16

How is God like a potter and the human heart like clay?

Like a potter makes pottery for different purposes, God shapes people's hearts according to His purposes, making some for honor and some for dishonor (Rom. 9:21).

What must one hear in order to call upon the Lord for salvation?

They must hear the gospel (Rom. 10:17).

The branch that was broken off of the olive tree represents who?

The Jews (Rom. 11:17).

The branch that was grafted into the olive tree represents who?

The Gentiles (Rom. 11:17).

What are some of the gifts that God gives to His people?

Prophecy, faith, ministry, teaching, and exhortation (Rom. 12:6–8).

Explain how love fulfills the law.

All the commandments are based on loving God and loving your neighbor (Rom. 13:10).

What are some things that a person who is weak in the faith might believe?

That certain foods should be avoided or that certain days must be observed (Rom. 14:2, 5).

Why is it important for Christians to be united with one another and not divided?

So that we might glorify God together (Rom. 15:6).

How should we treat divisive people in the church?

We should identify them and avoid them (Rom. 16:17)

What do we know about people who try to cause division in the church?

They serve their own fleshly appetites (Rom. 16:18).

O Word of God Incarnate

WORDS: William W. How, 1867; alt. MUSIC: "Munich"; Author unknown, pub.1693; har. by Felix Mendelssohn, 1847. Public Domain.

5 B.C.
Birth of Christ

30 A.D.
Crucifixion & Resurrection

95 A.D.
John Writes Revelation

Christ's Baptism & Ministry Start
26 A.D.

Paul's First Missionary Journey
48 A.D.

Journey through

1 & 2 Corinthians

THEME	AUTHOR	TIME OF WRITING
Called to be Saints	Paul	55–56 A.D.

MEMORY VERSE

"Now then, we are ambassadors for Christ, as though God were pleading through us: we implore you on Christ's behalf, be reconciled to God. For He made Him who knew no sin to be sin for us, that we might become the righteousness of God in Him."

2 Corinthians 5:20–21

OVERVIEW

The Corinthian letters are some of the most helpful documents to assist churches living in a pagan culture. The culture of immorality, the cult of personality, the atmosphere of litigation, and the culture of Christianity lite were rampant then and still are today. Our culture is very much like ancient Corinth - churches today lack discipline and are dominated by feminism, pagan philosophy, and idolatry. In both books, Paul answers various questions to help the church make its way through various issues that believers struggle with after salvation and through the process of sanctification.

In 2 Corinthians, after Paul's first 18-month visit to Corinth, the church fell into disarray and was subjected to false teachers who slandered Paul. Paul sent Titus to survey the situation and found that while the majority had repented, there were still some in opposition. Paul writes a very personal letter defending his apostleship and his message. Paul has many detractors in Corinth, and he goes to great length to answer the accusations of these detractors.

Top 5 Facts to Remember

1. God has made foolish the wisdom of this world though the preaching of the gospel (1 Cor. 1:20).
2. There are diversities of gifts, but the same Spirit (1 Cor. 12:4).
3. Spiritual gifts are useless if they are not accompanied by love (1 Cor. 13).
4. God "made Him who knew no sin to be sin for us, that we might become the righteousness of God in Him" (2 Cor. 5:21).
5. He who sows sparingly will also reap sparingly, and he who sows bountifully will also reap bountifully (2 Cor. 9:6).

Theme: Called to be Saints

In 1 & 2 Corinthians, God is glorifying Himself by calling the Corinthians to Christian conduct, so that He might demonstrate His superior goodness in the salvation sinners, the damnation of the wicked, and for the preservation of His people, for His eternal glory, and their eternal joy.

Author: Paul

"Paul, called to be an apostle of Jesus Christ through the will of God..." (1 Cor. 1:1).

"Now I, Paul, myself am pleading with you..." (2 Cor. 10:1).

Audience: The Church at Corinth

"To the church of God which is at Corinth, to those who are sanctified in Christ Jesus, called to be saints, with all who in every place call on the name of Jesus Christ our Lord, both theirs and ours" (1 Cor. 1:2).

"To the church of God which is at Corinth, with all the saints who are in all Achaia" (2 Cor. 1:1).

"Moreover I call God as witness against my soul, that to spare you I came no more to Corinth" (2 Cor. 1:23).

Key Verses

"For the message of the cross is foolishness to those who are perishing, but to us who are being saved it is the power of God. For it is written:

'I will destroy the wisdom of the wise,
And bring to nothing the understanding of the prudent.'

"Where is the wise? Where is the scribe? Where is the disputer of this age? Has not God made foolish the wisdom of this world? For since, in the wisdom of God, the world through wisdom did not know God, it pleased God through the foolishness of the message preached to save those who believe. For Jews request a sign, and Greeks seek after wisdom; but we preach Christ crucified, to the Jews a stumbling block and to the Greeks foolishness, but to those who are called, both Jews and Greeks, Christ the power of God and the wisdom of God. Because the foolishness of God is wiser than men, and the weakness of God is stronger than men."

1 Corinthians 1:18–25

"Do you not know that the unrighteous will not inherit the kingdom of God? Do not be deceived. Neither fornicators, nor idolaters, nor adulterers, nor homosexuals, nor sodomites, nor thieves, nor covetous, nor drunkards, nor revilers, nor extortioners will inherit the kingdom of God. And such were some of you. But you were washed, but you were sanctified, but you were justified in the name of the Lord Jesus and by the Spirit of our God."

1 Corinthians 6:9–11

"Do not be unequally yoked together with unbelievers. For what fellowship has righteousness with lawlessness? And what communion has light with darkness? And what accord has Christ with Belial? Or what part has a believer with an

unbeliever? And what agreement has the temple of God with idols? For you are the temple of the living God."

2 Corinthians 6:14–16

Lessons

1. God loves and praises the church in Corinth, even though it has some serious flaws.
2. Christ was made "to be sin for us, that we might become the righteousness of God in Him."
3. Christians are ambassadors for Christ.
4. Believers should not be yoked with unbelievers.
5. We ought to bring every thought captive to the obedience of Christ.

Outline

1 CORINTHIANS

I. **Divisions, (1 Cor. 1–4)**

II. **Fornication (1 Cor. 5)**

III. **Lawsuits (1 Cor. 6)**

IV. **Questions Answered, (1 Cor. 7–16)**

2 CORINTHIANS

I. **Paul's Reasons for Not Coming to Corinth (2 Cor. 1–7)**

II. **Paul's Experience with the Churches in Macedonia (2 Cor. 8–9)**

III. **Paul's Plans to Visit Corinth (2 Cor. 10–13)**

Study Questions

1 CORINTHIANS 1–8

What were some characteristics of the church in Corinth?

They possessed much knowledge and many spiritual gifts (1 Cor. 1:5–6).

How is God's wisdom different from human wisdom?

God's wisdom enables a person to understand spiritual things, while human wisdom does not (1 Cor. 2:13–14).

How will God test the works of Christians on the day of judgement?

In the fire of His presence (1 Cor. 3:13).

Why did Paul send Timothy to the church in Corinth?

To remind them of Paul's way of life so that they could imitate him as he imitated Christ (1 Cor. 4:17).

How did Paul instruct the church to deal with the sinful man?

To give him over to Satan (1 Cor. 5:5).

What kinds of people will not inherit the kingdom of God?

Fornicators, adulterers, idolaters, homosexuals, sodomites, thieves, covetous, drunkards, revilers, and extortioners (1 Cor. 6:9–10).

What is one benefit of remaining unmarried?

The single person can devote himself to the things of God (1 Cor. 7:32).

Which is more important in the sight of God: love or knowledge? How do you know?

Love. Paul says that knowledge puffs up, but love edifies. (1 Cor. 8:1).

1 CORINTHIANS 9–16

How is the Christian life like an athletic competition? How is it different?

The Christian and the athlete are both striving for a prize. The Christian's prize is eternal, while the athlete's prize is temporary (1 Cor. 9:24–27).

What lessons do we learn from the experience of the Israelites in the wilderness?

We learn how not to be idolaters (1 Cor. 10:6–8).

What does it mean to eat and drink of the Lord's Supper in an "unworthy manner" (1 Cor. 11:29)?

He eats and drinks judgement to himself (1 Cor. 11:29)

How is the church like a body?

It has different parts but each are part of one body (1 Cor. 12:12).

What is the greatest work of the Holy Spirit in a person's heart?

Love (1 Cor. 13:1–3).

Which gift did Paul encourage Christians to seek more than all others? Why do you think he valued it so much?

Prophecy. Because the gift of prophecy builds up the church (1 Cor. 14:3).

Why is Christ called the "firstfruits" of those who have died?

He was the first to be resurrected in His glorified body (1 Cor. 15:21).

What did Paul instruct the church to do when they gathered together on the first day of the week?

Take up a collection for Christians in need (1 Cor. 16:3).

2 CORINTHIANS 1–7

What was one way that God taught Paul not to trust in himself, but in God?

Persecution and suffering (2 Cor. 1:8).

How did Paul instruct the church to treat the one who had repented of his sin?

Forgive him and receive him back into the church (2 Cor. 2:7).

How does the New Covenant compare to the old?

The New Covenant is much more glorious than the old (2 Cor. 3:7–8).

What treasure is contained in "earthen vessels"?

The gospel (2 Cor. 4:6–7).

What does it mean to be reconciled to God?

To have peace with God through Christ's righteousness imputed to us (2 Cor. 5:19).

In what ways did Paul show himself to be a true apostle?

By preaching the true gospel, displaying divine power, and suffering for the name of Christ (2 Cor. 5:7–8).

How is godly sorrow different from worldly sorrow?

Godly sorrow "produces repentance" but worldly sorrow "produces death" (2 Cor. 7:10).

2 CORINTHIANS 8–13

Whose example did Paul want the Corinthians to follow in their giving?

The church in Macedonia (2 Cor. 8:1–2).

What is the right attitude to have when giving?

Cheerfulness (2 Cor. 9:7).

Where did Paul's authority over the Corinthian believers come from?

God (2 Cor. 10:13).

Why was Paul concerned for the Corinthian church?

He worried that they had been deceived and led away from Christ (2 Cor. 11:3–4).

Why didn't Jesus remove Paul's "thorn in the flesh"?

Christ's strength was being displayed in Paul's weakness (2 Cor. 12:9).

Why did Paul tell the Corinthian believers to "test" and "examine" themselves?

To make sure that they were true Christians (2 Cor. 13:5).

Day by Day

WORDS: Karolina W. Sandell-Berg, 1865; tr. by Andrew L. Skoog.
MUSIC: "Blott en Dag"; Oskar Ahnfelt, 1872. Public Domain.

5 B.C.
Birth of Christ

26 A.D.
Christ's Baptism & Ministry Start

30 A.D.
Crucifixion & Resurrection

48 A.D.
Paul's First Missionary Journey

95 A.D.
John Writes Revelation

Journey through

Galatians

THEME

Justification by Faith Alone

AUTHOR

Paul

TIME OF WRITING

49–50 A.D.

MEMORY VERSE

"I have been crucified with Christ; it is no longer I who live, but Christ lives in me; and the life which I now live in the flesh I live by faith in the Son of God, who loved me and gave Himself for me."

Galatians 2:20

OVERVIEW

In the book of Galatians, Paul was writing to a collection of churches in the Galatian region who had been led astray by a false gospel. Specifically, he addresses churches in the region of Antioch, Iconium, Lystra, and Derbe. A group known as the Judaizers (Phil. 3:2–6) had claimed that salvation depended upon works of righteousness. When the Galatians believed that keeping the law could save them, they were removed from Christ and all the blessings of His presence in their lives. The cold reality of claiming that salvation can be obtained by works, is that you are left alone to justify yourself.

Top 5 Facts to Remember

1. Paul did not receive his gospel from men, but through the revelation of Jesus Christ (Gal. 1:11–12).
2. Paul confronted Peter because of his compromise on the truth of the gospel (Gal. 2:14).
3. The law was added because of transgressions (Gal. 3:19).

4. Christians are no longer slaves to sin, but sons and heirs (Gal. 4:7).

5. The fruit of the Spirit is love, joy, peace, longsuffering, kindness, goodness, faithfulness, gentleness, and self-control (Gal. 5:22–23).

Theme: Justification by Faith Alone

In Galatians, God is glorifying Himself through the justification of believers by faith alone, so that He might demonstrate His superior goodness in the salvation sinners, the damnation of the wicked, and for the preservation of His people, for His eternal glory, and their eternal joy.

Author: Paul

"Paul, an apostle (not from men nor through man, but through Jesus Christ and God the Father who raised Him from the dead)..." (Gal. 1:1).

Audience: The Churches of Galatia

"To the churches of Galatia"

Galatians 1:2

Key Verses

I marvel that you are turning away so soon from Him who called you in the grace of Christ, to a different gospel, which is not another; but there are some who trouble you and want to pervert the gospel of Christ. But even if we, or an angel from heaven, preach any other gospel to you than what we have preached to you, let him be accursed.

Galatians 1:6–8

"Now the works of the flesh are evident, which are: adultery, fornication, uncleanness, lewdness, idolatry, sorcery, hatred, contentions, jealousies, outbursts of wrath, selfish ambitions, dissensions, heresies, envy, murders, drunkenness, revelries, and the like; of which I tell you beforehand, just as I also told you in time past, that those who practice such things will not inherit the kingdom of God.

"But the fruit of the Spirit is love, joy, peace, longsuffering, kindness, goodness, faithfulness, gentleness, self-control. Against such there is no law. And those who are Christ's have crucified the flesh with its passions and desires. If we live in the Spirit, let us also walk in the Spirit. Let us not become conceited, provoking one another, envying one another."

Galatians 5:19–26

"See with what large letters I have written to you with my own hand! As many as desire to make a good showing in the flesh, these would compel you to be circumcised, only that they may not suffer persecution for the cross of Christ. For not even those who are circumcised keep the law, but they desire to have you circumcised that they may boast in your flesh. But God forbid that I should boast except in the cross of our Lord Jesus Christ, by whom the world has been crucified to me, and I to the world. For in Christ Jesus neither circumcision nor uncircumcision avails anything, but a new creation."

Galatians 6:11–15

Lessons

1. Making works a precondition of justification results in a false gospel.
2. Those who try to obtain God's favor through the law are under the curse of the law, because they cannot keep it perfectly. Only Christ can redeem us from the curse of the law.
3. The law is fulfilled in loving your neighbor as yourself.

Outline

I. **Recognizing the Threat of Another Gospel (Gal. 1:1–10)**

II. **Making Known a Gospel Not from Man (Gal. 1:11–2:10)**

III. **Identifying the Conflicts from a False Gospel (Gal. 2:11–21)**

IV. **Bewitched by Another Gospel (Gal. 3:1–9)**

V. **Redeemed from the Curse of the Law (Gal. 3:10–26)**

VI. **Redeemed to Be Sons (Gal. 3:27–4:21)**

VII. **Casting out the Bondwoman – the Two Covenants (Gal. 4:22–31)**

VIII. **Standing Fast in the Liberty of the Gospel (Gal. 5:1–26)**

IX. **Walking in the Spirit of the Gospel (Gal. 6:1–10)**

X. **Boasting Only in the Cross (Gal. 6:11–18)**

Study Questions

What is the judgment that Paul warns will come to pass for those preaching a false gospel?

They will be accursed (Gal.1:8–9).

How is someone justified?

Through faith in Jesus Christ (Gal. 2:16).

Who are the children of Abraham, and what does this mean?

The children of Abraham are those who have faith in Christ, just as Abraham believed God and it was counted to him as righteousness (Gal. 3:6–9).

What was it that Paul's opponents attempted to persuade the Galatians to believe?

That they needed to adhere to the ceremonial law in order to be saved (Gal. 4:17–18, 21; 5:1–10).

What are the works of the flesh and what are the fruits of the Spirit?

"Now the works of the flesh are evident, which are: adultery, fornication, uncleanness, lewdness, idolatry, sorcery, hatred, contentions, jealousies, outbursts of wrath, selfish ambitions, dissensions, heresies, envy, murders, drunkenness, revelries, and the like... But the fruit of the Spirit is love, joy, peace, longsuffering, kindness, goodness, faithfulness, gentleness, self-control. Against such there is no law" (Gal. 5:19–23).

What did Paul's opponents boast in and what should believers boast in?

They boasted in being under the law and customs of Moses, but believers should boast in the cross of Christ (Gal. 6:12–15).

Grace Greater than Our Sin

WORDS: Julia H. Johnston, pub.1910. MUSIC: "Moody"; Daniel B. Towner, 1910. Public Domain

for more resources go to ***jttb.co/ephesians***

5 B.C.
Birth of Christ

26 A.D.
Christ's Baptism & Ministry Start

30 A.D.
Crucifixion & Resurrection

48 A.D.
Paul's First Missionary Journey

95 A.D.
John Writes Revelation

Journey through

Ephesians

THEME

Riches in Christ

AUTHOR

Paul

TIME OF WRITING

60–62 A.D.

MEMORY VERSE

"For by grace you have been saved through faith, and that not of yourselves; it is the gift of God, not of works, lest anyone should boast. For we are His workmanship, created in Christ Jesus for good works, which God prepared beforehand that we should walk in them."

Ephesians 2:8–10

OVERVIEW

Paul wants the saints in Ephesus to know that they are blessed with every spiritual blessing in Jesus Christ. They were rich in the glory of God's grace. He explains that to be "in Christ" is to be enriched. The Ephesian letter was written to explain the various manifestations of the glory of God displayed in the church. The letter is very clearly written to the rich – those blessed with every spiritual blessing. Do you have this sense of your own life – that you are rich? Do you identify yourself as someone who has been lavished with gifts from heaven?

Top 5 Facts to Remember

1. God has blessed us with every spiritual blessing in the heavenly places in Christ (Eph. 1:3).
2. We have redemption through the blood of Christ (Eph. 1:7).
3. We were once darkness, but now we are light in the Lord (Eph. 5:8).
4. Marriage is a picture of Christ's relationship with His church (Eph. 5:22–33).
5. We do not wrestle against flesh and blood, but against principalities, against powers, against the rulers of the darkness of this age, and against spiritual hosts of wickedness in the heavenly places (Eph. 6:12).

Theme: Riches in Christ

In Ephesians, God is glorifying Himself through the riches found in Christ, so that He might demonstrate His superior goodness in the salvation sinners, the damnation of the wicked, and for the preservation of His people, for His eternal glory, and their eternal joy.

Author: Paul

"Paul, an apostle of Jesus Christ by the will of God..."

Ephesians 1:1

"For this reason I, Paul, the prisoner of Christ Jesus for you Gentiles..."

Ephesians 3:1

Audience: The Saints in Ephesus

"To the saints who are in Ephesus, and faithful in Christ Jesus"

Ephesians 1:1

Key Verses

"In Him we have redemption through His blood, the forgiveness of sins, according to the riches of His grace which He made to abound toward us in all wisdom and prudence, having made known to us the mystery of His will, according to His good pleasure which He purposed in Himself, that in the dispensation of the fullness of the times He might gather together in one all things in Christ, both which are in heaven and which are on earth—in Him."

Ephesians 1:7–10

"Therefore be imitators of God as dear children. And walk in love, as Christ also has loved us and given Himself for us, an offering and a sacrifice to God for a sweet-smelling aroma."

Ephesians 5:1–2

"Finally, my brethren, be strong in the Lord and in the power of His might. Put on the whole armor of God, that you may be able to stand against the wiles of the devil. For we do not wrestle against flesh and blood, but against principalities, against powers, against the rulers of the darkness of this age, against spiritual hosts of wickedness in the heavenly places. Therefore take up the whole armor of God, that you may be able to withstand in the evil day, and having done all, to stand."

Ephesians 6:10–13

Lessons

1. God chose to save us before the foundation of the world.
2. Wives should submit to their husbands and husbands should love their wives, because marriage is a picture of Christ and the church.
3. Children should obey their parents.
4. Fathers should not provoke their children to wrath, but bring them up in the training and admonition of the Lord.
5. We are in a spiritual war with the devil.

Outline

I. **The Wealth of the Believer (Eph. 1–3)**

II. **The Walk of the Believer (Eph. 4–5)**

III. **The Warfare of the Believer (Eph. 6)**

Study Questions

What is the purpose for God's election and predestination of believers?

God's election and predestination of believers is according to the good pleasure of His will (Eph. 1:5,11).

How are people saved?

They are saved by grace through faith (Eph. 2:8–9).

What is the mystery about Christ that has now been revealed?

That Gentiles should be fellow heirs along with the Jews in the promise of Christ through the gospel (Eph. 3:6).

What does Paul tell the Ephesians to "put off"?

The old man, which grows corrupt according to the deceitful lusts (Eph. 4:22).

What is marriage a picture of?

Christ's relationship with the church (Eph. 5:22–33).

What blessing generally follows children who honor their parents?

Wellbeing and long life (Eph. 6:1–3).

I Am from Sin Set Free

WORDS: John Newton, pub 1774, ref. by H. R. Jeffrey, pub. 1885. MUSIC: H. R. J. Public Domain.

for more resources go to ***jttb.co/philippians***

5 B.C.
Birth of Christ

30 A.D.
Crucifixion & Resurrection

95 A.D.
John Writes Revelation

Christ's Baptism & Ministry Start
26 A.D.

Paul's First Missionary Journey
48 A.D.

Journey through

Philippians

THEME	AUTHOR	TIME OF WRITING
Joy in All Things	Paul	60–62 A.D.

MEMORY VERSE

"Finally, brethren, whatever things are true, whatever things are noble, whatever things are just, whatever things are pure, whatever things are lovely, whatever things are of good report, if there is any virtue and if there is anything praiseworthy—meditate on these things."

Philippians 4:8

OVERVIEW

The theme of the Philippian letter is joy. Paul believes that a relationship with Christ is a pipeline of joy and it produces a life of rejoicing. Paul is writing at the end of his life in a Roman prison, yet it is the most joyful book of the New Testament. Paul teaches us that in whatever prison we find ourselves, we can learn to rejoice. In whatever discontenting circumstance we encounter, we can learn to be content.

Top 5 Facts to Remember

1. Paul was able to rejoice whenever Christ was preached, regardless of the circumstances (Phil. 1:12–18).
2. God has highly exalted Christ and given Him the name which is above every name (Phil. 2:9).
3. Paul was willing to suffer the loss of all things for Christ (Phil. 3:7–11).
4. Paul described the enemies of the cross of Christ as those "who set their mind on earthly things" (Phil. 3:19).
5. Paul knew how to be content in whatever state he found himself (Phil. 4:11).

Theme: Joy in All Things

In Philippians, God is glorifying Himself through joy in the pursuit of Christ-likeness, so that He might demonstrate His superior goodness in the salvation sinners, the damnation of the wicked, and for the preservation of His people, for His eternal glory, and their eternal joy.

Author: Paul

"Paul and Timothy, bondservants of Jesus Christ..."

Philippians 1:1

Audience: The Saints in Philippi

"To all the saints in Christ Jesus who are in Philippi, with the bishops and deacons."

Philippians 1:1

Key Verses

"Let this mind be in you which was also in Christ Jesus, who, being in the form of God, did not consider it robbery to be equal with God, but made Himself of no reputation, taking the form of a bondservant, and coming in the likeness of men. And being found in appearance as a man, He humbled Himself and became obedient to the point of death, even the death of the cross. Therefore God also has highly exalted Him and given Him the name which is above every name, that at the name of Jesus every knee should bow, of those in heaven, and of those on earth, and of those under the earth, and that every tongue should confess that Jesus Christ is Lord, to the glory of God the Father."

Philippians 2:5–11

"Not that I have already attained, or am already perfected; but I press on, that I may lay hold of that for which Christ Jesus has also laid hold of me. Brethren, I do not count myself to have apprehended; but one thing I do, forgetting those things which are behind and reaching forward to those things which are ahead, I press toward the goal for the prize of the upward call of God in Christ Jesus."

Philippians 3:12–14

"Be anxious for nothing, but in everything by prayer and supplication, with thanksgiving, let your requests be made known to God; and the peace of God, which surpasses all understanding, will guard your hearts and minds through Christ Jesus."

Philippians 4:6–7

Lessons

1. Gaining Christ is worth losing all other things.
2. When we let God know our requests, He will give us peace that surpasses all understanding.
3. We ought to meditate on things that are noble, just, pure, lovely, of good report, virtuous and praiseworthy.

Outline

I. **Christ Is Our Life – Partakers of Christ (Phil. 1)**

II. **Christ Is Our Example – Humility of Christ and Ours (Phil. 2)**

III. **Christ Is Our Salvation – Pursuing Christ (Phil. 3)**

IV. **Christ Is Our Strength and Joy – the Power of Christ (Phil. 4)**

Study Questions

What does Paul mean in his statement, "For to me, to live is Christ, and to die is gain"?

This means while Paul lives, he labors to bear fruit for the Lord; if he dies, he departs to be immediately where Christ is, which is far better. (Phil. 1:22–23)

How did Christ display His humility?

He "made Himself of no reputation, taking the form of a bondservant, and coming in the likeness of men. And being found in appearance as a man, He humbled Himself and became obedient to the point of death, even the death of the cross" (Phil. 2:7–8).

How does a person receive righteousness from God?

By faith (Phil. 3:9).

How does Paul tell the church to handle anxiety?

Don't worry about anything but pray about everything (Philippians 4:6–7)

Where does true strength come from?

From Christ (Phil. 4:11–13).

Safe in the Arms of Jesus

WORDS: Frances J. Crosby, 1868. MUSIC: William H. Doane, 1868. Public Domain.

for more resources go to **jttb.co/colossians**

5 B.C.
Birth of Christ

30 A.D.
Crucifixion & Resurrection

95 A.D.
John Writes Revelation

Christ's Baptism & Ministry Start
26 A.D.

Paul's First Missionary Journey
48 A.D.

Journey through

Colossians

THEME

The Sufficiency of Christ

AUTHOR

Paul

TIME OF WRITING

60–62 A.D.

MEMORY VERSE

"He is the image of the invisible God, the firstborn over all creation. For by Him all things were created that are in heaven and that are on earth, visible and invisible, whether thrones or dominions or principalities or powers. All things were created through Him and for Him. And He is before all things, and in Him all things consist. And He is the head of the body, the church, who is the beginning, the firstborn from the dead, that in all things He may have the preeminence."

Colossians 1:15–18

OVERVIEW

The letter to the Colossians identifies Christ as the only sufficient Savior. He is the only reliable source of knowledge and guidance for your soul. You cannot trust in worldly philosophy. You cannot trust in your knowledge. You cannot trust in your abilities.

Christ is all-sufficient. We need nothing else. We need no one else.

Top 5 Facts to Remember

1. Paul teaches many of the same things in Colossians as he did in Ephesians.
2. Paul was imprisoned in Rome when he wrote this letter (cf. Acts 28).
3. The letter was written to refute a heresy which denied the sufficiency of Christ for salvation.
4. Colossae was a city in Asia Minor (Modern Turkey).
5. The city was destroyed by a massive earthquake in 61 A.D. shortly after the letter was written.

Theme: The Sufficiency of Christ

In Colossians, God is glorifying Himself through the sufficiency of Christ, so that He might demonstrate His superior goodness in the salvation sinners, the damnation of the wicked, and for the preservation of His people, for His eternal glory, and their eternal joy.

Author: Paul

"Paul, an apostle of Jesus Christ by the will of God..."

Colossians 1:1

"...of which I, Paul, became a minister"

Colossians 1:23

"This salutation by my own hand—Paul"

Colossians 4:18

Audience: The Saints in Colosse

"To the saints and faithful brethren in Christ who are in Colosse"

Colossians 1:2

Key Verses

"For it pleased the Father that in Him all the fullness should dwell, and by Him to reconcile all things to Himself, by Him, whether things on earth or things in heaven, having made peace through the blood of His cross.

"And you, who once were alienated and enemies in your mind by wicked works, yet now He has reconciled in the body of His flesh through death, to present you holy, and blameless, and above reproach in His sight—if indeed you continue in the faith, grounded and steadfast, and are not moved away from the hope of the gospel which you heard, which was preached to every creature under heaven, of which I, Paul, became a minister."

Colossians 1:19–23

"Beware lest anyone cheat you through philosophy and empty deceit, according to the tradition of men, according to the basic principles of the world, and not according to Christ. For in Him dwells all the fullness of the Godhead bodily; and you are complete in Him, who is the head of all principality and power."

Colossians 2:8–10

"Therefore, as the elect of God, holy and beloved, put on tender mercies, kindness, humility, meekness, longsuffering; bearing with one another, and forgiving one another, if anyone has a complaint against another; even as Christ forgave you, so you also must do. But above all these things put on love, which is the bond of perfection. And let the peace of God rule in your hearts, to which also you were called in one body; and be thankful. Let the word of Christ dwell in you richly in all wisdom, teaching and admonishing one another in psalms and hymns and spiritual songs, singing with grace in your hearts to the Lord. And whatever you do in word or deed, do all in the name of the Lord Jesus, giving thanks to God the Father through Him."

Colossians 3:12–17

Lessons

1. Christ is before all things and in Him all things hold together.
2. Since we have been raised with Christ, we ought to set our minds on things above.
3. We ought to continue earnestly in prayer, being vigilant in it with thanksgiving.

Outline

I. **Doctrine of Christ and His Absolute Sufficiency (Col. 1–2)**

   A. Paul's Joy and Gratitude Toward the Colossian Church (Col. 1:1–14)

   B. Doctrine of the Sufficiency of Christ (Col. 1:15–2:23)

II. **The Work of Christ as the Only Sufficient Work in Your Life (Col. 3–4)**

   A. Living a Resurrected Life (Col. 3:1–4:6)

   B. Final Greetings (Col. 4:7–15)

   C. Closing Exhortations and Blessings (Col. 4:16–18)

Study Questions

How did Christ reconcile sinners to God?

By His death on the cross (Col. 1:20, 22).

Why does Paul counsel against Christians submitting to man-made "regulations"?

Because Christ alone saves (Col. 2:8–14) and these regulations do not curb sin (Col. 2:20–23).

How should Christians live?

Setting our minds on heavenly things (Col. 3:1–4), turning from sin (vv. 5–11), and loving each other (vv. 12–25).

What two kinds of communication characterize the Christian?

Faithful prayer to God (Col. 4:2–4) and gracious speech to unbelievers (vv. 5–6).

The Love of God

WORDS: Frederick M. Lehman, 1917; v. 3 by Meir Ben Isaac Nehorai, 1050; v. 3 tr.
MUSIC: F. M. L., 1917; arr. by Claudia L. Mays. Public Domain.

5 B.C.
Birth of Christ

30 A.D.
Crucifixion & Resurrection

95 A.D.
John Writes Revelation

Christ's Baptism & Ministry Start
26 A.D.

Paul's First Missionary Journey
48 A.D.

Journey through

1 & 2 Thessalonians

THEME	AUTHOR	TIME OF WRITING
Stand Fast	Paul	51–52 A.D.

MEMORY VERSE

"For this reason we also thank God without ceasing, because when you received the word of God which you heard from us, you welcomed it not as the word of men, but as it is in truth, the word of God, which also effectively works in you who believe."

1 Thessalonians 2:13

OVERVIEW

These two letters to the Thessalonians demonstrate how the Thessalonian church was a model church in the things that really matter. It was a very young church that made a quick impact on their region. Their labors were motivated by love and stemmed from their faith. What a sweet and mighty church this was. The Thessalonian church was visited by men who were turning the world upside down and they turned their world upside down. These are very personal, grateful, and tender letters. Paul wrote this letter to provide the Thessalonian church with the encouragement to stand fast and stay the course.

Top 5 Facts to Remember

1. The first letter was written to the struggling church mentioned in Acts 17:1–9.
2. Paul's first letter was probably a response to a letter sent to him from Thessalonica (1 Thess. 4:9; 5:1, cf. 1 Cor. 7:1, 25; 8:1).
3. Apparently, some had accused Paul of fleeing when times got tough and so Paul defends his ministry in his first letter.

4. Thessalonica was a major port city and the most important city in Macedonia in the first century. Thus, Paul's readers were likely from a large church comprised of people from many ethnicities and social classes.

5. The main purpose of Paul's second letter was to clarify his eschatological teachings and to encourage the church in the face of persecution.

Theme: Stand Fast

In Thessalonians, God is glorifying Himself through the Thessalonian's steadfastness, so that He might demonstrate His superior goodness in the salvation sinners, the damnation of the wicked, and for the preservation of His people, for His eternal glory, and their eternal joy.

Author: Paul

"Paul, Silvanus, and Timothy…"

1 Thessalonians 1:1; 2 Thessalonians 1:1

"Therefore we wanted to come to you—even I, Paul, time and again—but Satan hindered us"

1 Thessalonians 2:18

"The salutation of Paul with my own hand, which is a sign in every epistle; so I write"

2 Thessalonians 3:17

Audience: The Church of the Thessalonians

"To the church of the Thessalonians in God the Father and the Lord Jesus Christ"

1 Thessalonians 1:1–2, Thessalonians 1:1

Key Verses

"Your faith toward God has gone out, so that we do not need to say anything. For they themselves declare concerning us what manner of entry we had to you, and how you turned to God from idols to serve the living and true God, and to wait for His Son from heaven, whom He raised from the dead, even Jesus who delivers us from the wrath to come."

1 Thessalonians 1:8–10

"But we are bound to give thanks to God always for you, brethren beloved by the Lord, because God from the beginning chose you for salvation through sanctification by the Spirit and belief in the truth, to which He called you by our gospel, for the obtaining of the glory of our Lord Jesus Christ. Therefore, brethren, stand fast and hold the traditions which you were taught, whether by word or our epistle."

2 Thessalonians 2:13–15

"But we command you, brethren, in the name of our Lord Jesus Christ, that you withdraw from every brother who walks disorderly and not according to the tradition which he received from us. For you yourselves know how you ought to follow us, for we were not disorderly among you; nor did we eat anyone's bread free of charge, but worked with labor and toil night and day, that we might not be a burden to any of you, not because we do not have authority, but to make ourselves an example of how you should follow us."

2 Thessalonians 3:6–9

Lessons

1. We do not need to sorrow without hope concerning those who have died, because we know that the dead in Christ will rise from the grave.
2. We ought to watch and be sober as we wait for the day of the Lord.
3. We should withdraw from every brother who walks disorderly.

Outline

1 THESSALONIANS

I. **Paul's Encouragement (1 Thess. 1–3)**

II. **Practical Exhortations (1 Thess. 4–5)**

2 THESSALONIANS

I. **The Coming Day of the Lord (2 Thess. 1)**

II. **The Revealing of the Son of Perdition (2 Thess. 2)**

III. **A Warning Against Idleness (2 Thess. 3)**

Study Questions

1 THESSALONIANS

What was the result of the Thessalonians believing the gospel?

They turned from idols to worship the true God (1 Thess. 1:9).

How should those who preach the gospel behave?

With boldness (1 Thess. 2:2), with honesty and integrity (v. 3), with the desire to please God not men (vv. 5–6), and with gentleness and affection (vv. 7–8).

How should the Christian react to affliction and persecution?

The Christian should remain steadfast in the faith and encourage one another, knowing God is in control (1 Thess. 3:2–4).

What two things does Paul tell them to do in order to please God?

Flee sexual immorality (1 Thess. 4:3–8) and love one another (vv. 9–12).

What is the believer's destiny?

To obtain salvation, not wrath (1 Thess. 5:9).

What will happen when Jesus returns?

He will punish those who persecute the church and give His people rest (2 Thess. 1:6–9).

What does Paul say will happen before the return of Jesus?

A great apostasy and the revealing of the "man of lawlessness" (2 Thess. 2:3).

What is the Christian view of work?

It is irresponsible to refuse to work (2 Thess. 3:7–9) and believers should work if they are able (vv. 10–12).

Onward, Christian Soldiers

WORDS: Sabine Baring-Gould, 1865. MUSIC: "St. Gertrude"; Arthur S. Sullivan, 1871. Public Domain.

5 B.C.
Birth of Christ

30 A.D.
Crucifixion & Resurrection

95 A.D.
John Writes Revelation

Christ's Baptism & Ministry Start
26 A.D.

Paul's First Missionary Journey
48 A.D.

Journey through

1 & 2 Timothy

THEME	AUTHOR	TIME OF WRITING
Fighting the Good Fight	Paul	62–67 A.D.

MEMORY VERSE

"All Scripture is given by inspiration of God, and is profitable for doctrine, for reproof, for correction, for instruction in righteousness, that the man of God may be complete, thoroughly equipped for every good work."

Timothy 3:16–17

OVERVIEW

In 1 and 2 Timothy, Paul writes to Timothy, a young pastor in the city of Ephesus, to teach him how to fight the good fight of faith and the importance of fostering faithful conduct in the house of God. Paul also instructs him how to manage the affairs of the church.

One of the realities of pastoral ministry is that pastors often encounter many varied challenges. Paul himself said, "I fought with beasts in Ephesus." Timothy was no different. He pastored in a pagan city and faced many difficulties. What is the solution? Hold fast to the Word of God which is "given by inspiration of God and is profitable" for everything.

Top 5 Facts to Remember

1. Timothy joined Paul in his missionary journeys prior to being appointed as an elder in Ephesus (Acts 16–20).
2. This is most likely the same Timothy in Hebrews 13:23 that is noted as having been imprisoned.
3. Not counting the letters addressed to him, Timothy is mentioned in eight of Paul's letters (nine if Hebrews is Pauline), often as coauthor: 2 Cor. 1:1; Phil. 1:1; Col. 1:1; 1 Thess. 1:1; 2 Thess. 1:1; Phm 1.
4. 1 Timothy arguably provides more information about church government than any other New Testament book.
5. 2 Timothy was Paul's last letter. He was martyred in Rome between 66–68 A.D. Perhaps due to his impending death, 2 Timothy is much more personal than Paul's other writings.

Theme: Fight the Good Fight

In 1 & 2 Timothy, God is glorifying Himself through Christians fighting the good fight, so that He might demonstrate His superior goodness in the salvation sinners, the damnation of the wicked, and for the preservation of His people, for His eternal glory, and their eternal joy.

Author: Paul

Paul, an apostle of Jesus Christ, by the commandment of God our Savior and the Lord Jesus Christ, our hope..."

1 Timothy 1:1

"Paul, an apostle of Jesus Christ by the will of God, according to the promise of life which is in Christ Jesus..."

2 Timothy 1:1

Audience: Timothy

"To Timothy, a true son in the faith"

1 Timothy 1:2

"This charge I commit to you, son Timothy..."

1 Timothy 1:18

"O Timothy! Guard what was committed to your trust..."

1 Timothy 6:20

"To Timothy, a beloved son"

2 Timothy 1:2

Key Verses

"This is a faithful saying and worthy of all acceptance, that Christ Jesus came into the world to save sinners, of whom I am chief. However, for this reason I obtained mercy, that in me first Jesus Christ might show all longsuffering, as a pattern to those who are going to believe on Him for everlasting life. Now to the King eternal, immortal, invisible, to God who alone is wise, be honor and glory forever and ever. Amen."

1 Timothy 1:15–17

"Therefore I exhort first of all that supplications, prayers, intercessions, and giving of thanks be made for all men, for kings and all who are in authority, that we may lead a quiet and peaceable life in all godliness and reverence."

1 Timothy 2:1–2

"Flee also youthful lusts; but pursue righteousness, faith, love, peace with those who call on the Lord out of a pure heart. But avoid foolish and ignorant disputes,

knowing that they generate strife. And a servant of the Lord must not quarrel but be gentle to all, able to teach, patient, in humility correcting those who are in opposition, if God perhaps will grant them repentance, so that they may know the truth, and that they may come to their senses and escape the snare of the devil, having been taken captive by him to do his will."

2 Timothy 2:22–26

Lessons

1. We should pray for those who are in authority.
2. When selecting elders and deacons, we should make sure that they have the proper qualifications.
3. We should regard Scripture as our ultimate authority, because it is God-breathed.

Outline

1 TIMOTHY

I. **Don't Give Up (1 Tim. 1)**

II. **Keep Praying (1 Tim. 2:1–8)**

III. **The Life and Adornment of Women in the Church (1 Tim. 2:9–15)**

IV. **The Office of Elder (1 Tim. 3:1–7)**

V. **The Office of Deacon (1 Tim. 3:8–13)**

VI. **Conduct in the House of God (1 Tim. 3:14–16)**

VII. **Be Holy in an Unholy World (1 Tim. 4:1–11)**

VIII. **Overcoming Obstacles (1 Tim. 4:12–16)**

IX. **Developing an Atmosphere of Honor in the Church (1 Tim. 5:1–6:10)**

A. Honor for Different Kinds of People in the Church (1 Tim. 5:1–2)

B. Honor for Widows (1 Tim. 5:3–16)

C. Honor for Elders (1 Tim. 5:17–21)

X. **Presumptuous Endorsing of Men (1 Tim. 5:22)**

XI. **Miscellaneous Instructions (1 Tim. 5:23–25)**

XII. **Honor of Masters and Contentment (1 Tim. 6:1–10)**

XIII. **The Good Confession of Men of God (1 Tim. 6:11–16)**

XIV. **Instructions for the Rich (1 Tim. 6:17–19)**

XV. **Final Appeal to Guard the Deposit (1 Tim. 6:20–21)**

2 TIMOTHY

I. **Hold on to Sound Doctrine and Do Not Give Up (2 Tim. 1)**

II. **Teach Sound Doctrine to Faithful Men (2 Tim. 2)**

III. **Preach Sound Doctrine in the Face of Opposition (2 Tim. 3–4)**

Study Questions

1 TIMOTHY

What changed Paul from being a blasphemer and enemy of the church into an apostle and missionary?

The mercy and grace of God (1 Tim. 1:13–16).

Who does Paul say Christians should pray for?

For all people (1 Tim. 2:1) and especially for those in authority (v. 2).

What are the two offices in the church?

Overseers (bishop/elders) and deacons (1 Tim. 3:1–13).

What three things are to occur in the church meeting?

Public reading of Scripture, exhortation, and teaching (1 Tim. 4:13).

How should other Christians in the church be treated?

Like family (older men as fathers, young women as sisters, etc.) (1 Tim. 5:1–2)

What is a root of all kinds of evil?

The love of money (1 Tim. 6:10).

2 TIMOTHY

What kind of spirit has God given to Christians?

One of power, love, and sound judgment – not fear (2 Tim. 1:7).

What should everyone who names the name of Christ do?

Depart from iniquity (2 Tim. 2:19).

What is Scripture profitable for?

For doctrine, for reproof, for correction, for instruction in righteousness, and to be equipped for good works (2 Tim. 3:16–17).

Why do people listen to false teachers?

Because the false teachers tell them what they want to hear (2 Tim. 4:3–4).

Amazing Grace

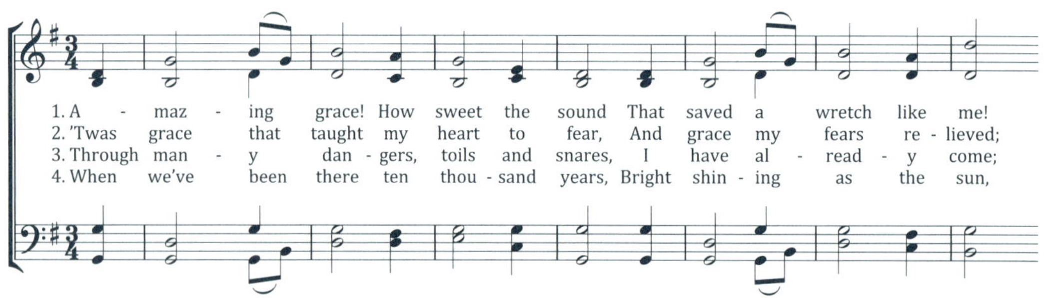

WORDS: John Newton, pub.1779; v. 4 Unknown, pub.1829.
MUSIC: "New Britain"; Unknown, pub.1829. Public Domain.

for more resources go to ***jttb.co/titus***

5 B.C.
Birth of Christ

26 A.D.
Christ's Baptism & Ministry Start

30 A.D.
Crucifixion & Resurrection

48 A.D.
Paul's First Missionary Journey

95 A.D.
John Writes Revelation

Journey through

Titus

THEME

Setting Things in Order

AUTHOR

Paul

TIME OF WRITING

62–64 A.D.

MEMORY VERSE

"For the grace of God that brings salvation has appeared to all men, teaching us that, denying ungodliness and worldly lusts, we should live soberly, righteously, and godly in the present age, looking for the blessed hope and glorious appearing of our great God and Savior Jesus Christ, who gave Himself for us, that He might redeem us from every lawless deed and purify for Himself His own special people, zealous for good works."

Titus 2:11–14

OVERVIEW

In his letter to Titus, a younger minister, Paul charges him to "set things in order." The interpretive key of the whole letter is found in Titus 1:5: "For this reason I left you in Crete, that you should set in order the things that are lacking." There were critical matters that needed to be settled to produce an orderly and godly expression of the church of Jesus Christ. Titus lived on one of the most beautiful islands in the Aegean Sea, inhabited by what someone referred to as some of the most bull-headed people you could ever meet in such a lovely spot. Paul's letter shows how sound doctrine leads to godly living.

Top 5 Facts to Remember

1. The book of Titus was most likely written between 1 and 2 Timothy, sometime between 60–68 A.D.

2. Along with Paul's letters to Timothy, the book of Titus is considered a "pastoral epistle" – a letter written to encourage and teach Titus and Timothy, both young pastors.

3. Though he is not mentioned in Acts, Titus clearly had a long history with Paul and is mentioned in other letters (cf. 2 Cor. 2:12–13; Gal. 2:1–5; 2 Tim. 4:10).

4. Since Titus is instructed to appoint elders in Crete, a work that "was left undone" (Tit. 1:5), it is probable that Titus evangelized the island with Paul and helped plant those churches.

5. As a Greek, Titus' partnership to share the gospel with Paul is an illustration of the reconciliation of both Jew and Gentile in Christ.

Theme: Setting Things in Order

In Titus, God is glorifying Himself through Christians setting things in order, so that He might demonstrate His superior goodness in the salvation sinners, the damnation of the wicked, and for the preservation of His people, for His eternal glory, and their eternal joy.

Author: Paul

"Paul, a bondservant of God and an apostle of Jesus Christ..."

Titus 1:1

Audience: Titus

"To Titus, a true son in our common faith"

Titus 1:4

Key Verses

"For this reason I left you in Crete, that you should set in order the things that are lacking, and appoint elders in every city as I commanded you—if a man is blameless, the husband of one wife, having faithful children not accused of dissipation or insubordination. For a bishop must be blameless, as a steward of God, not self-willed, not quick-tempered, not given to wine, not violent, not greedy for money, but hospitable, a lover of what is good, sober-minded, just, holy, self-controlled, holding fast the faithful word as he has been taught, that he may be able, by sound doctrine, both to exhort and convict those who contradict."

Titus 1:5–9

"But when the kindness and the love of God our Savior toward man appeared, not by works of righteousness which we have done, but according to His mercy He saved us, through the washing of regeneration and renewing of the Holy Spirit, whom He poured out on us abundantly through Jesus Christ our Savior, that having been justified by His grace we should become heirs according to the hope of eternal life."

Titus 3:4–7

"But avoid foolish disputes, genealogies, contentions, and strivings about the law; for they are unprofitable and useless. Reject a divisive man after the first and second admonition, knowing that such a person is warped and sinning, being self-condemned."

Titus 3:9–11

Lessons

1. As Christians, we should deny ungodliness and worldly lusts and live soberly, righteously, and in a godly manner in the present age.
2. We should be subject to rulers and authorities.
3. We should avoid foolish disputes.

Outline

I. **Set the Church on the Foundation of the Apostles (Tit. 1:1–4)**

II. **Select Qualified Elders (Tit. 1:5–9)**

III. **Correct the Insubordinate (Tit. 1:10–16)**

IV. **Speak Sound Doctrine for Sound Relationships in the Church (Tit. 2:1–15)**

- A. Older Men Who Are Sober (Tit. 2:2)
- B. Older Women Who Are Reverent (Tit. 2:3–5)
- C. Young Men Who Are a Pattern (Tit. 2:6–8)
- D. Bondservants Who Are Obedient (Tit. 2:9–10)
- E. Grace That Produces Good Works (Tit. 2:11–14)

V. **Be Obedient and Beneficial to Civil Authorities (Tit. 3:1–10)**

- A. The Behavior – Four Commands (Tit. 3:1–2)
- B. The Reasons for the Behavior (Tit. 3:3–8)
  1. Because of Who We Were (Tit. 3:3)
  2. Because of the Grace We Received (Tit. 3:4–7)
  3. To Fulfill a Faithful Saying (Tit. 3:8)

VI. **Avoid Dissension (Tit. 3:9–11)**

VII. **Meet Urgent Needs Together with Others (Tit. 3:12–14)**

VII. **Dwell in Grace (Tit. 3:15)**

Study Questions

Where are the qualifications for elders listed?

Titus 1:5–9

Why was Titus left in Crete?

To appoint elders in the churches in Crete (Tit. 1:5).

What were the Cretans known for in terms of their character?

"Cretans are always liars, evil beasts, lazy gluttons." (Tit. 1:12–13).

How are older men to behave?

"But as for you, speak the things which are proper for sound doctrine: that the older men be sober, reverent, temperate, sound in faith, in love, in patience" (Tit. 2:1–2).

What should older women encourage younger women to do?

"That they admonish the young women to love their husbands, to love their children, to be discreet, chaste, homemakers, good, obedient to their own husbands, that the word of God may not be blasphemed" (Tit. 2:4–5).

How are younger men to behave?

"Likewise, exhort the young men to be sober-minded, in all things showing yourself to be a pattern of good works; in doctrine showing integrity, reverence, incorruptibility, sound speech that cannot be condemned, that one who is an opponent may be ashamed, having nothing evil to say of you" (Tit. 2:6–8).

What is the Christian's "blessed hope"?

The appearing – the return – of Christ in glory (Tit. 2:13).

How does God save someone?

Not by their works but by His mercy (Tit. 3:5).

Immortal, Invisible, God Only Wise

WORDS: Walter C. Smith, pub.1876; alt.
MUSIC: "St. Denio"; Welsh melody, pub.1839. Public Domain.

5 B.C.
Birth of Christ

26 A.D.
Christ's Baptism & Ministry Start

30 A.D.
Crucifixion & Resurrection

48 A.D.
Paul's First Missionary Journey

95 A.D.
John Writes Revelation

Journey through

Philemon

THEME

Forgiveness and Restoration

AUTHOR

Paul

TIME OF WRITING

60–62 A.D.

MEMORY VERSE

"For perhaps he departed for a while for this purpose, that you might receive him forever, no longer as a slave but more than a slave—a beloved brother, especially to me but how much more to you, both in the flesh and in the Lord."

Philemon 15–16

OVERVIEW

The letter to Philemon shows how love works in the church when someone is wronged. Can there be love when someone steals from another church member or wrongs them in some way? Onesimus, the slave of Philemon in Colossae, was an unfaithful servant, a deserter, and an ungrateful thief who ran away from his master, Philemon. Can there be love between Philemon, a prominent and wealthy man with a church in his house, and Onesimus, a runaway slave?

Top 5 Facts to Remember

1. The book of Philemon was likely written between 62 A.D.
2. Internal evidence, found in both Colossians and Philemon, indicate that Philemon was a resident of Colossae.
3. Philemon and Colossians were likely written and sent together.
4. The letter of Philemon takes the concept of reconciliation with God in Colossians and applies it to the personal reconciliation of two individuals.
5. Philemon is Paul's shortest letter – only 335 words in Greek.

Theme: Forgiveness and Restoration

In Philemon, God is glorifying Himself through forgiveness and restoration, so that He might demonstrate His superior goodness in the salvation sinners, the damnation of the wicked, and for the preservation of His people, for His eternal glory, and their eternal joy.

Author: Paul

"Paul, a prisoner of Christ Jesus, and Timothy our brother"

Philemon 1:1

"Yet for love's sake I rather appeal to you—being such a one as Paul, the aged, and now also a prisoner of Jesus Christ"

Philemon 1:9

"I, Paul, am writing with my own hand. I will repay—not to mention to you that you owe me even your own self besides"

Philemon 1:19

Audience: Philemon

"To Philemon our beloved friend and fellow laborer, to the beloved Apphia, Archippus our fellow soldier, and to the church in your house"

Philemon 1:1–2

Key Verses

"I thank my God, making mention of you always in my prayers, hearing of your love and faith which you have toward the Lord Jesus and toward all the saints, that the sharing of your faith may become effective by the acknowledgment of every good thing which is in you in Christ Jesus."

Philemon 1:4–6

"I appeal to you for my son Onesimus, whom I have begotten while in my chains, who once was unprofitable to you, but now is profitable to you and to me."

Philemon 1:10–11

"If then you count me as a partner, receive him as you would me. But if he has wronged you or owes anything, put that on my account. I, Paul, am writing with my own hand. I will repay—not to mention to you that you owe me even your own self besides. Yes, brother, let me have joy from you in the Lord; refresh my heart in the Lord."

Philemon 1:17–20

Lessons

1. The gospel is for all classes, even slaves.
2. We should always be willing to forgive those who have wronged us.
3. Paul teaches us that it is often better to appeal to, rather than command those who are under our authority.

Outline

I. **Introductory Greetings (Philem. 1–3)**

II. **Prayers of Thanksgiving (Philem. 4–7)**

III. **Paul's Request - The Plea for Onesimus (Philem. 8–20)**

IV. **Paul Announces His Desire to Visit Philemon (Philem. 21–22)**

V. **A Personal Farewell Full of Love and Blessing (Philem. 23–25)**

Study Questions

Who was Philemon?

A friend and fellow laborer with Paul (Philem. 1:2).

Who was Onesimus?

Philemon's slave (Philem 1:16).

What happened to Onesimus when he was with Paul?

He was converted (Philem. 1:10).

Why did Paul want to keep Onesimus?

To minister to him and with him (Philem. 1:13).

How was Philemon told to treat his servant Onesimus?

As a beloved brother (Philem. 1:16).

I Love to Tell the Story

WORDS: Arabella K. Hankey, 1866. MUSIC: "Hankey"; William G. Fischer, pub.1869. Public Domain.

5 B.C.
Birth of Christ

26 A.D.
Christ's Baptism & Ministry Start

30 A.D.
Crucifixion & Resurrection

48 A.D.
Paul's First Missionary Journey

95 A.D.
John Writes Revelation

Journey through

Hebrews

THEME

A Superior Savior and Covenant

AUTHOR

Unknown

TIME OF WRITING

67–69 A.D.

MEMORY VERSE

"For Christ has not entered the holy places made with hands, which are copies of the true, but into heaven itself, now to appear in the presence of God for us."

Hebrews 9:24

OVERVIEW

The book of Hebrews shows us that a superior Savior brought a superior covenant resulting in a superior life. Throughout the letter, the author constantly argues for the supremacy of Christ over all things. This concept is present in every chapter and it is summarized in a very clear statement in Hebrews 8:1: "This is the main point of the things we are saying: We have such a High Priest, who is seated at the right hand of the throne of the Majesty in the heavens."

God gives us tremendous help in understanding the intended purpose of the book of Hebrews. Specifically, Hebrews ends with the words, "bear with the word of exhortation" (Hebrews 13:22). Hebrews is an exhortation for teaching and correction and for encouragement and comfort.

Top 5 Facts to Remember

1. The references to the Jewish temple and the still-functioning (but obsolete) priesthood and sacrificial system indicates that the letter was written before 70 A.D.

2. The letter's main purpose is to show the supremacy of Christ over all the Old Testament figures and religious system.

3. Though written in very complex and sophisticated Greek, the author seems to be Jewish and has a strong grasp of Old Testament theology and typology.

4. The author of Hebrews proclaimed Christ's divinity by applying the Psalms to Him—"Your throne, O God, is forever and ever," and "You, Lord, in the beginning laid the foundation of the earth" (Heb. 1:8–12).

5. Jesus Christ is referred to as our "High Priest" 11 times in the book of Hebrews (Heb. 2:17; 3:1; 4:14–15; 5:5, 10; 6:20; 7:26; 8:1; 9:11; 10:21).

Theme: A Superior Savior and Covenant

In Hebrews, God is glorifying Himself through a superior Savior and a better covenant, so that He might demonstrate His superior goodness in the salvation sinners, the damnation of the wicked, and for the preservation of His people, for His eternal glory, and their eternal joy.

Author: Unknown

Though often attributed to Paul, the letter is formally anonymous. The authorship has been debated since the early church. The reference to Timothy in Hebrews 13:23 indicates that the author may have been a companion of Paul, if not Paul himself.

Audience: The Hebrews

As both the title and the author's use of Old Testament imagery indicate, this letter was most likely sent to a Hebrew audience.

Key Verses

"God, who at various times and in various ways spoke in time past to the fathers by the prophets, has in these last days spoken to us by His Son, whom He has appointed heir of all things, through whom also He made the worlds; who being the brightness of His glory and the express image of His person, and upholding all things by the word of His power, when He had by Himself purged our sins, sat down at the right hand of the Majesty on high, having become so much better than the angels, as He has by inheritance obtained a more excellent name than they."

Hebrews 1:1–4

"Seeing then that we have a great High Priest who has passed through the heavens, Jesus the Son of God, let us hold fast our confession. For we do not have a High Priest who cannot sympathize with our weaknesses, but was in all points tempted as we are, yet without sin. Let us therefore come boldly to the throne of grace, that we may obtain mercy and find grace to help in time of need."

Hebrews 4:14–16

"These all died in faith, not having received the promises, but having seen them afar off were assured of them, embraced them and confessed that they were strangers and pilgrims on the earth. For those who say such things declare plainly that they seek a homeland. And truly if they had called to mind that country from which they had come out, they would have had opportunity to return. But now they desire a better, that is, a heavenly country. Therefore God is not ashamed to be called their God, for He has prepared a city for them."

Hebrews 11:13–16

Lessons

1. The writer of Hebrews is calling the church to its center—the gospel of Christ.
2. The author is concerned with teaching the proper doctrine of Christ.
3. Hebrews challenges us to know what it means to be saved.
4. Hebrews presents commands to a people who were experiencing many difficulties.
5. Hebrews was written to a people who were tempted to give up.
6. Hebrews teaches us much about angels (Heb. 1:15).
7. Hebrews declares Christ's objective for His children: "Bringing many sons to glory" (Heb. 2:10).
8. Hebrews instructs us on how to approach God: "Let us come boldly to the throne of grace" (Heb. 4:16).

Outline

I. **Christ is Superior (Heb. 1–6)**

II. **The Old Covenant is Fulfilled in Christ (Heb. 7–8)**

III. **The New Covenant is Complete (Heb. 9–10)**

IV. **The Life of Faith is Sweet (Heb. 11–13)**

Study Questions

CHAPTERS 1–6

Who is Jesus Christ as described in chapter 1?

He is "the brightness of His glory and the express image of His person, and upholding all things by the word of His power" (Heb. 1:3).

How did Christ defeat the Devil?

He took on flesh and blood and died for His people (Heb. 2:14–17).

Why is Christ worthy of more glory than Moses?

Because Moses was only God's servant and Jesus is God's Son (Heb. 3:5–6).

How does someone enter into God's rest?

By belief (Heb. 4:3).

Who made Jesus the High Priest for His people?

God the Father (Heb. 5:5–6, 10).

What happens to those who continually reject Christ?

They cannot be brought to repentance, and therefore must face God's judgement (Heb. 6:4–8).

Why is Jesus a better High Priest?

He was made a priest by God's oath (Heb. 7:20–21), guarantees a better covenant (v. 22), lives forever (vv. 23–25), and offered Himself as the final sacrifice for sins (v. 27).

What has happened to the Old Covenant?

It is obsolete and has vanished away (Heb. 8:13).

How did Christ secure redemption?

By His own blood (Heb. 9:12).

Why is Christ's sacrifice superior to the Old Testament sacrifices?

The blood of animals could never take away sin (Heb. 10:4), but the sacrifice of Christ does and was only offered once (vv. 11–12, 14).

How did people during the Old Testament live and please God?

By faith.

The Christian life is described as a race – how should we run it?

By laying aside every weight and sin and looking toward Jesus as our example (Heb. 12:1–2).

What are the sacrifices which please God?

Praise, doing good, and giving to those in need (Heb. 13:15–16).

Faith Is the Victory

WORDS: John H. Yates, 1891. MUSIC: "Sankey"; Ira D. Sankey, 1891. Public Domain.

5 B.C.
Birth of Christ

30 A.D.
Crucifixion & Resurrection

95 A.D.
John Writes Revelation

Christ's Baptism & Ministry Start
26 A.D.

Paul's First Missionary Journey
48 A.D.

Journey through

James

THEME	AUTHOR	TIME OF WRITING
Faith that Works	James	42–49 A.D.

MEMORY VERSE

"My brethren, count it all joy when you fall into various trials, knowing that the testing of your faith produces patience. But let patience have its perfect work, that you may be perfect and complete, lacking nothing."

James 1:2–4

OVERVIEW

Those who knew James called him "old camel's knees" because of the callouses on his knees from spending so much time in prayer. Perhaps it was his prayer life that gave him the wisdom to present the power of faith in everyday life in his letter to the twelve tribes scattered abroad. Some have called James "the Proverbs of the New Testament."

James desired that his readers understand that genuine faith will carry them through all of life and through any trial. In his letter, he declares the truth that genuine faith leads to action.

Top 5 Facts to Remember

1. The author is James, the half-brother of Jesus, also called "James the Just."
2. There are indications that the letter was likely written between 41–49 A.D.
3. James regularly alludes to Jesus' teachings as well as Old Testament instruction, thereby providing an example of how the Old and New Testaments work together.
4. The main purpose of the book is to show how true faith results in God-honoring good works in all areas of life.
5. James is a highly practical book with proverbial- style instruction throughout.

Theme: Faith that Works

In James, God is glorifying Himself through Christians displaying a faith that results in works, so that He might demonstrate His superior goodness in the salvation sinners, the damnation of the wicked, and for the preservation of His people, for His eternal glory, and their eternal joy.

Author: James

The author of the book is James, (Jam. 1:1) the brother of Jesus, known as "James the Just". "James, a bondservant of God and of the Lord Jesus Christ…" (Jam. 1:1).

Audience: The Jewish Christians Scattered Abroad

"To the twelve tribes which are scattered abroad"

James 1:1

Key Verses

My brethren, count it all joy when you fall into various trials, knowing that the testing of your faith produces patience. But let patience have its perfect work, that you may be perfect and complete, lacking nothing. If any of you lacks wisdom, let him ask of God, who gives to all liberally and without reproach, and it will be given to him. But let him ask in faith, with no doubting, for he who doubts is like a wave of the sea driven and tossed by the wind.

James 1:2–6

"But be doers of the word, and not hearers only, deceiving yourselves. For if anyone is a hearer of the word and not a doer, he is like a man observing his

natural face in a mirror; for he observes himself, goes away, and immediately forgets what kind of man he was. But he who looks into the perfect law of liberty and continues in it, and is not a forgetful hearer but a doer of the work, this one will be blessed in what he does."

James 1:22–25

"Who is wise and understanding among you? Let him show by good conduct that his works are done in the meekness of wisdom. But if you have bitter envy and self-seeking in your hearts, do not boast and lie against the truth. This wisdom does not descend from above, but is earthly, sensual, demonic. For where envy and self-seeking exist, confusion and every evil thing are there. But the wisdom that is from above is first pure, then peaceable, gentle, willing to yield, full of mercy and good fruits, without partiality and without hypocrisy. Now the fruit of righteousness is sown in peace by those who make peace."

James 3:13–18

Lessons

1. We should count it all joy when we fall into various trials.
2. We should be swift to hear, slow to speak, and slow to wrath.
3. We need to make sure that our wisdom is from above: pure, peaceable, gentle, willing to yield, full of mercy and good fruits, without partiality, and without hypocrisy, and that it is not demonic: full of bitter envy and self-seeking.

Outline

I. **Salutation (Jam. 1:1)**

II. **Enduring Trials and Temptations (Jam. 1:2–18)**

III. **Not Just Hearing, But Doing (Jam. 1:19–2:26)**

IV. **True Wisdom (Jam. 3)**

V. **True Humility (Jam. 4)**

VI. **Patience, Perseverance, and Prayer (Jam. 5)**

Study Questions

How should Christians respond to God's Word?

By being doers of it and not only hearers (Jam. 1:22).

What is the evidence of a true, living faith?

Good works (Jam. 2:14–26).

Why should not many Christians become teachers?

Because teachers will be judged more strictly (Jam. 3:1).

What is the result of being a friend of the world?

Becoming an enemy of God (Jam. 4:4).

What should a Christian patiently wait for?

The coming of the Lord (Jam. 5:7–8).

What is the difference between the wisdom from the world and the wisdom that is from God?

The wisdom from heaven is pure and peaceable while the wisdom from the world is earthly, sensual and demonic (Jam. 3:15–18).

I Sing the Mighty Power of God

WORDS: Isaac Watts, pub.1715. MUSIC: "Ellacombe"; Gesangbuch der H. W. K. Hofkapelle, 1784; arr., har. by William H. Monk, 1868. Public Domain.

for more resources go to ***jttb.co/peter***

5 B.C.
Birth of Christ

30 A.D.
Crucifixion & Resurrection

95 A.D.
John Writes Revelation

Christ's Baptism & Ministry Start
26 A.D.

Paul's First Missionary Journey
48 A.D.

Journey through

1 & 2 Peter

THEME

God's Protection of the Persecuted

AUTHOR

Peter

TIME OF WRITING

64–68 A.D.

MEMORY VERSE

"For we did not follow cunningly devised fables when we made known to you the power and coming of our Lord Jesus Christ, but were eyewitnesses of His majesty."

2 Peter 1:16

OVERVIEW

In 1 and 2 Peter, Peter is writing to a despised and persecuted people. On July 19, 64 A.D., a fire broke out in Rome. The flames licked up large parts of the city and both mansions and hovels were destroyed. The fires burned for three days and three nights. There were rumors that Nero had his men all over town trying to hinder people from putting out the fires. Nero identified a scapegoat – the Christians. A savage outbreak of persecution ensued. In view of these circumstances, Peter instructs these "pilgrims of the dispersion" to pursue holiness and truth. He encourages them that they are protected by the power of God.

Top 5 Facts to Remember

1. Men wither away like grass, but the word of the Lord endures forever (1 Pet. 1:22–25).
2. We are a chosen generation, a royal priesthood, a holy nation, God's own special people (1 Pet. 2:9).
3. Christ suffered once for sins, the just for the unjust, that He might bring us to God (2 Pet. 3:18).
4. The apostles did not follow cunningly devised fables when they spoke of Jesus Christ, but were eyewitnesses of His majesty (2 Pet. 1:16–18).
5. The Lord is not slack concerning His promises, but longsuffering, not willing that any should perish but that all should come to repentance (2 Pet. 3:9).

Theme: God's Protection of the Persecuted

In 1 & 2 Peter, God is glorifying Himself through holiness and truth, so that He might demonstrate His superior goodness in the salvation sinners, the damnation of the wicked, and for the preservation of His people, for His eternal glory, and their eternal joy.

Author: Peter

"Peter, an apostle of Jesus Christ..."

1 Peter 1:1

"Simon Peter, a bondservant and apostle of Jesus Christ..."

2 Peter 1:1

Audience: The Pilgrims of the Dispersion

1 Peter is addressed to "the pilgrims of the Dispersion in Pontus, Galatia, Cappadocia, Asia, and Bithynia" (1 Pet. 1:1). While 2 Peter does not contain as specific an introduction, it appears to be a follow-up letter to the same recipients (2 Pet. 3:1).

Key Verses

"In this you greatly rejoice, though now for a little while, if need be, you have been grieved by various trials, that the genuineness of your faith, being much more precious than gold that perishes, though it is tested by fire, may be found to praise, honor, and glory at the revelation of Jesus Christ, whom having not seen you love. Though now you do not see Him, yet believing, you rejoice with joy inexpressible and full of glory, receiving the end of your faith—the salvation of your souls."

1 Peter 1:6–9

"Be sober, be vigilant; because your adversary the devil walks about like a roaring lion, seeking whom he may devour. Resist him, steadfast in the faith, knowing that the same sufferings are experienced by your brotherhood in the world. But may the God of all grace, who called us to His eternal glory by Christ Jesus, after you have suffered a while, perfect, establish, strengthen, and settle you. To Him be the glory and the dominion forever and ever. Amen."

1 Peter 5:8–11

"And so we have the prophetic word confirmed, which you do well to heed as a light that shines in a dark place, until the day dawns and the morning star rises in your hearts; knowing this first, that no prophecy of Scripture is of any private interpretation, for prophecy never came by the will of man, but holy men of God spoke as they were moved by the Holy Spirit."

2 Peter 1:19–21

Lessons

1. We ought to abstain from fleshly lusts which war against the soul.
2. Wives should be submissive to their husbands and husbands should be understanding and give honor to their wives.
3. We should remember that the Scriptures were written by men who spoke from God as they were carried along by the Holy Spirit.

Outline

1 PETER

I. **Greeting to the Elect Pilgrims (1 Pet. 1:1–2)**

II. **A Heavenly Inheritance and the Fullness of Salvation (1 Pet. 1:3–25)**

III. **Growing Like Newborn Babes (1 Pet. 2:1–10)**

IV. **Living Before the World and Enduring Suffering (1 Pet. 2:11–4:19)**

V. **Elders, Shepherd the Flock (1 Pet. 5:1–8)**

VI. **Be on Guard - the Devil Walks Like a Roaring Lion (1 Pet. 5:8–11)**

VII. **Farewell (1 Pet. 5:12–14)**

2 PETER

I. **Greeting the Faithful (2 Pet. 1:1–2)**

II. **What God Has Provided for His Children (2 Pet. 1:3–21)**

III. **How God Governs All Things (2 Pet. 2:1–3:13)**

IV. **Final Call to Be Steadfast (2 Pet. 3:14–18)**

Study Questions

1 PETER

What are we supposed to rest our hope upon?

The grace that is to be brought to us at the revelation of Jesus Christ (1 Pet. 1:13).

How do we put to silence the ignorance of foolish men?

By doing good (1 Pet. 2:15).

What should we always be ready to do when asked about our hope?

Give a defense (1 Pet. 3:15).

What does love cover?

A multitude of sins (1 Pet. 4:8).

What kind of animal does Peter compare the devil to?

A roaring lion (1 Pet. 5:8).

What did Peter and the other apostles hear God the Father say on the holy mountain?

"This is My beloved Son, in whom I am well pleased" (2 Pet. 1:17).

While false teachers promise liberty, what are they themselves slaves of?

Corruption (2 Pet. 2:19).

As what will the day of the Lord come?

A thief in the night (2 Pet. 3:10).

My Jesus, I Love Thee

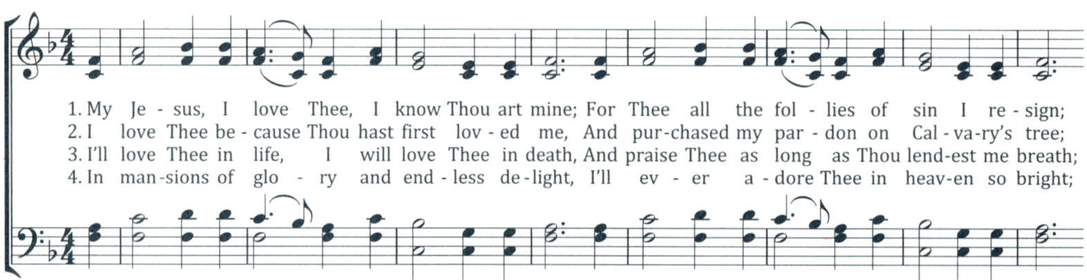

WORDS: William R. Featherston, 1864. MUSIC: "Gordon"; Adoniram J. Gordon, 1876. Public Domain.

5 B.C.
Birth of Christ

30 A.D.
Crucifixion & Resurrection

95 A.D.
John Writes Revelation

Christ's Baptism & Ministry Start
26 A.D.

Paul's First Missionary Journey
48 A.D.

Journey through

1, 2, & 3 John

THEME	AUTHOR	TIME OF WRITING
Fellowship with God and One Another	Paul	90–95 A.D.

MEMORY VERSE

"Do not love the world or the things in the world. If anyone loves the world, the love of the Father is not in him. For all that is in the world—the lust of the flesh, the lust of the eyes, and the pride of life—is not of the Father but is of the world. And the world is passing away, and the lust of it; but he who does the will of God abides forever."

John 2:15–17

OVERVIEW

John's theme in each of his three letters is the treasure of fellowship with God the Father, His Son Jesus Christ, and the Holy Spirit. He writes to combat false teaching, to provide reassurance, to constrain sin, and to make the joy of his audience complete.

Top 5 Facts to Remember

1. "[I]f anyone sins, we have an Advocate with the Father, Jesus Christ the righteous" (1 Jo. 2:1).
2. "For this purpose the Son of God was manifested, that He might destroy the works of the devil" (1 Jo. 3:8).
3. "He who does not love does not know God, for God is love" (1 Jo. 4:8).
4. "[I]f we ask anything according to God's will, He hears us" (1 Jo. 5:14).
5. "[M]any deceivers have gone out into the world who do not confess Jesus Christ as coming in the flesh" (2 Jo. 1:7).

Theme: Fellowship with God and One Another

In 1, 2, & 3 John, God is glorifying Himself through our fellowship with Himself and believers with one another, so that He might demonstrate His superior goodness in the salvation sinners, the damnation of the wicked, and for the preservation of His people, for His eternal glory, and their eternal joy.

Author: John

The author is the apostle John, "the disciple whom Jesus loved," and one of the "sons of thunder" whom Jesus charged with the care of His mother Mary while on the cross. He also wrote the Gospel of John and the book of Revelation.

Audience

1 John – People Who Need Assurance of Salvation (1 John 1:3).

2 John – The Elect Lady and Her Children (2 Jo. 1:1, 5).[1]

3 John – Gaius (3 Jo. 1:1).

Key Verses

"Beloved, let us love one another, for love is of God; and everyone who loves is born of God and knows God. He who does not love does not know God, for God is love. In this the love of God was manifested toward us, that God has sent His only begotten Son into the world, that we might live through Him. In this is love,

1. The "elect lady" is thought by some to be a metaphorical reference to a particular church, rather than a literal reference to an individual Christian woman.

not that we loved God, but that He loved us and sent His Son to be the propitiation for our sins. Beloved, if God so loved us, we also ought to love one another."

1 John 4:7–11

"And now I plead with you, lady, not as though I wrote a new commandment to you, but that which we have had from the beginning: that we love one another. This is love, that we walk according to His commandments. This is the commandment, that as you have heard from the beginning, you should walk in it."

2 John 5–6

"I wrote to the church, but Diotrephes, who loves to have the preeminence among them, does not receive us. Therefore, if I come, I will call to mind his deeds which he does, prating against us with malicious words. And not content with that, he himself does not receive the brethren, and forbids those who wish to, putting them out of the church. "Beloved, do not imitate what is evil, but what is good. He who does good is of God, but he who does evil has not seen God."

3 John 9–11

Lessons

1. If we profess to know God, then we should keep His commandments.
2. If we love God, then we should love our brother also.
3. We should not believe those who claim to be speaking God's truth if they deny that Jesus Christ has come in the flesh.

Outline

1 JOHN

I. **The Incarnation (1 Jo. 1:1–4)**

II. **Fellowship with God and One Another (1 Jo. 1:5–2:17)**

III. **False Teachers (1 Jo. 2:18–27)**

IV. **Eschatological Hope (1 Jo. 2:28–3:10)**

V. **Loving the Brethren (1 Jo. 3:11–24)**

VI. **False Spirits (1 Jo. 4:1–6)**

VII. **God is Love (1 Jo. 4:7–21)**

VIII. **Faith that Overcomes (1 Jo. 5:1–12)**

IX. **Confidence in Prayer (1 Jo. 5:13–21)**

2 JOHN

I. **Salutation (2 Jo. 1:1–3)**

II. **Walking in Love Is Obeying His Commandments (2 Jo. 1:4–6)**

III. **Beware of Antichrist Deceivers (2 Jo. 1:7–11)**

IV. **Farewell Message (2 Jo. 1:12–13)**

I. **Greeting (3 Jo. 1:1)**

II. **Joy in Children Walking in Truth (3 Jo. 1:2–4)**

III. **Gaius Commended for Faithfulness and Hospitality (3 Jo. 1:5–8)**

IV. **Diotrephes, the Divisive Man Who Does Not See God (3 Jo. 1:9–11)**

V. **Imitate Demetrius (3 Jo. 1:12)**

VI. **Farewell Message (3 Jo. 1:13)**

Study Questions

How can we know whether we know God?

If we keep His commandments (1 Jo. 2:3).

By what act of God do we know love?

The laying down of His life for us (1 Jo. 3:16).

Why did the elder rejoice in his letter to the elect lady?

Because he had found some of her children walking in truth (2 Jo. 1:4).

What was it that Diotrephes loved to have?

The preeminence (2 Jo. 1:9).

Stand Up, Stand Up for Jesus

WORDS: George Duffield, Jr., 1858. MUSIC: "Webb"; George J. Webb, 1830. Public Domain.

for more resources go to ***jttb.co/jude***

5 B.C. Birth of Christ

30 A.D. Crucifixion & Resurrection

95 A.D. John Writes Revelation

Christ's Baptism & Ministry Start 26 A.D.

Paul's First Missionary Journey 48 A.D.

Journey through

Jude

THEME

Earnestly Contend for the Faith

AUTHOR

Jude

TIME OF WRITING

68–70

MEMORY VERSE

"Beloved, while I was very diligent to write to you concerning our common salvation, I found it necessary to write to you exhorting you to contend earnestly for the faith which was once for all delivered to the saints. For certain men have crept in unnoticed, who long ago were marked out for this condemnation, ungodly men, who turn the grace of our God into lewdness and deny the only Lord God and our Lord Jesus Christ."

Jude 3–4

OVERVIEW

Jude wants his readers to defend the faith. Therefore, his letter is designed to be an apologetic for apologists. Jude is writing to those in the church who are facing the attacks of the Devil. He is appealing that they would "contend earnestly for the faith." He makes the argument why every Christian should be well versed in apologetics. There are people within the church who are abandoning the faith, reinventing the faith, and using the faith for their own desires. Specifically, he is speaking of those who are like this and stay in the church and become defiling influences within the church. He identifies them as "[S]pots in your love feasts" (Jude 1:12).

Top 5 Facts to Remember

1. Jude found it necessary to write in defense of the faith because certain men had turned the grace of God into lewdness (Jude 1:3–4).
2. After the Lord saved some out of Egypt, He destroyed those who did not believe (Jude 1:5).
3. Sodom, Gomorrah, and the cities around them were destroyed for giving themselves over to immorality (Jude 1:7).
4. The men that Jude spoke about had become like brute beasts in their corruption (Jude 1:10).
5. God is able to keep us from stumbling (Jude 1:24–25).

Theme: Earnestly Contend for the Faith

In Jude, God is glorifying Himself through Christians earnestly contending for the faith, so that He might demonstrate His superior goodness in the salvation sinners, the damnation of the wicked, and for the preservation of His people, for His eternal glory, and their eternal joy.

Author: Jude

He is the brother of Jesus, and "Jude, a bondservant of Jesus Christ, and brother of James..." (Jude 1:1).

Audience: Unknown

Jude addresses his letter "to those who are called, sanctified by God the Father, and preserved in Jesus Christ" (Jude 1:1).

Key Verses

"But I want to remind you, though you once knew this, that the Lord, having saved the people out of the land of Egypt, afterward destroyed those who did not believe. And the angels who did not keep their proper domain, but left their own abode, He has reserved in everlasting chains under darkness for the judgment of the great day; as Sodom and Gomorrah, and the cities around them in a similar manner to these, having given themselves over to sexual immorality and gone after strange flesh, are set forth as an example, suffering the vengeance of eternal fire."

Jude 5–7

"But you, beloved, building yourselves up on your most holy faith, praying in the Holy Spirit, keep yourselves in the love of God, looking for the mercy of our Lord Jesus Christ unto eternal life."

Jude 20–21

"Now to Him who is able to keep you from stumbling,
And to present you faultless
Before the presence of His glory with exceeding joy,
To God our Savior,
Who alone is wise,
Be glory and majesty,
Dominion and power,
Both now and forever.
Amen."

Jude 24–25

Lessons

1. We ought to contend earnestly for the faith.
2. We should beware of those who use the name of Christ to serve their own lusts.
3. We should keep ourselves in the love of God.

Outline

I. **Greeting (Jude 1:1–2)**

II. **Contend Earnestly for the Faith (Jude 1:3–4)**

III. **The Ungodly Will Be Judged (Jude 1:5–19)**

IV. **Keep Yourselves in the Love of God (Jude 1:20–23)**

V. **Glory to God (Jude 1:24–25)**

Study Questions

What three evil men from the Old Testament does Jude mention?

Cain, Balaam, and Korah (Jude 1:11).

To what kind of clouds does Jude compare the men who had crept into the church?

Clouds without water, carried about by the winds (Jude 1:12).

Who does Jude quote as having prophesied against these men?

Enoch (Jude 1:14).

Holy, Holy, Holy

WORDS: Reginald Heber, 1826. MUSIC: "Nicaea"; John B. Dykes, *pub.* 1861. Public Domain.

5 B.C.
Birth of Christ

30 A.D.
Crucifixion & Resurrection

95 A.D.
John Writes Revelation

Christ's Baptism & Ministry Start
26 A.D.

Paul's First Missionary Journey
48 A.D.

Journey through

Revelation

THEME

Christ's Victory

AUTHOR

John

TIME OF WRITING

94–96 A.D.

MEMORY VERSE

"And there shall be no more curse, but the throne of God and of the Lamb shall be in it, and His servants shall serve Him. They shall see His face, and His name shall be on their foreheads. There shall be no night there: They need no lamp nor light of the sun, for the Lord God gives them light. And they shall reign forever and ever."

Revelation 22:3–5

OVERVIEW

John shows us Jesus in His power and glory. Beholding the face of Jesus Christ is the most life-giving thing a human being can experience. This is what John brings us in this powerful and enlightening book.

Further, from a practical standpoint, Revelation is a book for people who are struggling to have hope in their present experience. It is for people who need to hear about the power and glory of the Triune God, particularly God's sovereignty over all things and His unstoppable plan to wipe every tear from our eyes. While we may experience consternation on our journey, Revelation teaches us that a glorious consummation awaits us. He is the King of Kings and Lord of Lords.

Top 5 Facts to Remember

1. John was on the Island of Patmos when he received the vision that he recorded in the book of Revelation (Rev. 1:9–11).

2. In John's vision, only the Lamb was worthy enough to take and open the scroll (Rev. 5).

3. In his vision, John saw God sitting on a great white throne, where all the dead were judged. Anyone not found written in the Book of Life was cast into the lake of fire (Rev. 20:11–15).

4. John saw a new heaven and new earth, where God would dwell with His people (Rev. 21:1–4).

5. John was rebuked by an angel when he fell down at his feet to worship, who told him that he was simply a fellow servant (Rev. 22:8–9).

Theme: Christ's Victory

In Revelation, God is glorifying Himself through Christ's victory over all things, so that He might demonstrate His superior goodness in the salvation sinners, the damnation of the wicked, and for the preservation of His people, for His eternal glory, and their eternal joy.

Author: John

"And He sent and signified it by His angel to His servant John"

Revelation 1:1–2

"John, to the seven churches which are in Asia"

Revelation 1:4

"I, John ... was on the island that is called Patmos..."

Revelation 1:9

"Now I, John, saw and heard these things"

Revelation 22:8

Audience: The Seven Churches in Asia

John addressed the book of Revelation "to the seven churches which are in Asia;" (Rev. 1:4.) located in Ephesus (Rev. 2:1), Smyrna (Rev. 2:8), Pergamos (Rev. 2:12), Thyatira (Rev. 2:18), Sardis (Rev. 3:1), Philadelphia (Rev. 3:7), and Laodicea (Rev. 3:14).

Key Verses

"Whenever the living creatures give glory and honor and thanks to Him who sits on the throne, who lives forever and ever, the twenty-four elders fall down before Him who sits on the throne and worship Him who lives forever and ever, and cast their crowns before the throne, saying:

'You are worthy, O Lord,
To receive glory and honor and power;
For You created all things,
And by Your will they exist and were created.' "

Revelation 4:9–11

"After these things I looked, and behold, a great multitude which no one could number, of all nations, tribes, peoples, and tongues, standing before the throne and before the Lamb, clothed with white robes, with palm branches in their hands, and crying out with a loud voice, saying, 'Salvation belongs to our God who sits on the throne, and to the Lamb!' "

Revelation 7:9–10

"He who testifies to these things says, 'Surely I am coming quickly.' Amen. Even so, come, Lord Jesus!"

Revelation 22:20

Lessons

1. We ought always to be prepared for the coming of Christ.
2. We should warn unbelievers of the eternal destruction that awaits them if they do not turn to Christ.
3. We should rejoice in the eternal life that is promised to those who have trusted in Christ for salvation.

Outline

I. **Introduction (Rev. 1)**

II. **Letters to the Seven Churches (Rev. 2–3)**

III. **The Throne Scene (Rev. 4–5)**

IV. **The Seven Seals (Rev. 6:1–8:6)**

V. **The Seven Trumpets (Rev. 8:7–11:19)**

VI. **The Great Conflict (Rev. 12–14)**

VII. **The Seven Bowls of Wrath (Rev. 15–16)**

VIII. **The Fall of Babylon (Rev. 17:1–19:10)**

IX. **The Lamb is Victorious (Rev. 19:11–20:15)**

X. **Eternal Life for the Redeemed (Rev. 21:1–22:5)**

XI. **Conclusion (Rev. 22:6–21)**

Study Questions

How many churches did John write to?

Seven (Rev. 1:4).

What is the most repeated number in the book of Revelation?

Seven

What was the name of the wicked city that was destroyed?

Babylon (Rev. 14:8).

Why was there no temple in the New Jerusalem?

Because the Lord God Almighty and the Lamb are its temple (Rev. 21:22).

Why was there no need for the sun or the moon in the New Jerusalem?

Because the glory of God illuminated it, and the Lamb is its light (Rev. 21:23).

What will happen to the person who adds to God's prophecy?

God will add to him the plagues that are written in His book (Rev. 22:18).

At what speed is Christ coming?

Quickly (Rev. 22:20).

Resources

The Bible *in* Chronological Order

OLD TESTAMENT

Job	Unknown
Genesis	1445–1405 B.C.
Exodus	1445–1405 B.C.
Leviticus	1445–1405 B.C.
Numbers	1445–1405 B.C.
Deuteronomy	1445–1405 B.C.
Psalms	1410–450 B.C.
Joshua	1405–1385 B.C.
Judges	1043 B.C.
Ruth	1030–1010 B.C.
Song of Solomon	971–965 B.C.
Proverbs	971–686 B.C.
Ecclesiastes	940–931 B.C.
1 Samuel	931–722 B.C.
2 Samuel	931–722 B.C.

Obadiah	850–840 B.C.
Joel	835–796 B.C.
Jonah	775 B.C.
Amos	750 B.C.
Hosea	750–710 B.C.
Micah	735–710 B.C.
Isaiah	700–681 B.C.
Nahum	650 B.C.
Zephaniah	635–625 B.C.
Habakkuk	615–605 B.C.
Ezekiel	590–570 B.C.
Lamentations	586 B.C.
Jeremiah	586–570 B.C.
1 Kings	561–538 B.C.
2 Kings	561–538 B.C.
Daniel	536–530 B.C.
Haggai	520 B.C.
Zechariah	480–470 B.C.
Ezra	457–444 B.C.
1 Chronicles	450–430 B.C.
2 Chronicles	450–430 B.C.
Esther	450–331 B.C.
Malachi	433–424 B.C.
Nehemiah	424–400 B.C.

NEW TESTAMENT

James	42–49 A.D.
Galatians	49–50 A.D.
Mark	50–60 A.D.
Matthew	50–60 A.D.
1 Thessalonians	51 A.D.
2 Thessalonians	51–52 A.D.
1 Corinthians	55 A.D.
2 Corinthians	55–56 A.D.
Romans	56 A.D.
Luke	60–61 A.D.
Ephesians	60–62 A.D.
Philippians	60–62 A.D.

Philemon	60–62 A.D.
Colossians	60–62 A.D.
Acts	62 A.D.
1 Timothy	62–64 A.D.
Titus	62–64 A.D.
1 Peter	64–65 A.D.
2 Timothy	66–67 A.D.
2 Peter	67–68 A.D.
Hebrews	67–69 A.D.
Jude	68–70 A.D.
John	80–90 A.D.
1 John	90–95 A.D.
2 John	90–95 A.D.
3 John	90–95 A.D.
Revelation	94–96 A.D.

Old & New Testament Together Plan

JANUARY

1 Mt 1-2; Gen 1-2

2 Mt 3-4; Gen 3-5

3 Mt 5; Gen 6-8

4 Mt 6; Gen 9-11

5 Mt 7-8; Gen 12-14

6 Mt 9; Gen 15-17

7 Mt 10; Gen 18-19

8 Mt 11; Gen 20-22

9 Mt 12; Gen 23-24

10 Mt 13; Gen 25

11 Mt 14; Gen 26-27

12 Mt 15; Gen 28-29

13 Mt 16-17; Gen 30

14 Mt 18; Gen 31-32

15 Mt 19; Gen 33-35

16 Mt 20-21; Gen 36-37

17 Mt 22; Gen 38-39

18 Mt 23; Gen 40-41

19 Mt 24; Gen 42

20 Mt 25; Gen 43-44

21 Mt 26; Gen 45-46

22 Mt 27; Gen 47-49

23 Mt 28; Gen 50-Ex 1

24 Mk 1; Ex 2-4

25 Mk 2; Ex 5-6

26 Mk 3; Ex 7-8

27 Mk 4; Ex 9-10

28 Mk 5; Ex 11-12

29 Mk 6; Ex 13-14

30 Mk 7; Ex 15-16

31 Mk 8; Ex 17-18

FEBRUARY

1 Mk 9; Ex 19-21
2 Mk 10; Ex 22-23
3 Mk 11; Ex 24-25
4 Mk 12; Ex 26-27
5 Mk 13; Ex 28-29
6 Mk 14; Ex 30-31
7 Mk 15; Ex 32-33
8 Mk 16; Ex 34
9 Lk 1; Ex 35-36
10 Lk 2; Ex 37-38
11 Lk 3; Ex 39-Lev 1
12 Lk 4; Lev 2-3
13 Lk 5; Lev 4-5
14 Lk 6; Lev 6-7
15 Lk 7; Lev 8-9
16 Lk 8; Lev 10-11
17 Lk 9; Lev 12-13
18 Lk 10; Lev 14
19 Lk 11; Lev 15
20 Lk 12; Lev 16-18
21 Lk 13; Lev 19-20
22 Lk 14; Lev 21-22
23 Lk 15; Lev 23
24 Lk 16; Lev 24-25
25 Lk 17; Lev 26
26 Lk 18; Lev 27-Num 1
27 Lk 19; Num 2-3
28 Lk 20; Num 4

MARCH

1 Lk 21; Num 5-6
2 Lk 22; Num 7
3 Lk 23; Num 8-9
4 Lk 24; Num 10-11
5 Jn 1; Num 12-13
6 Jn 2; Num 14-15
7 Jn 3; Num 16
8 Jn 4; Num 17-18
9 Jn 5; Num 19-20
10 Jn 6; Num 21-22
11 Jn 7; Num 23-25
12 Jn 8; Num 26
13 Jn 9; Num 27-28
14 Jn 10; Num 29-30
15 Jn 11; Num 31-32
16 Jn 12; Num 33-34
17 Jn 13; Num 35-36
18 Jn 14; Deut 1-2
19 Jn 15; Deut 3
20 Jn 16; Deut 4-5
21 Jn 17; Deut 6-7
22 Jn 18; Deut 8-9
23 Jn 19-20; Deut 10-11
24 Jn 21; Deut 12-13
25 Acts 1; Deut 14-15
26 Acts 2; Deut 16-18
27 Acts 3-4; Deut 19-20
28 Acts 5; Deut 21-23
29 Acts 6; Deut 24-25
30 Acts 7; Deut 26-27
31 Acts 8; Deut 28

APRIL

1 Acts 9; Deut 29-30
2 Acts 10; Deut 31-32
3 Acts 11; Deut 33-34
4 Acts 12; Josh 1-3
5 Acts 13-14; Josh 4-5
6 Acts 15; Josh 6-7
7 Acts 16; Josh 8-9
8 Acts 17; Josh 10
9 Acts 18; Josh 11-13
10 Acts 19; Josh 14-15
11 Acts 20; Josh 16-18
12 Acts 21; Josh 19-20
13 Acts 22; Josh 21
14 Acts 23-24; Josh 22-23
15 Acts 25; Josh 24-Judg 1
16 Acts 26; Judg 2-3
17 Acts 27; Judg 4-5
18 Acts 28; Judg 6
19 Rom 1-2; Judg 7-8
20 Rom 3-4; Judg 9
21 Rom 5; Judg 10-11
22 Rom 6-7; Judg 12-14
23 Rom 8; Judg 15-16
24 Rom 9-10; Judg 17-18
25 Rom 11; Judg 19
26 Rom 12-14; Judg 20-21
27 Rom 15; Ruth 1-3
28 Rom 16-1 Cor 1; Ruth 4-1 Sam 1
29 1 Cor 2-3; 1 Sam 2-3
30 1 Cor 4-5; 1 Sam 4-6

MAY

1 1 Cor 6-7; 1 Sam 7-9
2 1 Cor 8-9; 1 Sam 10-11
3 1 Cor 10; 1 Sam 12-13
4 1 Cor 11-12; 1 Sam 14
5 1 Cor 13-14; 1 Sam 15-16
6 1 Cor 15; 1 Sam 17
7 1 Cor 16; 1 Sam 18-19
8 2 Cor 1-2; 1 Sam 20-21
9 2 Cor 3-4; 1 Sam 22-23
10 2 Cor 5-7; 1 Sam 24-25
11 2 Cor 8-9; 1 Sam 26-27
12 2 Cor 10-11; 1 Sam 28-30
13 2 Cor 12; 1 Sam 31-2 Sam 1
14 2 Cor 13-Gal 2; 2 Sam 2-3
15 Gal 3; 2 Sam 4-6
16 Gal 4-5; 2 Sam 7-8
17 Gal 6-Eph 1; 2 Sam 9-11
18 Eph 2-3; 2 Sam 12-13
19 Eph 4-5; 2 Sam 14
20 Eph 6-Phil 1; 2 Sam 15-16
21 Phil 2-3; 2 Sam 17-18
22 Phil 4; 2 Sam 19
23 Col 1-2; 2 Sam 20-21
24 Col 3-1 Thess 1; 2 Sam 22-23
25 1 Thess 2-3; 2 Sam 24
26 1 Thess 4-2 Thess 1; 1 Kings 1
27 2 Thess 2-3; 1 Kings 2-3
28 1 Tim 1-3; 1 Kings 4-5
29 1 Tim 4-5; 1 Kings 6-7
30 1 Tim 6-2 Tim 1; 1 Kings 8
31 2 Tim 2-4; 1 Kings 9

JUNE

1 Titus 1-2; 1 Kings 10-11
2 Titus 3-Heb 1; 1 Kings 12
3 Heb 2-3; 1 Kings 13-14
4 Heb 4-6; 1 Kings 15
5 Heb 7-8; 1 Kings 16-17
6 Heb 9; 1 Kings 18-19
7 Heb 10; 1 Kings 20
8 Heb 11; 1 Kings 21-22
9 Heb 12-13; 2 Kings 1
10 Jas 1-2; 2 Kings 2-3
11 Jas 3-4; 2 Kings 4-5
12 Jas 5-1 Pet 1; 2 Kings 6-7
13 1 Pet 2-3; 2 Kings 8
14 1 Pet 4-5; 2 Kings 9-10
15 2 Pet 1-2; 2 Kings 11-12
16 2 Pet 3-1 Jn 1; 2 Kings 13-14
17 1 Jn 2-3; 2 Kings 15
18 1 Jn 4-5; 2 Kings 16-17
19 2 Jn 1-3 Jn 1; 2 Kings 18
20 Jude 1-Rev 1; 2 Kings 19-20
21 Rev 2; 2 Kings 21-22
22 Rev 3-5; 2 Kings 23-24
23 Rev 6-7; 2 Kings 25-1 Chr 1
24 Rev 8-9; 1 Chr 2-3
25 Rev 10-11; 1 Chr 4-5
26 Rev 12-13; 1 Chr 6-7
27 Rev 14-15; 1 Chr 8-9
28 Rev 16-17; 1 Chr 10-11
29 Rev 18-19; 1 Chr 12-14
30 Rev 20; 1 Chr 15-16

JULY

1 Rev 21-22; 1 Chr 17-20
2 Mt 1-2; 1 Chr 21-22
3 Mt 3-4; 1 Chr 23-25
4 Mt 5; 1 Chr 26-27
5 Mt 6; 1 Chr 28-29
6 Mt 7-8; 2 Chr 1-3
7 Mt 9; 2 Chr 4-5
8 Mt 10; 2 Chr 6-7
9 Mt 11; 2 Chr 8-9
10 Mt 12; 2 Chr 10-12
11 Mt 13; 2 Chr 13-16
12 Mt 14; 2 Chr 17-18
13 Mt 15; 2 Chr 19-20
14 Mt 16-17; 2 Chr 21-23
15 Mt 18; 2 Chr 24-25
16 Mt 19; 2 Chr 26-27
17 Mt 20; 2 Chr 28-29
18 Mt 21; 2 Chr 30-31
19 Mt 22-23; 2 Chr 32
20 Mt 24; 2 Chr 33-34
21 Mt 25; 2 Chr 35-36
22 Mt 26; Ezra 1-2
23 Mt 27; Ezra 3-5
24 Mt 28; Ezra 6-7
25 Mk 1; Ezra 8-9
26 Mk 2; Ezra 10-Neh 1
27 Mk 3; Neh 2-3
28 Mk 4; Neh 4-6
29 Mk 5; Neh 7-8
30 Mk 6; Neh 9
31 Mk 7; Neh 10-11

AUGUST

1 Mk 8; Neh 12-13
2 Mk 9; Esth 1 1-2
3 Mk 10; Esth 1 3-5
4 Mk 11; Esth 1 6-9
5 Mk 12; Job 1-4
6 Mk 13; Job 5-8
7 Mk 14; Job 9-12
8 Mk 15; Job 13-16
9 Mk 16; Job 17-20
10 Lk 1; Job 21-24
11 Lk 2; Job 25-29
12 Lk 3; Job 30-33
13 Lk 4; Job 34-36
14 Lk 5; Job 37-39
15 Lk 6; Job 40-Psalm 3
16 Lk 7; Psalm 4-9
17 Lk 8; Psalm 10-17
18 Lk 9; Psalm 18-21
19 Lk 10; Psalm 22-27
20 Lk 11; Psalm 28-32
21 Lk 12; Psalm 33-36
22 Lk 13; Psalm 37-41
23 Lk 14; Psalm 42-46
24 Lk 15; Psalm 47-52
25 Lk 16; Psalm 53-58
26 Lk 17; Psalm 59-64
27 Lk 18; Psalm 65-68
28 Lk 19; Psalm 69-73
29 Lk 20; Psalm 74-77
30 Lk 21; Psalm 78-80
31 Lk 22; Psalm 81-87

SEPTEMBER

1 Lk 23; Psalm 88-90
2 Lk 24; Psalm 91-98
3 Jn 1; Psalm 99-104
4 Jn 2; Psalm 105-106
5 Jn 3; Psalm 107-110
6 Jn 4; Psalm 111-118
7 Jn 5; Psalm 119
8 Jn 6; Psalm 120-126
9 Jn 7; Psalm 127-136
10 Jn 8; Psalm 137-143
11 Jn 9; Psalm 144-150
12 Jn 10; Prov 1-4
13 Jn 11; Prov 5-7
14 Jn 12; Prov 8-11
15 Jn 13; Prov 12-14
16 Jn 14; Prov 15-18
17 Jn 15; Prov 19-21
18 Jn 16; Prov 22-24
19 Jn 17; Prov 25-28
20 Jn 18; Prov 29-31
21 Jn 19; Eccl 1-3
22 Jn 20; Eccl 4-7
23 Jn 21-Acts 1; Eccl 8-11
24 Acts 2; Eccl 12-Song 4
25 Acts 3; Song 5-8
26 Acts 4; Isa 1-3
27 Acts 5-6; Isa 4-6
28 Acts 7; Isa 7-9
29 Acts 8; Isa 10-12
30 Acts 9; Isa 13-16

OCTOBER

1 Acts 10; Isa 17-20
2 Acts 11; Isa 21-23
3 Acts 12; Isa 24-27
4 Acts 13; Isa 28-29
5 Acts 14; Isa 30-32
6 Acts 15; Isa 33-35
7 Acts 16; Isa 36-37
8 Acts 17; Isa 38-40
9 Acts 18; Isa 41-43
10 Acts 19-20; Isa 44-45
11 Acts 21; Isa 46-48
12 Acts 22; Isa 49-51
13 Acts 23; Isa 52-54
14 Acts 24; Isa 55-58
15 Acts 25; Isa 59-61
16 Acts 26-27; Isa 62-64
17 Acts 28; Isa 65-Jer 1
18 Rom 1; Jer 2-3
19 Rom 2-3; Jer 4-5
20 Rom 4; Jer 6
21 Rom 5-6; Jer 7-9
22 Rom 7; Jer 10-11
23 Rom 8-9; Jer 12-14
24 Rom 10; Jer 15-16
25 Rom 11-12; Jer 17-18
26 Rom 13-14; Jer 19-21
27 Rom 15-16; Jer 22-23
28 1 Cor 1; Jer 24-25
29 1 Cor 2-4; Jer 26-27
30 1 Cor 5-6; Jer 28-29
31 1 Cor 7; Jer 30-31

NOVEMBER

1 1 Cor 8-9; Jer 32
2 1 Cor 10-11; Jer 33-34
3 1 Cor 12; Jer 35-36
4 1 Cor 13-14; Jer 37-39
5 1 Cor 15; Jer 40-41
6 1 Cor 16-2 Cor 1; Jer 42-44
7 2 Cor 2-3; Jer 45-47
8 2 Cor 4-5; Jer 48
9 2 Cor 6-7; Jer 49-50
10 2 Cor 8-9; Jer 51
11 2 Cor 10-11; Jer 52
12 2 Cor 12-13; Lam 1-2
13 Gal 1-2; Lam 3-4
14 Gal 3-4; Lam 5-Ezek 2
15 Gal 5-6; Ezek 3-5
16 Eph 1-2; Ezek 6-8
17 Eph 3-4; Ezek 9-11
18 Eph 5; Ezek 12-13
19 Eph 6-Phil 1; Ezek 14-15
20 Phil 2-3; Ezek 16-17
21 Phil 4-Col 1; Ezek 18-19
22 Col 2-3; Ezek 20
23 Col 4-1 Thess 1; Ezek 21-22
24 1 Thess 2-4; Ezek 23-24
25 1 Thess 5-2 Thess 1; Ezek 25-26
26 2 Thess 2-1 Tim 1; Ezek 27-28
27 1 Tim 2-4; Ezek 29-31
28 1 Tim 5-6; Ezek 32-33
29 2 Tim 1-2; Ezek 34
30 2 Tim 3-4; Ezek 35-36

DECEMBER

1 Titus 1-3; Ezek 37-38
2 Phil 1-Heb 1; Ezek 39-40
3 Heb 2-4; Ezek 41-42
4 Heb 5-6; Ezek 43-44
5 Heb 7-8; Ezek 45
6 Heb 9; Ezek 46-47
7 Heb 10; Ezek 48-Dan 1
8 Heb 11-12; Dan 2-3
9 Heb 13; Dan 4
10 Jas 1-2; Dan 5-6
11 Jas 3-5; Dan 7
12 1 Pet 1; Dan 8-9
13 1 Pet 2-3; Dan 10-11
14 1 Pet 4-5; Dan 12-Hos 2
15 2 Pet 1-2; Hos 3-7
16 2 Pet 3-1 Jn 1; Hos 8-11
17 1 Jn 2-3; Hos 12-Joel 1
18 1 Jn 4-5; Joel 2-Am 1
19 2 Jn 1-Jude 1; Am 2-5
20 Rev 1; Am 6-8
21 Rev 2-3; Am 9-Jon 2
22 Rev 4-5; Jon 3-Mic 3
23 Rev 6-7; Mic 4-6
24 Rev 8-9; Mic 7-Nah 3
25 Rev 10-11; Hab 1-Zeph 1
26 Rev 12-13; Zeph 2-Hag 1
27 Rev 14-15; Zech 1-4
28 Rev 16-17; Zech 5-8
29 Rev 18-19; Zech 9-11
30 Rev 20; Zech 12-14
31 Rev 21-22; Mal 1-4

The McCheyne Reading Plan

JANUARY

1 Gn 1; Mt 1; Ezra 1; Act 1

2 Gn 2; Mt 2; Ezra 2; Act 2

3 Gn 3; Mt 3; Ezra 3; Act 3

4 Gn 4; Mt 4; Ezra 4; Act 4

5 Gn 5; Mt 5; Ezra 5; Act 5

6 Gn 6; Mt 6; Ezra 6; Act 6

7 Gn 7; Mt 7; Ezra 7; Act 7

8 Gn 8; Mt 8; Ezra 8; Act 8

9 Gn 9-10; Mt 9; Ezra 9; Act 9

10 Gn 11; Mt 10; Ezra 10; Act 10

11 Gn 12; Mt 11; Neh 1; Act 11

12 Gn 13; Mt 12; Neh 2; Act 12

13 Gn 14; Mt 13; Neh 3; Act 13

14 Gn 15; Mt 14; Neh 4; Act 14

15 Gn 16; Mt 15; Neh 5; Act 15

16 Gn 17; Mt 16; Neh 6; Act 16

17 Gn 18; Mt 17; Neh 7; Act 17

18 Gn 19; Mt 18; Neh 8; Act 18

19 Gn 20; Mt 19; Neh 9; Act 19

20 Gn 21; Mt 20; Neh 10; Act 20

21 Gn 22; Mt 21; Neh 11; Act 21

22 Gn 23; Mt 22; Neh 12; Act 22

23 Gn 24; Mt 23; Neh 13; Act 23

24 Gn 25; Mt 24; Esth 1; Act 24

25 Gn 26; Mt 25; Esth 2; Act 25

26 Gn 27; Mt 26; Esth 3; Act 26

27 Gn 28; Mt 27; Esth 4; Act 27

28 Gn 29; Mt 28; Esth 5; Act 28

29 Gn 30; Mk 1; Esth 6; Ro 1

30 Gn 31; Mk 2; Esth 7; Ro 2

31 Gn 32; Mk 3; Esth 8; Ro 3

FEBRUARY

1 Gn 33; Mk 4; Esth 9-10; Ro 4

2 Gn 34; Mk 5; Job 1; Ro 5

3 Gn 35-36; Mk 6; Job 2; Ro 6

4 Gn 37; Mk 7; Job 3; Ro 7

5 Gn 38; Mk 8; Job 4; Ro 8

6 Gn 39; Mk 9; Job 5; Ro 9

7 Gn 40; Mk 10; Job 6; Ro 10

8 Gn 41; Mk 11; Job 7; Ro 11

9 Gn 42; Mk 12; Job 8; Ro 12

10 Gn 43; Mk 13; Job 9; Ro 13

11 Gn 44; Mk 14; Job 10; Ro 14

12 Gn 45; Mk 15; Job 11; Ro 15

13 Gn 46; Mk 16; Job 12; Ro 16

14 Gn 47; Lk 1:1-38; Job 13; 1Co 1

15 Gn 48; Lk 1:39-80; Job 14; 1Co 2

16 Gn 49; Lk 2; Job 15; 1Co 3

17 Gn 50; Lk 3; Job 16-17; 1Co 4

18 Ex 1; Lk 4; Job 18; 1Co 5

19 Ex 2; Lk 5; Job 19; 1Co 6

20 Ex 3; Lk 6; Job 20; 1Co 7

21 Ex 4; Lk 7; Job 21; 1Co 8

22 Ex 5; Lk 8; Job 22; 1Co 9

23 Ex 6; Lk 9; Job 23; 1Co 10

24 Ex 7; Lk 10; Job 24; 1Co 11

25 Ex 8; Lk 11; Job 25-26; 1Co 12

26 Ex 9; Lk 12; Job 27; 1Co 13

27 Ex 10; Lk 13; Job 28; 1Co 14

28 Ex 11:1-12:21; Lk 14; Job 29; 1Co 15

MARCH

1 Ex 12:22-51; Lk 15; Job 30; 1Co 16

2 Ex 13; Lk 16; Job 31; 2Co 1

3 Ex 14; Lk 17; Job 32; 2Co 2

4 Ex 15; Lk 18; Job 33; 2Co 3

5 Ex 16; Lk 19; Job 34; 2Co 4

6 Ex 17; Lk 20; Job 35; 2Co 5

7 Ex 18; Lk 21; Job 36; 2Co 6

8 Ex 19; Lk 22; Job 37; 2Co 7

9 Ex 20; Lk 23; Job 38; 2Co 8

10 Ex 21; Lk 24; Job 39; 2Co 9

11 Ex 22; Jn 1; Job 40; 2Co 10

12 Ex 23; Jn 2; Job 41; 2Co 11

13 Ex 24; Jn 3; Job 42; 2Co 12

14 Ex 25; Jn 4; Pr 1; 2Co 13

15 Ex 26; Jn 5; Pr 2; Gal 1

16 Ex 27; Jn 6; Pr 3; Gal 2

17 Ex 28; Jn 7; Pr 4; Gal 3

18 Ex 29; Jn 8; Pr 5; Gal 4

19 Ex 30; Jn 9; Pr 6; Gal 5

20 Ex 31; Jn 10; Pr 7; Gal 6

21 Ex 32; Jn 11; Pr 8; Eph 1

22 Ex 33; Jn 12; Pr 9; Eph 2

23 Ex 34; Jn 13; Pr 10; Eph 3

24 Ex 35; Jn 14; Pr 11; Eph 4

25 Ex 36; Jn 15; Pr 12; Eph 5

26 Ex 37; Jn 16; Pr 13; Eph 6

27 Ex 38; Jn 17; Pr 14; Phil 1

28 Ex 39; Jn 18; Pr 15; Phil 2

29 Ex 40; Jn 19; Pr 16; Phil 3

30 Lv 1; Jn 20; Pr 17; Phil 4

31 Lv 2-3; Jn 21; Pr 18; Col 1

APRIL

1 Lv 4; Ps 1-2; Pr 19; Col 2

2 Lv 5; Ps 3-4; Pr 20; Col 3

3 Lv 6; Ps 5-6; Pr 21; Col 4

4 Lv 7; Ps 7-8; Pr 22; 1Th 1

5 Lv 8; Ps 9; Pr 23; 1Th 2

6 Lv 9; Ps 10; Pr 24; 1Th 3

7 Lv 10; Ps 11-12; Pr 25; 1Th 4

8 Lv 11-12; Ps 13-14; Pr 26; 1Th 5

9 Lv 13; Ps 15-16; Pr 27; 2Th 1

10 Lv 14; Ps 17; Pr 28; 2Th 2

11 Lv 15; Ps 18; Pr 29; 2Th 3

12 Lv 16; Ps 19; Pr 30; 1Ti 1

13 Lv 17; Ps 20-21; Pr 31; 1Ti 2

14 Lv 18; Ps 22; Eccl 1; 1Ti 3

15 Lv 19; Ps 23-24; Eccl 2; 1Ti 4

16 Lv 20; Ps 25; Eccl 3; 1Ti 5

17 Lv 21; Ps 26-27; Eccl 4; 1Ti 6

18 Lv 22; Ps 28-29; Eccl 5; 2Ti 1

19 Lv 23; Ps 30; Eccl 6; 2Ti 2

20 Lv 24; Ps 31; Eccl 7; 2Ti 3

21 Lv 25; Ps 32; Eccl 8; 2Ti 4

22 Lv 26; Ps 33; Eccl 9; Tit 1

23 Lv 27; Ps 34; Eccl 10; Tit 2

24 Nu 1; Ps 35; Eccl 11; Tit 3

25 Nu 2; Ps 36; Eccl 12; Philemon

26 Nu 3; Ps 37; Song 1; He 1

27 Nu 4; Ps 38; Song 2; He 2

28 Nu 5; Ps 39; Song 3; He 3

29 Nu 6; Ps 40-41; Song 4; He 4

30 Nu 7; Ps 42-43; Song 5; He 5

MAY

1 Nu 8; Ps 44; Song 6; He 6

2 Nu 9; Ps 45; Song 7; He 7

3 Nu 10; Ps 46-47; Song 8; He 8

4 Nu 11; Ps 48; Is 1; He 9

5 Nu 12-13; Ps 49; Is 2; He 10

6 Nu 14; Ps 50; Is 3-4; He 11

7 Nu 15; Ps 51; Is 5; He 12

8 Nu 16; Ps 52-54; Is 6; He 13

9 Nu 17-18; Ps 55; Is 7; Jas 1

10 Nu 19; Ps 56-57; Is 8:1-9:7; Jas 2

11 Nu 20; Ps 58-59; Is 9:8-10:4; Jas 3

12 Nu 21; Ps 60-61; Is 10:5-34; Jas 4

13 Nu 22; Ps 62-63; Is 11-12; Jas 5

14 Nu 23; Ps 64-65; Is 13; 1Pe 1

15 Nu 24; Ps 66-67; Is 14; 1Pe 2

16 Nu 25; Ps 68; Is 15; 1Pe 3

17 Nu 26; Ps 69; Is 16; 1Pe 4

18 Nu 27; Ps 70-71; Is 17-18; 1Pe 5

19 Nu 28; Ps 72; Is 19-20; 2Pe 1

20 Nu 29; Ps 73; Is 21; 2Pe 2

21 Nu 30; Ps 74; Is 22; 2Pe 3

22 Nu 31; Ps 75-76; Is 23; 1 Jn 1

23 Nu 32; Ps 77; Is 24; 1 Jn 2

24 Nu 33; Ps 78:1-37; Is 25; 1 Jn 3

25 Nu 34; Ps 78:38-72; Is 26; 1 Jn 4

26 Nu 35; Ps 79; Is 27; 1 Jn 5

27 Nu 36; Ps 80; Is 28; 2Jn 1

28 Dt 1; Ps 81-82; Is 29; 3 Jn 1

29 Dt 2; Ps 83-84; Is 30; Jude

30 Dt 3; Ps 85; Is 31; Rev 1

31 Dt 4; Ps 86-87; Is 32; Rev 2

JUNE

1 Dt 5; Ps 88; Is 33; Rev 3

2 Dt 6; Ps 89; Is 34; Rev 4

3 Dt 7; Ps 90; Is 35; Rev 5

4 Dt 8; Ps 91; Is 36; Rev 6

5 Dt 9; Ps 92-93; Is 37; Rev 7

6 Dt 10; Ps 94; Is 38; Rev 8

7 Dt 11; Ps 95-96; Is 39; Rev 9

8 Dt 12; Ps 97-98; Is 40; Rev 10

9 Dt 13-14; Ps 99-101; Is 41; Rev 11

10 Dt 15; Ps 102; Is 42; Rev 12

11 Dt 16; Ps 103; Is 43; Rev 13

12 Dt 17; Ps 104; Is 44; Rev 14

13 Dt 18; Ps 105; Is 45; Rev 15

14 Dt 19; Ps 106; Is 46; Rev 16

15 Dt 20; Ps 107; Is 47; Rev 17

16 Dt 21; Ps 108-109; Is 48; Rev 18

17 Dt 22; Ps 110-111; Is 49; Rev 19

18 Dt 23; Ps 112-113; Is 50; Rev 20

19 Dt 24; Ps 114-115; Is 51; Rev 21

20 Dt 25; Ps 116; Is 52; Rev 22

21 Dt 26; Ps 117-118; Is 53; Mt 1

22 Dt 27:1-28:19; Ps 119:1-24; Is 54; Mt 2

23 Dt 28:20-68; Ps 119:25-48; Is 55; Mt 3

24 Dt 29; Ps 119:49-72; Is 56; Mt 4

25 Dt 30; Ps 119:73-96; Is 57; Mt 5

26 Dt 31; Ps 119:97-120; Is 58; Mt 6

27 Dt 32; Ps 119:121-144; Is 59; Mt 7

28 Dt 33-34; Ps 119:145-176; Is 60; Mt 8

29 Jsh 1; Ps 120-122; Is 61; Mt 9

30 Jsh 2; Ps 123-125; Is 62; Mt 10

JULY

1 Jsh 3; Ps 126-128; Is 63; Mt 11

2 Jsh 4; Ps 129-131; Is 64; Mt 12

3 Jsh 5:1-6:5; Ps 132-134; Is 65; Mt 13

4 Jsh 6:6-27; Ps 135-136; Is 66; Mt 14

5 Jsh 7; Ps 137-138; Jer 1; Mt 15

6 Jsh 8; Ps 139; Jer 2; Mt 16

7 Jsh 9; Ps 140-141; Jer 3; Mt 17

8 Jsh 10; Ps 142-143; Jer 4; Mt 18

9 Jsh 11; Ps 144; Jer 5; Mt 19

10 Jsh 12-13; Ps 145; Jer 6; Mt 20

11 Jsh 14-15; Ps 146-147; Jer 7; Mt 21

12 Jsh 16-17; Ps 148; Jer 8; Mt 22

13 Jsh 18-19; Ps 149-150; Jer 9; Mt 23

14 Jsh 20-21; Act 1; Jer 10; Mt 24

15 Jsh 22; Act 2; Jer 11; Mt 25

16 Jsh 23; Act 3; Jer 12; Mt 26

17 Jsh 24; Act 4; Jer 13; Mt 27

18 Jdg 1; Act 5; Jer 14; Mt 28

19 Jdg 2; Act 6; Jer 15; Mk 1

20 Jdg 3; Act 7; Jer 16; Mk 2

21 Jdg 4; Act 8; Jer 17; Mk 3

22 Jdg 5; Act 9; Jer 18; Mk 4

23 Jdg 6; Act 10; Jer 19; Mk 5

24 Jdg 7; Act 11; Jer 20; Mk 6

25 Jdg 8; Act 12; Jer 21; Mk 7

26 Jdg 9; Act 13; Jer 22; Mk 8

27 Jdg 10:1-11:11; Act 14; Jer 23; Mk 9

28 Jdg 11:12-40; Act 15; Jer 24; Mk 10

29 Jdg 12; Act 16; Jer 25; Mk 11

30 Jdg 13; Act 17; Jer 26; Mk 12

31 Jdg 14; Act 18; Jer 27; Mk 13

AUGUST

1 Jdg 15; Act 19; Jer 28; Mk 14

2 Jdg 16; Act 20; Jer 29; Mk 15

3 Jdg 17; Act 21; Jer 30-31; Mk 16

4 Jdg 18; Act 22; Jer 32; Ps 1-2

5 Jdg 19; Act 23; Jer 33; Ps 3-4

6 Jdg 20; Act 24; Jer 34; Ps 5-6

7 Jdg 21; Act 25; Jer 35; Ps 7-8

8 Ruth 1; Act 26; Jer 36,45; Ps 9

9 Ruth 2; Act 27; Jer 37; Ps 10

10 Ruth 3-4; Act 28; Jer 38; Ps 11-12

11 1Sa 1; Ro 1; Jer 39; Ps 13-14

12 1Sa 2; Ro 2; Jer 40; Ps 15-16

13 1Sa 3; Ro 3; Jer 41; Ps 17

14 1Sa 4; Ro 4; Jer 42; Ps 18

15 1Sa 5-6; Ro 5; Jer 43; Ps 19

16 1Sa 7-8; Ro 6; Jer 44; Ps 20-21

17 1Sa 9; Ro 7; Jer 46; Ps 22

18 1Sa 10; Ro 8; Jer 47; Ps 23-24

19 1Sa 11; Ro 9; Jer 48; Ps 25

20 1Sa 12; Ro 10; Jer 49; Ps 26-27

21 1Sa 13; Ro 11; Jer 50; Ps 28-29

22 1Sa 14; Ro 12; Jer 51; Ps 30

23 1Sa 15; Ro 13; Jer 52; Ps 31

24 1Sa 16; Ro 14; La 1; Ps 32

25 1Sa 17; Ro 15; La 2; Ps 33

26 1Sa 18; Ro 16; La 3; Ps 34

27 1Sa 19; 1Co 1; La 4; Ps 35

28 1Sa 20; 1Co 2; La 5; Ps 36

29 1Sa 21-22; 1Co 3; Eze 1; Ps 37

30 1Sa 23; 1Co 4; Eze 2; Ps 38

31 1Sa 24; 1Co 5; Eze 3; Ps 39

SEPTEMBER

1 1Sa 25; 1Co 6; Eze 4; Ps 40-41

2 1Sa 26; 1Co 7; Eze 5; Ps 42-43

3 1Sa 27; 1Co 8; Eze 6; Ps 44

4 1Sa 28; 1Co 9; Eze 7; Ps 45

5 1Sa 29-30; 1Co 10; Eze 8; Ps 46-47

6 1Sa 31; 1Co 11; Eze 9; Ps 48

7 2Sa 1; 1Co 12; Eze 10; Ps 49

8 2Sa 2; 1Co 13; Eze 11; Ps 50

9 2Sa 3; 1Co 14; Eze 12; Ps 51

10 2Sa 4-5; 1Co 15; Eze 13; Ps 52-54

11 2Sa 6; 1Co 16; Eze 14; Ps 55

12 2Sa 7; 2Co 1; Eze 15; Ps 56-57

13 2Sa 8-9; 2Co 2; Eze 16; Ps 58-59

14 2Sa 10; 2Co 3; Eze 17; Ps 60-61

15 2Sa 11; 2Co 4; Eze 18; Ps 62-63

16 2Sa 12; 2Co 5; Eze 19; Ps 64-65

17 2Sa 13; 2Co 6; Eze 20; Ps 66-67

18 2Sa 14; 2Co 7; Eze 21; Ps 68

19 2Sa 15; 2Co 8; Eze 22; Ps 69

20 2Sa 16; 2Co 9; Eze 23; Ps 70-71

21 2Sa 17; 2Co 10; Eze 24; Ps 72

22 2Sa 18; 2Co 11; Eze 25; Ps 73

23 2Sa 19; 2Co 12; Eze 26; Ps 74

24 2Sa 20; 2Co 13; Eze 27; Ps 75-76

25 2Sa 21; Gal 1; Eze 28; Ps 77

26 2Sa 22; Gal 2; Eze 29; Ps 78:1-37

27 2Sa 23; Gal 3; Eze 30; Ps 78:38-72

28 2Sa 24; Gal 4; Eze 31; Ps 79

29 1Ki 1; Gal 5; Eze 32; Ps 80

30 1Ki 2; Gal 6; Eze 33; Ps 81-82

OCTOBER

1 1Ki 3; Eph 1; Eze 34; Ps 83-84

2 1Ki 4-5; Eph 2; Eze 35; Ps 85

3 1Ki 6; Eph 3; Eze 36; Ps 86

4 1Ki 7; Eph 4; Eze 37; Ps 87-88

5 1Ki 8; Eph 5; Eze 38; Ps 89

6 1Ki 9; Eph 6; Eze 39; Ps 90

7 1Ki 10; Phil 1; Eze 40; Ps 91

8 1Ki 11; Phil 2; Eze 41; Ps 92-93

9 1Ki 12; Phil 3; Eze 42; Ps 94

10 1Ki 13; Phil 4; Eze 43; Ps 95-96

11 1Ki 14; Col 1; Eze 44; Ps 97-98

12 1Ki 15; Col 2; Eze 45; Ps 99-101

13 1Ki 16; Col 3; Eze 46; Ps 102

14 1Ki 17; Col 4; Eze 47; Ps 103

15 1Ki 18; 1Th 1; Eze 48; Ps 104

16 1Ki 19; 1Th 2; Dn 1; Ps 105

17 1Ki 20; 1Th 3; Dn 2; Ps 106

18 1Ki 21; 1Th 4; Dn 3; Ps 107

19 1Ki 22; 1Th 5; Dn 4; Ps 108-109

20 2Ki 1; 2Th 1; Dn 5; Ps 110-111

21 2Ki 2; 2Th 2; Dn 6; Ps 112-113

22 2Ki 3; 2Th 3; Dn 7; Ps 114-115

23 2Ki 4; 1Ti 1; Dn 8; Ps 116

24 2Ki 5; 1Ti 2; Dn 9; Ps 117-118

25 2Ki 6; 1Ti 3; Dn 10; Ps 119:1-24

26 2Ki 7; 1Ti 4; Dn 11; Ps 119:25-48

27 2Ki 8; 1Ti 5; Dn 12; Ps 119:49-72

28 2Ki 9; 1Ti 6; Ho 1; Ps 119:73-96

29 2Ki 10; 2Ti 1; Ho 2; Ps 119:97-120

30 2Ki 11-12; 2Ti 2; Ho 3-4; Ps 119:121-144

31 2Ki 13; 2Ti 3; Ho 5-6; Ps 119:145-176

NOVEMBER

1 2Ki 14; 2Ti 4; Ho 7; Ps 120-122

2 2Ki 15; Tit 1; Ho 8; Ps 123-125

3 2Ki 16; Tit 2; Ho 9; Ps 126-128

4 2Ki 17; Tit 3; Ho 10; Ps 129-131

5 2Ki 18; Phil; Ho 11; Ps 132-134

6 2Ki 19; He 1; Ho 12; Ps 135-136

7 2Ki 20; He 2; Ho 13; Ps 137-138

8 2Ki 21; He 3; Ho 14; Ps 139

9 2Ki 22; He 4; Joel 1; Ps 140-141

10 2Ki 23; He 5; Joel 2; Ps 142

11 2Ki 24; He 6; Joel 3; Ps 143

12 2Ki 25; He 7; Am 1; Ps 144

13 1Ch 1-2; He 8; Am 2; Ps 145

14 1Ch 3-4; He 9; Am 3; Ps 146-147

15 1Ch 5-6; He 10; Am 4; Ps 148-150

16 1Ch 7-8; He 11; Am 5; Lk 1:1-38

17 1Ch 9-10; He 12; Am 6; Lk 1:39-80

18 1Ch 11-12; He 13; Am 7; Lk 2

19 1Ch 13-14; Jas 1; Am 8; Lk 3

20 1Ch 15; Jas 2; Am 9; Lk 4

21 1Ch 16; Jas 3; Ob 1; Lk 5

22 1Ch 17; Jas 4; Jon 1; Lk 6

23 1Ch 18; Jas 5; Jon 2; Lk 7

24 1Ch 19-20; 1Pe 1; Jon 3; Lk 8

25 1Ch 21; 1Pe 2; Jon 4; Lk 9

26 1Ch 22; 1Pe 3; Mic 1; Lk 10

27 1Ch 23; 1Pe 4; Mic 2; Lk 11

28 1Ch 24-25; 1Pe 5; Mic 3; Lk 12

29 1Ch 26-27; 2Pe 1; Mic 4; Lk 13

30 1Ch 28; 2Pe 2; Mic 5; Lk 14

DECEMBER

1 1Ch 29; 2Pe 3; Mic 6; Lk 15

2 2Ch 1; 1 Jn 1; Mic 7; Lk 16

3 2Ch 2; 1 Jn 2; Nah 1; Lk 17

4 2Ch 3-4; 1 Jn 3; Nah 2; Lk 18

5 2Ch 5:1-6:11; 1 Jn 4; Nah 3; Lk 19

6 2Ch 6:12-42; 1 Jn 5; Hab 1; Lk 20

7 2Ch 7; 2Jn 1; Hab 2; Lk 21

8 2Ch 8; 3 Jn 1; Hab 3; Lk 22

9 2Ch 9; Jude; Zph 1; Lk 23

10 2Ch 10; Rev 1; Zph 2; Lk 24

11 2Ch 11-12; Rev 2; Zph 3; Jn 1

12 2Ch 13; Rev 3; Hag 1; Jn 2

13 2Ch 14-15; Rev 4; Hag 2; Jn 3

14 2Ch 16; Rev 5; Zech 1; Jn 4

15 2Ch 17; Rev 6; Zech 2; Jn 5

16 2Ch 18; Rev 7; Zech 3; Jn 6

17 2Ch 19-20; Rev 8; Zech 4; Jn 7

18 2Ch 21; Rev 9; Zech 5; Jn 8

19 2Ch 22-23; Rev 10; Zech 6; Jn 9

20 2Ch 24; Rev 11; Zech 7; Jn 10

21 2Ch 25; Rev 12; Zech 8; Jn 11

22 2Ch 26; Rev 13; Zech 9; Jn 12

23 2Ch 27-28; Rev 14; Zech 10; Jn 13

24 2Ch 29; Rev 15; Zech 11; Jn 14

25 2Ch 30; Rev 16; Zech 12:1-13:1; Jn 15

26 2Ch 31; Rev 17; Zech 13:2-9; Jn 16

27 2Ch 32; Rev 18; Zech 14; Jn 17

28 2Ch 33; Rev 19; Mal 1; Jn 18

29 2Ch 34; Rev 20; Mal 2; Jn 19

30 2Ch 35; Rev 21; Mal 3; Jn 20

31 2Ch 36; Rev 22; Mal 4; Jn 21

Time *of* Events

DATE	EVENT	SOURCE
4004 B.C.	Creation	Gen. 1–2.
4004 B.C.	The Fall	Gen. 3.
4004–3074 B.C.	Adam	Created in the beginning (Gen. 1:26–2:25). Lived 930 years (Gen. 5:5).
3874–2962 B.C.	Seth	Born when Adam was 130 years old (Gen. 5:3). Lived 912 years (Gen. 5:8).
3769–2864 B.C.	Enos	Born when Seth was 105 years old (Gen. 5:6). Lived 905 years (Gen. 5:11).

DATE	EVENT	SOURCE
3679–2769 B.C.	Cainan	Born when Enos was 90 years old (Gen. 5:9). Lived 910 years (Gen. 5:14).
3609–2714 B.C.	Mahalalel	Born when Cainan was 70 years old (Gen. 5:12). Lived 892 years (Gen. 5:17).
3544–2582 B.C.	Jared	Born when Mahalalel was 65 years old (Gen. 5:15). Lived 962 years (Gen. 5:20).
3382–3017 B.C.	Enoch	Born when Jared was 162 years old (Gen. 5:18). Lived 365 years (Gen. 5:23–24).
3317–2349 B.C.	Methuselah	Born when Enoch was 65 years old (Gen. 5:21). Lived 969 years (Gen. 5:27).
3130–2353 B.C.	Lamech	Born when Methuselah was 187 years old (Gen. 5:25). Lived 777 years (Gen. 5:31).
2948–1998 B.C.	Noah	Born when Lamech was 182 years old (Gen. 5:29). Lived 950 years (Gen. 9:28–29).
2349–2348 B.C.	The Flood	Began when Noah was 600 years old (Gen. 7:6). He left the ark at the age of 601 (Gen. 8:13–19).
2242 B.C.	The Tower of Babel	Gen. 11.
2000–1825 B.C.	Abraham	Lived 175 years (Gen. 25:7–8).

DATE	EVENT	SOURCE
1900–1720 B.C.	Isaac	Born when Abraham was 100 years old (Gen. 21:5). Lived 180 years (Gen. 35:28–29).
1840–1693 B.C.	Jacob	Born when Isaac was 60 years old (Gen. 25:24–26). Lived 147 years (Gen. 47:28).
1749–1639 B.C.	Joseph	Lived 110 years (Gen. 50:22, 26).
1710 B.C.	Jacob Moves to Egypt	He was 130 years old (Gen. 47:9).
1525–1405 B.C.	Moses	He was 80 years old at the time of the Exodus (Ex. 7:7). Lived 120 years (Deut. 34:7).
1445 B.C.	The Exodus	Ex. 13–18.
1445–1405 B.C.	Moses Writes the Pentateuch	Ex. 24:4, 7; Num. 33:2; Deut. 17:18; 28:58, 61; 29:20–21, 27; 30:10; 31:9–13, 22, 24–26.
1410–1405 B.C.	Moses Writes Psalm 90	Ps. 90.
1405–1385 B.C.	Joshua Writes His Book	Josh. 1–24.
1043 B.C.	Book of Judges Written	Judg. 1–21.
1030–1010 B.C.	Book of Ruth Written	Ruth 1–4.
1010–970 B.C.	David Reigns Over Israel and Judah	Was 30 when he began to reign, and reigned 40 years (2 Sam. 5:4; 1 Kings 2:11).

DATE	EVENT	SOURCE
971–965 B.C.	Solomon Writes the Song of Solomon	Song of Solomon 1:1.
971–686 B.C.	Book of Proverbs Written	Prov. 1:1; 10:1; 22:17; 24:23; 25:1; 30:1; 31:1.
940–931 B.C.	Solomon Writes Ecclesiastes	Eccl. 1:1.
931–722 B.C.	Book of 1 & 2 Samuel Written	1 Sam. 1–31; 2 Sam. 1–24.
850–840 B.C.	Obadiah Writes His Book	Obad. 1:1.
835–796 B.C.	Joel Writes His Book	Joel 1:1.
775 B.C.	Jonah Writes His Book	Jon. 1–4.
750 B.C.	Amos Writes His Book	Amos 1:1.
750–710 B.C.	Hosea Writes His Book	Hos. 1:1.
735–710 B.C.	Micah Writes His Book	Mic. 1:1.
722 B.C.	Sennacherib Invades Judah	2 Kings 1;, Isa. 36; 2 Chron. 32.
700–681 B.C.	Isaiah Writes His Book	Isa. 1:1; 2:1; 13:1.
663 B.C.	Fall of Thebes (No Amon)	Nah. 3:8–10.
650 B.C.	Nahum Writes His Book	Nah. 1:1.

DATE	EVENT	SOURCE
641–609 B.C.	Josiah Reigns Over Judah	Began reigning at 8 years old, and reigned 31 years (2 Kings 22:1, 2 Chron. 34:1).
635–625 B.C.	Zephaniah Writes His Book	Zeph. 1:1
615–605 B.C.	Habakkuk Writes His Book	Hab. 1:1; 3:1.
612 B.C.	Destruction of Nineveh	Nah. 1–3.
605 B.C.	Daniel Taken Captive by Babylon	Dan. 1.
597 B.C.	Jehoichin Taken Captive by Nebuchadnezzar	2 Kings 24:8–16.
590–570 B.C.	Ezekiel Writes His Book	Ezek. 1:1–3.
586 B.C.	Nebuchadnezzar Destroys Jerusalem	The 19th year of Nebuchadnezzar's reign (2 Kings 25:8).
586 B.C.	Jeremiah Writes Lamentations	Lam. 1–5.
561 B.C.	Jehoichin Released from Prison	2 Kings 25:27–29; Jer. 52:31–33.
586–570 B.C.	Jeremiah Writes the Book of Jeremiah	Jer. 1:1.
538–537 B.C.	Cyrus Orders the Rebuilding of the Temple	The 1st year of Cyrus' reign (2 Chron. 36:22; Ezra 1:1; 5:13; 6:3).
536–530 B.C.	Daniel Writes His Book	Dan. 7:1–2, 15, 28; 8:1, 15, 27; 9:2, 22; 10:2, 7, 11–12; 12:4–5, 9.

DATE	EVENT	SOURCE
561–538 B.C.	Jeremiah Writes 1 & 2 Kings	1 Kings 1–22; 2 Kings 1–25.
520–519 B.C.	Haggai Delivers His Prophecy	The 2nd year of Darius' reign (Hag. 1:1; 2:1; 2:10; 2:20).
520–519 B.C.	Zechariah Begins to Prophesy	The 2nd year of Darius' reign (Zech. 1:1, 7).
520 B.C.	Haggai Writes His Book	Hag. 1:1.
518–517 B.C.	Zechariah's Last Prophecy (Most Likely)	The 4th year of Darius' reign (Zech. 7:1).
516 B.C.	Temple Rebuilt	The 6th year of Darius' reign (Ezra 6:15).
480–470 B.C.	Zechariah Writes His Book	Zech. 1:1.
458–457 B.C.	Ezra Arrives in Jerusalem	The 7th year of Artaxerxes' reign (Ezra 7:7–8).
457–444 B.C.	Ezra Writes His Book	Ezra 1–10.
450 B.C.	Book of Psalms Completed	Ps. 1–150.
450–430 B.C.	Ezra Writes 1 & 2 Chronicles	Written 8 generations after Jehoiachin (aka Jeconiah; 1 Chron. 3:17–24), who was taken to Babylon in 597 B.C.
450–331 B.C.	Book of Esther Written	Esth. 1–10.

DATE	EVENT	SOURCE
445–444 B.C.	Nehemiah Arrives in Jerusalem	The 20th year of Artaxerxes' reign (Neh. 1:1; 2:1; 5:14).
433–432 B.C.	Nehemiah Returns to Artaxerxes	The 32nd year of Artaxerxes' reign (Neh. 5:14; 13:6).
433–424 B.C.	Malachi Writes His Book	Mal. 1:1.
424–400 B.C.	Book of Nehemiah Written	Neh. 1–13.
5 B.C.	Christ's Birth	Matt. 1; Mark 1; Luke 2:6; John 1:14.
27 A.D.	Christ's Baptism	Matt. 3:13; Mark 1:9; Luke 3:21.
30 A.D.	Christ's Death	Matt. 27; Mark 15; Luke 23; John 18; 19.
30 A.D.	Christ's Resurrection	Matt. 28; Mark 16; Luke 24; John 20, 21.
30 A.D.	The Ascension	Acts 1.
30 A.D.	Matthias Chosen by Lot	Acts 1:12.
30 A.D.	The Holy Spirit Comes at Pentecost	Acts 2.
30 A.D.	Peter Heals and Preaches	Acts 3.
30 A.D.	Peter and John Arrested and Released	Acts 4.
30 A.D.	Believers Share All	Acts 4:32.

DATE	EVENT	SOURCE
30 A.D.	Deaths of Ananias and Sapphira	Acts 5.
30 A.D.	Apostles Preach and Heal	Acts 5:11.
31 A.D.	Stephen's Speech, Stoning and Death	Acts 6–7.
31 A.D.	Saul Persecutes the Church	Acts 8.
31 A.D.	Philip in Samaria	Acts 8:3.
31 A.D.	Simon the Sorcerer	Acts 8:9.
31 A.D.	Philip and the Ethiopian	Acts 8:26.
34 A.D.	Saul's Conversion	Acts 9.
37 A.D.	Peter Preaches to the Gentiles	Acts 10–11.
42–49 A.D.	James Writes His Letter	James 1:1.
42 A.D.	Barnabas Sent to Antioch	Acts 11:22.
42 A.D.	Peter Led from Prison by the Angel	Acts 12.
44 A.D.	Herod Agrippa Dies	Acts 12:20.
48 A.D.	Paul's First Missionary Journey	Acts 13.

DATE	EVENT	SOURCE
48 A.D.	Paul preaches in Pisidian Antioch	Acts 13:14.
48 A.D.	Paul and Barnabas in Iconium	Acts 14.
48 A.D.	Paul and Barnabas in Lystra and Derbe	Acts 14:8.
48 A.D.	Paul and Barnabas Return to Syrian Antioch	Acts 14:21.
48 A.D.	Return to Syrian Antioch	Acts 14:24.
48 A.D.	The Council at Jerusalem	Acts 15.
49 A.D.	Paul's Second Missionary Journey	Acts 15:36.
49–50 A.D.	Paul Writes Galatians	Gal. 1:1.
49 A.D.	Paul in Philippi	Acts 16.
49 A.D.	Paul in Thessalonica, Berea, Athens	Acts 17.
50–60 A.D.	Mark Writes His Gospel	Mark 1–16.
50–60 A.D.	Matthew Writes His Gospel	Matthew 1–28.
51 A.D.	Paul in Corinth	Acts 18.

DATE	EVENT	SOURCE
51 A.D.	Paul Writes 1 Thessalonians	1 Thess. 1:1.
51–52 A.D.	Paul Writes 2 Thessalonians	2 Thess. 1:1.
55 A.D.	Paul Writes 1 Corinthians	1 Cor. 1:1.
55–56 A.D.	Paul Writes 2 Corinthians	2 Cor. 1:1.
56 A.D.	Paul Writes Romans	Rom. 1:1.
60–61 A.D.	Luke Writes His Gospel	Luke 1–24.
60–62 A.D.	Paul Writes Ephesians	Eph 1:1.
60–62 A.D.	Paul Writes Philippians	Phil. 1:1.
60–62 A.D.	Paul Writes Philemon	Philemon 1:1.
60–62 A.D.	Paul Writes Colossians	Col. 1:1.
62 A.D.	Luke Writes Acts	Acts 1–28.
62–64 A.D.	Paul Writes 1 Timothy	1 Tim. 1:1.
62–64 A.D.	Paul Writes Titus	Tit. 1:1.

DATE	EVENT	SOURCE
64–65 A.D.	Peter Writes 1 Peter	1 Pet. 1:1.
66–67 A.D.	Paul Writes 2 Timothy	2 Tim. 1:1.
67–68 A.D.	Peter Writes 2 Peter	2 Pet. 1:1.
67–69 A.D.	Book of Hebrews Written	Heb. 1–13.
68–70 A.D.	Jude Writes His Letter	Jude 1:1.
80–90 A.D.	John Writes His Gospel	John 1–21.
90–95 A.D.	John Writes 1, 2, & 3 John	1 John 1–5; 2 John 1; 3 John 1.
94–96 A.D.	John Writes Revelation	Rev. 1–22.

Weights & Measures

MONEY			
Denarius	Day's wage		Matthew 20:2
Drachma	Est. 0.035 oz silver	Est. 1 g silver	Luke 15:8
Didrachma (2 drach)	Est. 0.07 oz silver	Est. 2 g silver	Matthew 17:24
Talent, silver	≈ 100 lb	≈ 45.4 kg	Ezra 8:26
Talent, silver (Alternate)	≈ 50 lb	≈ 22.7 kg	Ezra 8:26
Talent, gold	≈ 120 lb	≈ 54.4 kg	1 Kings 9:28
Talent, gold (Alternate)	≈ 60 lb	≈ 27.2 kg	1 Kings 9:28

LENGTHS

Finger	0.73 in	1.85 cm	Jeremiah 52:21
Handbreadth (4 fingers)	2.92 in	7.4 cm	Exodus 25:25
Span	9 in	22.86 cm	Exodus 28:16
Cubit	18 in	45.72 cm	Matthew 6:27
Long Cubit	20.4 in	51.9 cm	Ezekiel 40:5
Fathom	6 ft	1.829 m	Acts 27:28
Reed (6 cubits)	8.75 ft	2.73 m	Ezekiel 40:5
Furlong	1/8 mi, 660 ft	201.2 m	Revelation 14:20
Stadion	697 ft	185.4 m	Luke 24:13
Sabbath day's journey	3/5 mi	0.9656 km	Acts 1:12
Day's journey	20 mi	32.19 km	1 Kings 19:4

WEIGHTS

Gerah	1/50 oz	0.567 g	Ezekiel 45:12
Bekah (10 gerahs)	1/5 oz	5.67 g	Genesis 24:22
Pim (2/3 shekel)	1/3 oz	9.45 g	1 Samuel 13:21

WEIGHTS

Shekel (2 bekahs)	2/5 oz	11.34 g	Exodus 30:23
Mina (50 shekels)	1.25 lb	0.567 kg	Ezra 2:69
Talent (60 minas)	75 lb	34.02 kg	Ezra 8:26
Liquid Measures			
Log	0.65 pt	0.31 L	Leviticus 14:10
Kab (4 logs)	2.6 pt	1.2 L	2 Kings 6:25
Hin (12 logs)	0.98 gal	3.7 L	Numbers 15:4
Bath (6 hins)	5.9 gal	22 L	Isaiah 5:10
Homer (10 baths)	59 gal	220 L	Ezekiel 45:11
Kor (10 baths)	59 gal	220 L	Ezekiel 45:11
Metretes	10 gal	37.85 L	John 2:6

DRY MEASURES

Kab (1/18 ephah)	2.6 pt	1.2 L	2 Kings 6:25
Omer (1/10 ephah)	2.3 qt	2.2 L	Exodus 16:36

DRY MEASURES

Seah (1/3 ephah)	7.7 qt	7.3 L	2 Kings 7:1
Ephah (10 omers)	5.9 gal	22 L	Ruth 2:17
Lethech (5 ephaths)	29 gal	110 L	Hosea 3:2
Homer (10 ephaths)	59 gal	220 L	Leviticus 27:16
Kor (10 ephaths)	59 gal	220 L	Ezekiel 45:14

TIME

Sunrise	6:00 am	6:00	Mark 16:2
First hour	7:00 am	7:00	
Second hour	8:00 am	8:00	
Third hour	9:00 am	9:00	Matthew 20:3
Fourth hour	10:00 am	10:00	
Fifth hour	11:00 am	11:00	
Sixth hour	12:00 pm	12:00	Matthew 27:45
Seventh hour	1:00 pm	13:00	John 4:52
Eighth hour	2:00 pm	14:00	

TIME

Ninth hour	3:00 pm	15:00	Acts 3:1
Tenth hour	4:00 pm	16:00	John 1:39
Eleventh hour	5:00 pm	17:00	Matthew 20:6–9
Sunset	6:00 pm	18:00	Luke 4:40
First watch of night	6 pm - 9 pm	18:00 - 21:00	
Second watch	9 pm - midnight	21:00 - 00:00	Luke 12:38
Third watch	Midnight - 3 am	00:00 - 03:00	Luke 12:38
Fourth watch	3 am - 6 am	03:00 - 06:00	Matthew 14:25